INTO THE

Reed Timmer

with Andrew Tilin

 NEW AMERICAN LIBRARY

STORM

VIOLENT TORNADOES, KILLER HURRICANES, AND DEATH-DEFYING ADVENTURES IN EXTREME WEATHER

For my mom

...

NEW AMERICAN LIBRARY
Published by New American Library, a division of
Penguin Group (USA) Inc., 375 Hudson Street,
New York, New York 10014, USA

Penguin Group (Canada), 90 Eglinton Avenue East, Suite 700, Toronto, Ontario M4P 2Y3, Canada (a division
of Pearson Penguin Canada Inc.); Penguin Books Ltd., 80 Strand, London WC2R 0RL, England; Penguin
Ireland, 25 St. Stephen's Green, Dublin 2, Ireland (a division of Penguin Books Ltd.); Penguin Group (Aus-
tralia), 250 Camberwell Road, Camberwell, Victoria 3124, Australia (a division of Pearson Australia Group
Pty. Ltd.); Penguin Books India Pvt. Ltd., 11 Community Centre, Panchsheel Park, New Delhi - 110 017, India;
Penguin Group (NZ), 67 Apollo Drive, Rosedale, Auckland 0632, New Zealand (a division of Pearson New
Zealand Ltd.); Penguin Books (South Africa) (Pty.) Ltd., 24 Sturdee Avenue, Rosebank, Johannesburg 2196,
South Africa

Penguin Books Ltd., Registered Offices:
80 Strand, London WC2R 0RL, England

Published by New American Library, a division of Penguin Group (USA) Inc. Previously published in a
Dutton edition.

First New American Library Printing, September 2011
10 9 8 7 6 5 4 3 2 1

REGISTERED TRADEMARK—MARCA REGISTRADA

New American Library Trade Paperback ISBN: 978-0-451-23459-9

The Library of Congress has cataloged the hardcover edition of this title as follows:
Timmer, Reed.
  Into the storm: violent tornadoes, killer hurricanes, and death-defying adventures in extreme weather/
Reed Timmer with Andrew Tilin.
    p. cm.
  ISBN 978-0-525-95193-3 (hardcover)
  1. Severe storms—Miscellanea. 2. Storm chasers—Psychology. 3. Storm chasers—United States.
I. Tilin, Andrew. II. Title.
  QC941.8.T56 2010
  551.55092—dc22   2010033101

Set in Celeste with ITC Officina
Designed by Daniel Lagin

Printed in the United States of America

PUBLISHER'S NOTE
Penguin is committed to publishing works of quality and integrity. In that spirit, we are proud to offer this
book to our readers; however the story, the experiences and the words are the author's alone.

While the author has made every effort to provide accurate telephone numbers and Internet addresses
at the time of publication, neither the publisher nor the author assumes any responsibility for errors, or for
changes that occur after publication. Further, publisher does not have any control over and does not assume
any responsibility for author or third-party Web sites or their content.

CONTENTS

INTRODUCTION:

STORM OF MY DREAMS

. . .

*T*he dream starts with a breeze. When I envision the complex creation of the most violent and mysterious weather phenomenon of all—a three-hundred-mile-per-hour, landscape-churning, damage-scale-topping tornado—it starts with a soothing breeze.

Here in central Oklahoma, where I really do live, and where tornadoes rated the maximum F5 on meteorology's Fujita Scale truly have gouged the earth time and time again, the breeze comes out of the south. The air is sultry—moist and warm. When it reaches your skin, it's as thick as lotion, and it makes you feel like you've been transported somewhere exotic. You almost have. The breeze originates in the Gulf of Mexico, where it once washed over beachgoers.

In my mind, I watch how this special air flows—meteorologists call this movement the low-level jet—as if it were a river, a thousand feet in the sky, extending halfway across the continent to the Great Plains. When the tropical air reaches the likes of Texas, Oklahoma, Nebraska, or Kansas, something curious happens. And the air is no longer a quiet, soothing breeze.

Near the Earth's surface, moist air collides with different kinds of air coming from different directions. Hot, dry air from the American Southwest and northern Mexico. Cold air from the north, blown southward across Canada, all the way from the Arctic. Such a convergence doesn't happen everywhere, but in central Oklahoma it's hardly a freak event. The Great Plains—which weather nuts like me call Tornado Alley—is a rare, natural intersecting point for all this wind. About 90 percent of all tornadoes reported annually in the United States—some eight hundred or more per year—touch down in Tornado Alley.

In the birth of my envisioned F5, all of that clashing air follows a meteorological script. The hot, dry air injects the atmosphere with heat that serves as a springboard for the now warm, moist air to rise. As kids, we were taught that hot air rises—hot air molecules agitate more than cold air molecules, and, needing lots of room to move, the hot air expands upward. When an F5 forms over Tornado Alley, this ascension is violent, sometimes moving at over one hundred miles per hour. The surrounding cold air only helps matters. Cold air forces neighboring hot air to rise faster.

Then, approximately a mile above the ground, the moisture in the rising air condenses into a mist. This is the meteorological equivalent of a shark fin popping out of the ocean water. It marks the beginnings of a storm cloud. It's the first visible sign of danger.

Usually the rising air in a cloud quickly cools as it ascends, and the cloud stops moving up. But not during the formation of an F5. The rising air—the *updraft*—won't die. Condensation continues, and the traces of ascending mist accumulate, not unlike the way a snowball gathers more snow as it rolls downhill. But in the case of an F5, the "snowball" is climbing toward the heavens. On a humid spring day, folks in Tornado Alley can turn their backs on the sky for just minutes, to mow a lawn or wash a car, and when they look up again, what was a cloud-free sky before has become blemished—more like *dominated*—by a lone sunlit, bright white, ominous cloud.

The crisp cloud in my mind rapidly grows from a height of hundreds of feet to thousands to tens of thousands, blasting through the troposphere and into the stratosphere until it's thirteen miles tall. This is a

cumulonimbus cloud, and in its most radical, towering form, people say that it looks like the mushroom cloud that's associated with a nuclear explosion. Considering what an F5 tornado can do to both property and people, the metaphor isn't too far-fetched.

According to the Fujita Scale upon which the F5 classification is based, such a tornado can flatten homes, turn cars into airborne missiles, and debark trees. The Fujita Scale is a widely accepted "damage scale" for categorizing tornadoes that's based on the havoc they wreak, and F5 is used only to identify the most destructive rotating winds—those that spin anywhere from an estimated 261 to 318 miles per hour. Created by University of Chicago meteorologist Tetsuya "Ted" Fujita in 1971, the scale's other five categories also use damage characteristics and estimated speeds to classify every other tornado: F0 (under 73 miles per hour); F1 (73 to 112 miles per hour); F2 (113 to 157 miles per hour); F3 (158 to 206 miles per hour); and F4 (207 to 260 miles per hour). In 2007, the F-scale was supplanted by a slightly modified Enhanced Fujita Scale, or EF-scale (for consistency I've stuck with the F-scale, which was in use for most of my early days of storm chasing, throughout this book). Whichever scale you use, to suggest F5 is to suggest almost unfathomable power.

Sure enough, near the base of this imaginary and towering cumulonimbus cloud, forces are at work. Winds howl through the cloud at varying elevations, directions, and speeds. One gale from the southwest might blow at fifty miles per hour at an elevation of six thousand feet; another blows at sixty miles per hour from the west, at ten thousand feet; a third gust maintains twenty miles per hour near the earth's surface. This phenomenon is called wind shear. The conflicting and contrasting winds push and pull the air inside the cloud until, finally, that air moves in a uniform, circular current. Ultimately the air inside the cloud begins to rotate on a horizontal axis, much the same way that laundry rotates inside a clothes dryer.

The turbulence, however, has only just begun. The force of the updraft inside the cumulonimbus cloud acts like a crane, yanking and tilting the cylinder of rotating air inside the cloud as if it were a pipe that had to ultimately stand on one end. By the time the updraft inside the cloud is finished repositioning this cylinder of air, it spins vertically, like a barber pole.

Then the mesocyclone comes alive. I can picture it now—although anyone who is in the vicinity of such a cloud can't miss it. The mesocyclone, which is the rotating and rising air inside the cloud, is so powerful that it forces part, if not all, of the cloud to also turn. There's more to the spectacle, too. Miles in the sky, the warm and moist air that fed the growth of the cumulonimbus cloud has finally cooled, causing an upper layer of ice crystals to spread in all directions like a pancake. Now that same guy who was washing his car might look up and see a massive, glistening, flying-saucer-shaped, rotating cloud. If I were him, and this storm were real, I wouldn't be turning my back on the sky anymore.

The rogue cloud structure is now known as a supercell thunderstorm. Pregnant with moisture, wind, and both the warm air coming in and the cooling air spewing out its top and trickling down, the storm roars forth. Thunder. Lightning. Torrential rain. Cold cloud droplets turn into hail and get swept back into the updraft, only to attract more moisture and freeze again, cycling through until the hailstones grow as big as baseballs. Then they finally fall from the sky, kill livestock, smash windshields, and put holes in the roofs of buildings.

I imagine something else dropping from the storm's belly: a wall cloud. It's a signature, block-shaped mass of condensation produced close to the heart of the storm's twisting and ascending updraft. A wall cloud might be only hundreds of feet off the ground, and it can spin like a top.

Here the tornado science gets fuzzy. For reasons that aren't fully known, the wall cloud sprouts a thinner funnel that features an intensified rotation. Responding to pressure and temperature changes, the funnel lowers to the ground even as it sucks air upward. The spinning cloud might get longer and thinner, or it might not. Tornadoes can look like elephant trunks, stovepipes, drill bits, or wedges. They can be straight or crooked. They can range anywhere from three hundred feet to over two miles wide and can spin for a couple of minutes or an hour. They can glisten white in the sun or appear black in the shadows, although they can also turn shades of red, yellow, brown, and pink, depending on the color of the dirt and man-made materials they pull off the ground.

The F5 of my dreams doesn't do colossal damage to people and their property. I've seen all manner of such destruction: rain gutters peeled off by sixty-five-mile-per-hour F0s, large trees snapped in half by hundred-and-twenty-mile-per-hour F2s, and neighborhoods reduced to sticks and stones by a three-hundred-mile-per-hour F5. I've encountered semitrucks that have been lifted onto their noses and houses that exploded under the force of the storm.

The F5 I imagine—a bright white stovepipe—spins in the open fields. I get close enough to hear its unmistakable jet-engine *whoosh*. I smell the earth as the tornado slashes through shrubbery and trees like some giant-size lawn mower generating the unmistakable aroma of fresh-cut grass. I watch as the lone, imperfect cylinder unpredictably moves one way and then skips another.

When there's no more warm, moist air in the pipeline and the F5 has strangled itself by sucking in its own cold air, the once huge tornado turns into an ever-thinning, twisting rope before disappearing into the ether.

This collision of air and water is what rules my life. It fills my thoughts. It pushes me to take risks and put myself in positions that some view with awe but many view with suspicion. And chasing tornadoes is how I want to spend the rest of my life. Honestly, I'm not sure I have a choice.

CHAPTER 1

FRESHMAN PERSPECTIVE

...

I t's an interesting proposition, seeking happiness from tornadoes. For those few of us who are unquestionably mesmerized by them, chasing tornadoes can be the most fantastic experience in the world. Tornado chasing taxes your intellect and puts you at one with incredible, spectacular forces of nature. Chasing is also a fix for any adrenaline junkie and, if you do it often enough, can become your career.

But an obsession with stalking tornadoes can kill or maim you, too, and even if chasing doesn't leave you with physical scars or a need for crutches, it's hard to escape unscathed. You'll witness death and destruction of property that sickens your stomach and saddens your heart. Your family will worry about you. Significant others will grow tired of playing second fiddle. Peers will disagree with the way you chase, and you'll lose friends to your obsession.

So when it comes to shadowing tornadoes, you have to ask yourself: What is chasing those violent, crazy, beautiful dreams—and I do mean *chasing* them—worth to you?

Twelve years ago, even before I'd experienced the highs and lows, before I'd seen what tornadoes were truly capable of, chasing them became everything to me.

I remember exactly when the dreams started crowding my mind.

I was a naive eighteen-year-old, still eight months shy of a huge storm-chasing rite of passage—intercepting a stunning, gigantic, and deadly F5 tornado.

I was in college, a smart and quirky freshman, and I sat in a lecture hall full of aspiring meteorologists. Back then nobody—myself included—thought my name would become synonymous with tornadoes and severe weather. In fact, back then I stood out only because I appeared to be the student least likely to succeed.

I remember one fellow student's sentiments toward me in particular. Honestly, she thought I was a fool.

It was a Tuesday afternoon, weeks into the fall semester of 1998. I was sitting next to my new friend Rick during a class held in sprawling Dale Hall on the University of Oklahoma campus in Norman. The course was Meteorology 1111, a prerequisite for all OU freshmen pursuing a meteorology degree. Rick and I spent class exchanging messages and sketches about things we found more interesting than the boring lecture. This day was no different. After I'd written something on the back of a paper napkin and handed it to him, Rick softly yet enthusiastically pounded the armrest with his fist.

That's when the blond student sitting in the row ahead of us turned around and gave us a dismissive glance. Without saying a thing, I understood her glare. It said, "Please pay attention."

I didn't appreciate being told—even silently—what to do. I wanted to ignore her. But instead I gave the young woman an acknowledging nod. Three minutes later, Rick accidentally knocked a notebook off his desk while returning the napkin to mine. The notebook hit the floor with a thud.

This time the blond turned around and clearly mouthed this message to me: "Why do you show up?"

Judging from her attitude, the woman sitting in front of me apparently thought it was only a matter of time before I was looking for a new

major or a new school. Meteorology is a complicated and difficult science. For starters, understanding the earth's atmosphere and weather—what we can understand, I should say—requires learning a lot of math and physics, especially fluid dynamics and thermodynamics. Back when I was a high school senior and an OU applicant, I was interviewed as part of Oklahoma's School of Meteorology's admissions process. I was told that Oklahoma had one of the most prestigious meteorology programs in the country. I was also told that I would likely be humbled. Approximately three of every four people in the program leave or fail before graduating.

She was like some other students in the lecture hall that day: good-looking and polished. Sitting right behind her, I could see that her thick hair was perfectly styled, as if she'd prepared herself to appear in front of a camera. And maybe that's exactly what she'd done. In 1998, college meteorology programs across the country were enjoying a wave of popularity. A lot of credit went to Helen Hunt and the movie *Twister,* which had been a major blockbuster only two years earlier. The movie romanticized weather in general and storm chasing in particular. Hunt, who of course is also blond and good-looking, turned the act of pursuing and witnessing severe weather—specifically tornadoes—into a combination of science, romance, and thrill ride. The movie was a megahit, and meteorology was suddenly sexy. A lot of kids came out of high school thinking that they'd make a career of it. There were a couple hundred students in my Meteorology 1111 class, and I'd have bet that some of them—maybe even the woman sitting in front of me—were there with the hopes of becoming "weather celebrities." That is, they wanted to become high-profile weathermen and weatherwomen with big-bucks jobs on national TV networks.

Rick and I didn't carry ourselves like celebrities *at all.* We couldn't, really. Rick was tall, gangly, and something of an introvert, courtesy of a quiet, religious upbringing back east in Delaware. I was your average scrawny, young-looking freshman—I didn't have much of a beard to go with my blue eyes and mop of brown hair, and I still had a boy's huge metabolism as well as a complete indifference to fashion. On that Tuesday I wore what I wore practically every day that fall—khaki shorts, a white T-shirt that I'd stained baby blue in the wash, and my black and white in-line skates.

As a kid growing up in Grand Rapids, Michigan, I may have been too small and geeky to play high school team sports, but I had skated in more than my share of neighborhood street hockey games. Now the wheels were coming in handy as a means for getting around campus quickly. I didn't care if they were dorky. The skates were what got me to class on time.

Well, almost on time. Because I was frequently preoccupied with whatever I was doing—like reading a book or listening to music—I was habitually tardy for just about everything at OU, including Meteorology 1111. Which is why, after a while, I stopped taking off my skates when I entered the lecture hall for class. I'd show up in a sweat after hustling, speed-skater style, from my dorm. Then I'd clomp into the hall, sit down next to Rick, continue to sweat (I swear, I was born to sweat), and take out my notebook right after the professor started talking.

But Rick and I never paid attention for long. I'd met Rick soon after arriving in Norman for school. We lived in the same dorm. Initially he kept to himself, but once I got him talking he became very friendly, and I realized that he was quite smart. We both liked playing pickup basketball and following college sports. In fact, Rick and I together became dedicated OU football fans—two of the crazies who painted their torsos and faces Oklahoma Sooner crimson for every home game. And what the woman sitting in front of me on that Tuesday in Meteorology 1111 couldn't know was that we were both complete weather nerds.

Growing up, Rick and I had both watched the Weather Channel whenever we could and had bolted outside any time conditions turned sour. In our budding friendship, we almost always talked about the weather—especially horrendous weather, like thunder, lightning, hurricanes, and tornadoes. We agreed that the worse the weather, the more we were mesmerized by its beauty and chaos. Attending OU, we both admitted, had little to do with career opportunities. We'd both come to OU for a pilgrimage to the Great Plains—to experience Tornado Alley. Norman is the severe-weather capital of the world, and that is why we were there.

Meteorology 1111 was an introductory class. We already knew all of the information in the reading assignments. Rick and I didn't need to hear the whats and whys of anemometers or fair-weather cumulus clouds. We'd both learned about that stuff as weather-obsessed kids.

And those notes we passed definitely weren't about kids' stuff.

Rick silently laid the napkin back on my desk, so as not to disturb the irritable blond in front of me. What he passed me was a fantasy graph illustrating conditions that might produce a huge thunderstorm. The graph's vertical axis measured height into the sky, and the horizontal axis measured temperature and moisture. Called a skew-T plot, the chart gauges instability in the atmosphere. Rick had plotted a line on the chart that would indicate the rise of hot and moist air, which meant prime conditions for massive tornadoes—and for getting my blood flowing.

I studied it, nodded, and whispered to Rick, "Wouldn't that be sweet!"

Unfortunately, my whisper is pretty loud—I don't do many things quietly, to be honest. The blond turned around again, this time looking me up and down. She inventoried my skates, stained shirt, beardless face, and smug grin, although it wasn't directed at her. I was envisioning Rick's fantasy skew-T becoming reality.

The student in front of me slowly shook her head, no doubt silently wondering if I was the least bit serious about meteorology.

In that moment, I couldn't tell her how serious I was.

I didn't draw imaginary tornadoes just to fantasize about how they

might look. I didn't chart unstable atmospheres simply to pass the time. I drew tornadoes in Meteorology 1111 because that was the next best thing to seeing them live.

. . .

In those first few weeks at OU, I wished that I could scribble on the sky what I could on napkins and paper. But Oklahoma storm chasing, I'd soon discover, wasn't nearly so easy.

For one thing, the weather wasn't on my side. Storm season in Tornado Alley (which runs approximately from Central Texas north, beyond Oklahoma, Kansas, and Nebraska, all the way into the Canadian prairie) typically starts in early spring, peaks around late spring and early summer, and enjoys a resurgence in the fall before hibernating for the winter. I was dying for a fall sampler before the long wait until March, April, or May. But so far, no luck.

"Nothing on the radar," I said, sitting on the bed in my dorm room, watching the latest televised forecasts on the Weather Channel. The door to my room was wide open, and Rick was leaning against the doorjamb. It was a couple days after our encounter with the blond woman in Meteorology 1111.

"All blue sky," I added, looking out the window.

"There's definitely something in the air," said Rick, who grabbed his nose and held it before turning away from my room. "I'll be on my floor if you need me. My odor-free floor."

I crossed my arms, finding the joke only mildly funny. Then I surveyed my messy room and inhaled. The smell *was* funky.

I'd known there would be a problem with my living situation shortly after I set down my suitcases. My dorm room itself was fine—small but windowed, on the eighth floor of a twelve-story brick structure called the Johnson Tower. My roommate, however, was a sloppy, huge, and particularly pungent (albeit very nice) kid from West Virginia, and I was terrible about putting away my clothes—there always seemed to be something better to do, like tuning in to the Weather Channel. One friend in the building could stay in my room—which he said smelled like sour milk—for only minutes at a time.

I had other quirks, too, besides the inability to put away my laundry. One big one in particular.

It had to do with music, which had played a huge role in my childhood. My parents divorced when I was young, and once my schoolteacher mother became the family's primary caregiver, she repeatedly instilled the importance of education and culture in my two sisters and me. When my sisters and I were young, my mom regularly took us to the symphony. When I was ten years old, I told my mom that I liked the sound of the oboe. Soon she put one in my hands.

At first my mom pushed me to play. But that didn't last long, because I quickly pushed myself even harder. It would be a recurring theme in my young life, my highly motivated mother encouraging me to do something and then frequently standing back to marvel as I'd turn hobbies into passions bordering on obsessions.

So long as I'd obsess over things like my studies or classical music, my mom didn't discourage me. Why should she have? In due time I became pretty accomplished at the oboe, to the point that I turned into the oddball high schooler who went to music camps and preferred classical songs over pop tunes. When I applied for college, OU gave me a partial scholarship to play, which I did throughout my undergraduate days.

But when I arrived at my dormitory in Norman, I quickly got an earful of pop music from my dormmates' stereos. At first I found myself humming along. Then I bought a few rock albums. Then it was like a switch went off inside of me. The pop music started to sound *really* good, and I couldn't get enough of it.

During those early days at OU, I was the young and previously sheltered, borderline obsessive-compulsive kid who was growing up and busting out—painting myself and partying for every football game, and trading Vivaldi and Mozart for rap and classic rock. And much to the annoyance of my dormmates, I'd play my favorite songs over and over.

One Sunday afternoon in late September, I picked up the phone in my room. I dialed Rick's number. He lived three floors above me.

"Hello," he said, and before I responded, I hit the pause button on my stereo's CD player. I was listening to Bruce Springsteen's "Glory Days" for the ninth straight time.

"It's Reed," I said. "You want to go downstairs and play some Ultimate?"

I was sure that my roommate could've used the break from me, as well as Springsteen. Plus I needed some fresh air. I had to blow off some steam after OU's football team had lost the previous night. Bare-chested and coated in Oklahoma crimson from waist to scalp, Rick and I had screamed and cheered for hours at the game.

The grass field in front of my dorm was spacious and sat under a big sky. The area was perfect for wide-open pickup games of Ultimate Frisbee, and, of course, perfect for aspiring meteorologists like me and Rick who wanted to keep tabs on the clouds.

Halfway through the game I looked up and noticed something unusual developing to the north. I stopped in my tracks.

"Look at that," I said to Rick, pointing to a lone, bright white cloud formation in the sky. He stopped, too. Most of the other players kept moving.

"That," he said, still breathing heavily from running, "looks interesting."

Minutes later Rick and I, along with another player named Chuck, walked back toward our dorm, in search of a radio, TV, or computer that could answer our burning question: Would that lone, skyscraper-tall, cauliflower-shaped cloud formation to the north produce a tornado? Rick and I had never seen a tornado in person, but we'd both watched plenty of tornado videos on television. And tornadoes often came from storms with dramatic, stand-alone cloud structures.

We didn't have to go farther than the ground-floor cafeteria to get the news. Regular television programming was being interrupted by tornado warnings.

"Let's go after it," I said to Rick and Chuck. Chuck wasn't a meteorology student but an OU freshman who lived in a nearby dorm and was more than mildly intrigued by our preoccupation with the weather. As for Rick and me, we needed someone like Chuck to come along on our maiden Oklahoma storm chase. Chuck had wheels. Rick and I didn't have cars at school.

In minutes we were traveling northeast on Interstate 44 in Chuck's beater SUV. The body showed more rust than paint.

"Maybe it'll look like a stovepipe," I said excitedly, imagining one of the classic, thick and straight shapes of a tornado. "Or an elephant trunk." An elephant trunk is skinny and crooked.

"How about a giant wedge?" said Rick wishfully from the backseat. Wedge tornadoes are wider than they are tall.

Chuck, a round, jovial guy, looked over at me riding alongside him. He saw me craning my neck to look up at the sky through the windshield and briefly looked up, too. In the day's fading light, that giant, black and ice-blue cylindrical cloud still stood against a pale sky.

"Does that weird thing have a name?" he asked.

"It's a cumulonimbus cloud," I said with a smile, having come across them many times before in books and on television. But I'd never seen such a cloud in person. "Cumulonimbus loosely translates to 'heaped-up rain cloud' in Latin," I added. "It can be a precursor to what's called a supercell thunderstorm."

A cumulonimbus cloud, I explained to Chuck, forms when a stream of particularly warm and moist air develops in an atmosphere otherwise full of colder air. This warm, moist air is lighter than the surrounding, colder air, and it wants to flow upward rapidly. In fact, the leading edge of warm air bolts upward.

"Not unlike one of those big hot-air balloons flying toward the sun," I added, and then went on to explain how the column of warm and moist air ultimately created more cold air, which aided in the upward movement of the warm air.

"The cloud feeds off itself. It gets bigger and fiercer," I said.

Chuck nodded, but slowly and without conviction. Afraid I was losing him, I cut to the chase. I told him that the supercell thunderstorm was a cumulonimbus cloud containing rising and rotating winds.

"Sometimes there's violent rain and hail, too," I said. "More importantly, supercells can spawn tornadoes."

Chuck nodded again, this time more enthusiastically.

A couple hours into the drive we still hadn't seen any tornadoes. But in the fading light, a huge lightning bolt appeared. The ensuing thunderclap was louder than any I'd ever heard.

"Woo-hoo!" yelled Rick. "Welcome to Oklahoma!"

"Incredible!" I said. "Keep going!"

Chuck gamely motored on for a while longer. Lightning continued to strike all around us, and as night fell we saw bolts hit the land and spark grass fires. In a surreal scene, the orange flames gave the sky an ominous purple-black tint, and I felt like we'd exited Tornado Alley and entered some sort of underworld. Then the weather grew even more biblical. We drove directly into the deluge of a forceful rainstorm, and Chuck had to slow down to a crawl because the windshield wipers couldn't move fast enough to sweep away the water. That was followed by monstrous hail. The hailstones were bigger than quarters—twice as big as anything I'd seen growing up in Michigan.

"This is a Michigan thunderstorm on steroids," I shouted over the crash of hail pounding the windshield and roof.

"How long will it last?" Chuck yelled back. His SUV would emerge from that storm with significant hail damage. The truck ended up as dimpled as a golf ball.

"Oh man!" shouted Rick, looking out his passenger window.

I wasn't exactly sure that Chuck and Rick were as excited as me about the violent weather, but I was overcome by a huge surge of happiness and adrenaline. I truly felt like we were on an incredible amusement park ride.

"Insane!" I shouted. I couldn't help myself.

After the hail let up we drove a bit farther, only for the storm to weaken and the sunlight to evaporate completely. Chasing tornadoes in the dark is very dangerous, because you can't see them. You could drive right into a funnel's path.

We finally turned around. But the multihour drive back to Norman didn't feel long to me. It felt like a victory lap.

In terms of trying to spot a tornado, we'd done plenty wrong. Rick and I didn't know what subtleties to look for in the structure of the supercell. We weren't armed with much of the valuable meteorological data that might have helped us deconstruct the storm's behavior. We didn't even have a weather radio or a good map. We hadn't yet learned about the detailed maps showing secondary roads that storm chasers frequently depend on to both pursue and escape from tornadoes.

Instead, Rick, Chuck, and I were mostly storm-chasing blind—that is, with enthusiasm, bits of knowledge gleaned from years of watching televised weather reports, and the rusted steel of a now thoroughly dented sport-utility vehicle. Add it all up, and we didn't have the right stuff to see a tornado.

But I was still thoroughly energized. We'd witnessed the most severe conditions I'd ever encountered. Although I hadn't yet lived in Oklahoma for a month, I knew I was in the right place. The weather there fascinated me. It was like a wild and crazed animal. With my obsessive sensibilities already kicking in, I was dying to learn how to stalk it.

• • •

First things first—I had to become more tech savvy. At OU, my dorm-mates informed me that the Internet held many secrets to successful storm chasing. Certainly I already knew plenty about the Web. But when I was growing up, my mom heavily discouraged screen time (although she often looked the other way when I tuned in to TV weather reports). She made sure that her kids' interests were in not just music and culture but science and the outdoors too.

At OU, however, it seemed like everyone had been born with a mouse in his hand. My dormmates, many of them meteorology and computer science students, seemingly knew every corner of the Internet. They took apart and reassembled their computers. For fun. They were addicted to interactive war games.

"Get up here," Rick said with urgency after I picked up the phone on the third ring in my dorm room. It was a couple of weeks after we'd storm-chased with Chuck—midmorning on Sunday, October 4.

"What's going on?" I said, turning down my CD player. I was working toward hearing Jay-Z and Jermaine Dupri sing "Money Ain't a Thang" twenty-seven times in a row.

"Come see what's up on my screen. It's incredible," he said.

My roommate was out—which is why I had the Weather Channel blasting on the TV *and* my music playing. I turned everything off. As I walked down the hall, I thought about what I'd seen only hours before . . .

Some buddies and I had been barbecuing, out in front of the dorms and late into the night, when the skies above us got interesting. A long line of ghostly clouds, suspended just a thousand feet above the ground, were heading north past the moon with amazing speed—traveling about as fast as cars roll down a highway. Those clouds were part of the low-level jet stream, which is that virtual river of summertime wind that often flows at a fast clip right through the Great Plains. The presence of that strong-running low-level jet (LLJ) suggested that thunderstorms would follow. During tornado season, the LLJ frequently transports the warm, moist, southern air to Tornado Alley. That tropical air, as I'd tried to explain to Chuck on our first storm chase, is a key to subsequent explosive weather.

Rick's excitement had to be related to the LLJ. I mean, Sooner football was enduring a down year. What else could have him so worked up?

Rick was sitting where he usually sat in his dorm room: in front of his computer. It was a hulking desktop model, with a 1990s-era big-box monitor. I crouched beside him. Rick was on a Web site that displayed a map of some of the plains. There was a yellow, misshapen circle marked around a few states. The line went around north-central and northeastern Oklahoma.

"The SPC says big things could happen today," said Rick. "It issued a convective outlook. Moderate risk."

"Really?" I said with a lift in my voice. "Tell me again. Where did you find this information?"

Rick blinked slowly.

"Let's review," he said with a sigh. He'd already given me a tour (or three) of weather-related Web sites.

Rick told me to bookmark the Web site of the SPC, or Storm Prediction Center. The SPC is a branch of the National Weather Service that's located in Norman for pretty much the same reason that Rick and I were in Norman. The spot is ground zero for the nation's most extreme convective weather. The SPC's primary role is to provide daily forecasts of convective severe weather in the United States. Convective severe weather is weather that's shaped by rising hot air and includes thunderstorms that produce brutal straight-line (nonrotating) winds, large hail, and, of course, tornadoes.

I knew that SPC meteorologists and researchers never want to cry wolf—they issue serious forecasts only when they're genuinely concerned that the conditions they're tracking will produce a storm. Even the "moderate risk" forecast that Rick spoke of meant that a tornado outbreak was truly possible—and the SPC's warnings grow increasingly dire from there. The broad-based "convective outlook" forecasts, which often focus on a region of the United States, can also be upgraded to "high risk." These outlooks could be followed by something called a "mesoscale discussion," and then a "watch." With each step, the predictions are sterner, and the focus is on a smaller geographic area. The most dire forecast—a "warning"—is issued by individual National Weather Service forecast offices that are spread out across the country. A warning (like a tornado warning or severe thunderstorm warning) implies that damaging weather is imminent or ongoing for specified counties.

"See that yellow line?" said Rick, pointing to the map on the screen. The line encircled portions of central Oklahoma. "Inside of it?" he continued. "That's the moderate-risk area. Predicted for this afternoon."

I studied the image for a minute. I was beginning to understand why Rick was glued to his screen and why he already had about two dozen weather-related Web sites bookmarked. The Internet could reveal up-to-the-minute information about the weather—and a lot more than could be gleaned by simply looking at the sky.

"At first all the details available on the Web can feel like information overload," he said, resting an elbow on his desk and cradling his forehead in his hand as he clicked from one screen to another within the SPC Web site. "But once you get a feel for how to organize the data, you realize how valuable it really is. Then it's like a drug. You can't live without it."

Rick was right, of course. In coming years I would also become a major Web geek and look back at my first electronic storm-tracking resources—television updates and broadcasts on a portable weather radio—as primitive chasing tools.

Nonetheless, on that early October day, Rick's tutorial left my head swimming with details and terminology. I wanted to get moving.

"So what are the chances of a tornado touching down today?" I said, crossing my arms.

Rick clicked through some pages on the SPC's Web site.

"About fifteen percent," he said.

My heart started to pound.

"When are we leaving?" I asked.

Rick looked at me and shook his head.

"I'm watching from here today," he said, pointing at the screen. "I don't want to chase them all."

But I wanted to pursue this storm. I wanted to pursue them all.

"Don't you want that same rush we felt a few weeks ago?" I asked Rick. "That hail? That thunder? Who wants to be stuck behind four walls when you can experience the weather in 3-D?"

Rick shrugged.

"Sometimes I'm content to see the show from here," he said.

Over time I'd discover that Rick's perspective was widely shared. It turned out that many of my college meteorology peers, even if they were passionate about severe weather, would often find enough pleasure in tracking foul-weather outbreaks and tornado threats on-screen. Besides, they'd sometimes argue, the odds were strongly against actually inter-cepting an individual tornado. Or occasionally they'd pass on chasing because they insisted that they'd found some discouraging wrinkle of data about the storm. Or they'd simply confess that storm chasing took up too much time.

In the years to come, I decided that the pessimism and apathy didn't make sense—skipping a storm chase was like not scratching an itch or passing on the chance to sit courtside at a basketball game because the game *might* be a blowout. What if the contest went into overtime and you were stuck watching it on TV, fuming because you could've been there?

For all of its usefulness, I'd never think of the Internet as anything more than a fantastic convenience; it is a poor substitute for the real thing.

I said good-bye to Rick and quickly returned to my dorm. I picked up the phone and dialed Chuck's number.

"Up for another storm chase?" I said to him.

"I don't know, Reed," he said. "I have homework."

"The Storm Prediction Center says this could be an incredible day," I said, exaggerating. I told him that I had the latest forecast information. I'm not sure he bought it.

"This might be a once-in-a-lifetime opportunity," I added. Believe it or not, the more I chased, the more I'd ultimately come to feel this way about every chase.

But Chuck was from Oklahoma. He said that he'd seen tornadoes. I argued that there was a difference between hiding from them and hunting them in order to witness their splendor.

"I'll meet you at my car," he finally said.

Thirty minutes later we were blasting north up Interstate 35 in Chuck's beater SUV.

"The SPC says that the storms are northwest of us. They'll be moving northeast," I said, trying to sound as authoritative as I was giddy while cocking my head to look at the sky through the windshield. But honestly, this was only my second chase in Tornado Alley. I was suppressing pure youthful excitement. When it came to storm chasing, I was still a rank amateur. Chuck, however, didn't need to know that.

"We should be able to get ahead of the storms," I said to him, putting my hands behind my neck before resting my back against the car seat. "Then we'll reposition ourselves so that we can watch the tornadoes touch down."

The Oklahoma sky quickly rewarded us for venturing out that day. Early on during the drive, we encountered mammatus clouds. These alien-looking clouds appear to hang off higher clouds, and their pouch-like silhouettes resemble cow udders (hence the name). Mammatus clouds are created by pockets of sinking motion in high horizontal clouds that are blown downwind off the top of a storm. They aren't dangerous, or solid indicators of approaching thunderstorms or tornadoes. But they're suspended from clouds that sometimes have extended from distant thunderstorms. Unquestionably, mammatus clouds are beautiful and exotic.

"I've only seen clouds like these in textbooks," I said after making Chuck pull over so that we could drink up the sights. "You're so lucky to be from here."

A bit farther down the road, the sights got even better.

To our west was an incredible cloud formation. The thunderstorm's body had a telltale vertical element, which was accompanied by a "shelf cloud." The name alone gives one an idea of this cloud structure: A shelf cloud extends horizontally, well beyond a thunderstorm's vertical cloud structure. But this "shelf" can also be smooth and circular like a flying saucer, or even serpentine, like an otherworldly snake dreamed up for an *Avatar* sequel.

Indeed, blue men could have popped out from behind the layered, twisting shelf cloud that Chuck and I encountered. The thing was white, black, and green.

Had the SPC delivered, or what?

"There's a tornado!" I shouted as I simultaneously pointed out the window.

Chuck abruptly hit the brakes.

"Sorry," I said, before losing myself in the thrill of the moment again.

"Another one!" I said, pointing at the leading edge of the shelf cloud. The cloud was just west of us. It had a creepy rolling motion.

"Where? Where?" said Chuck, trying to drive.

"Another!" I said, pointing farther left to a spot in the cloud.

Chuck pulled over.

Several small and nearly invisible vortices, or circular flows of wind, appeared and disappeared in front of the cloud. Then I realized that the shelf cloud and trailing storm system was headed straight for us.

"We have to find cover," I said in a semi-panicky voice, and soon Chuck was caught up in my anxiety. He punched the car's accelerator and drove crazy fast until we came to an overpass. He pulled over and turned off the engine. We scrambled up one of the structure's embankments until we could cling to its steel girders.

Rain came, and howling winds drove the precipitation straight at us, even though we were under the overpass. But there wasn't a tornado in sight.

"Actually, I'm not sure that what we saw earlier were tornadoes," I admitted to Chuck after the rain relented. Waiting out the storm under the overpass, I'd given the sightings some thought. My conclusion? False alarm. What we'd seen were called "gustnadoes," or small, harmless rotating winds that kick up dust at the turbulent leading edge of a storm.

Completely soaked, we got back in the car. Chuck didn't immediately fire up the engine. He seemed annoyed.

"What do we do now?" he asked, leaning back in the driver's seat, his arms crossed. "Which way?"

I needed guidance. I could've really used the SPC, and someone like Rick to tell me exactly what to look for on the SPC Web site. But would the Internet have all the answers? For all his Web savvy, Rick hadn't led us to a tornado on our last chase.

"Head south," I said, being decisive if not smart. "If there are more supercells behind this storm, we'll be southbound on I-35. Perfect positioning for intercepts."

I wiped the water that was dripping from my hair to my face. "Tornadoes are on the southern sides of the storms."

I didn't quite know if this last statement was always true. But Chuck needed direction. Plus south was the way home.

We tuned in to an AM radio news station. I thought luck was with us. There were tornado warnings for several cities south of our location.

"We'll drive through the storms' hail and rain," I said as Chuck accelerated. We were near the Oklahoma-Kansas border. "Tornadoes are often just on the other side of the heavy precipitation."

Thank God my advice didn't get us killed. Tornadoes can closely follow the heavy rain and hail that come out of the same storm. Many storm chasers refuse to blast through a supercell thunderstorm's heavy precipitation—a strategy that the chaser community calls "punching the core"—because the storm's hail can destroy windshields and dent every inch of a car's body. Even worse, you can drive blind right into a tornado, which might be wrapped inside a storm's precipitation.

Later on in my storm-chasing career, I'd be more judicious about when I punched the core. But developing that level of intuition was still years away. Chuck and I were poised to drive right into a funnel cloud.

We narrowly missed the possibility of seeing a tornado (and being sucked into the sky) near the small Oklahoma town of Tonkawa. Chuck drove through more rain and hail before we passed by the even smaller Perry. Soon afterward, I looked east.

"What are those?" I said, pointing to a pair of dark funnels maybe eight miles away.

"Those, my friend, are tornadoes," said Chuck.

"Pull over!" I yelled.

From our vantage point, the two tornadoes were skinny little things— thin vertical lines on the horizon. But I had a rich imagination and was still thoroughly fueled by their distant power. Chuck and I stood on the side of the road, and I gave him a bunch of celebratory high fives.

Soon we lost the daylight and blithely continued to dodge bullets all the way home. When Chuck finally dropped me off at my dorm, I wanted to run inside and get some news. I was eager to find out what I could about the day's storms. Had the SPC steered me right? How many tornadoes had

there been? But before I got very far, I encountered a wall of people. They were leaving the building.

"Everyone to the basement," one of the resident advisers barked. "Tornado warning. The campus might be hit."

The basement? No way.

I resisted the RA's command. That was nothing new. I'd once convinced a schoolteacher to leave me in a classroom when everyone else evacuated on account of stormy weather. And the way I used to stalk venomous snakes and climb to the tops of thirty-foot trees drove my mother insane with worry.

So while my OU dormmates went underground, I took off. I ended up within spitting distance of the dorms, as the only customer inside a pizzeria that had inexplicably remained open. Soon I was chomping on pepperoni pizza and looking out the restaurant's window with great anticipation, as if nothing more threatening than a Fourth of July parade was about to roll down the street.

· · ·

The late-night tornado that I stubbornly waited for, which could've struck Norman, my dorm, and the pizza joint? It never materialized. As for the pair of tornadoes I saw, they were only two of twenty-eight to touch down that day in the state, making October 4, 1998, noteworthy. The date marks the largest autumnal outbreak of tornadoes ever recorded in Oklahoma. Yet I missed almost all of them. I still had so much to learn.

When I woke up on October 5 and heard about the size of the outbreak, I had one question for myself. Where *were* those tornadoes?

"It was cone shaped. Huge. An incredible thing to witness," said Danny, a fellow freshman in the meteorology department who wore glasses, a soul patch on his chin, and his ego on his sleeve. He got a good look at one of the day's big tornadoes outside of the Oklahoma town of Dover. "I thought I was watching a claw tear at the ground," he added.

Danny and I, and a couple dozen other meteorology students, were gathered in a room known as the Map Room, on the fourteenth floor of a building called Sarkeys Energy Center. Sarkeys is a brick monolith housing offices, labs, classrooms, and a library, and it's located near the northeastern corner of OU's campus. At the time, the then seven-year-old structure hosted the school's meteorology department, and the Map Room was the unofficial gathering spot for the department's students. Every day, someone from meteorology tacked up a computer graphic of the forecasted weather for the state. Then all afternoon, and well into the night, weather geeks would come and go, filling the room with the smells of take-out Mexican food, littering the floor with empty Coke bottles, and covering its whiteboards with physics equations. The Map Room had computers and a panoramic view of the southwest. From almost any desk, you could see storms coming from sixty miles away.

The Map Room also hosted endless conversations about severe weather—how it develops, what it can do, and how best to witness it.

"The funnel was perfect, just like you'd imagine it," Danny added, drawing a picture of the tornado he saw on a whiteboard for a small cluster of students. "It was beautiful and scary. Awesome, too."

Danny turned to me.

"Hey, Reed," he said. "What'd you see?"

I briefly recalled the twin dark stripes that I'd spotted a good ways away. I wasn't nearly close enough to see clawed earth or offer a lot of detail.

Danny had taken what I'd later realize was a textbook approach to beginner storm chasing. He'd ventured out the day before with much more experienced people. I'm sure he'd learned a lot from them, and he'd come back to the Map Room with an incredible war story. I'd taken a different approach. I was the beginner storm chaser working with a chase partner who knew less than me. Chuck was prelaw.

Chasing as Danny had—with seasoned storm chasers—would likely have netted me better results too. But there was that stubborn part of me that wanted to chase my way. I hadn't wanted my mom telling me which snake to stalk or (foolish as I might have been) a dorm RA telling me to hide in a basement. I didn't want a fellow storm chaser putting me on a leash, either. I wanted to figure out storm chasing and the weather on my own. It was just my personality.

Fortunately, time was on my side. The October 4 outbreak represented a bookend to the 1998 season, and I had a long winter ahead of me.

During that stretch, I kept returning to the Map Room. I wasn't afraid to engage in conversations with upperclassmen and OU faculty in the meteorology department. Some of my teachers, after all, had storm-chased for decades. I wrapped my head around advanced concepts like "CAPE," which stands for "convective available potential energy" and measures the buoyancy of a parcel of air. CAPE helps chasers know the existing potential for warm air to rise—and thus the potential for thunderstorms to develop—in the atmosphere. I learned to appreciate the significance of the dew point, too—that's the temperature at which water vapor changes to liquid. A dew point in the sixties, I learned, means there's enough moisture in the air to catch the attention of storm chasers—and, I figured, to fuel a tornado.

I threw myself at my schoolwork, too. I'd beg, borrow, and steal time on computers wherever I could find them to learn what meteorology-related information was available on the Internet. Meanwhile, Rick and I regularly pushed each other into the early hours of the morning to master the material for Meteorology 1004, which was the grueling antithesis of the basic (to us anyway) Meteorology 1111. Met 1004 was a lot of math and physics, and I watched other students' eyes glaze over as we all studied long and involved thermodynamics cycles and wind equations.

Feeling increasingly confident about my weather-related knowledge and forecasting skills, in the spring of 1999 I entered a biweekly online game called the National Collegiate Weather Forecast Contest that was played nationwide. The points-based contest required that the approximately one thousand entrants predict high and low temperatures, as well as precipitation amounts, for selected cities across the country. For a while I flailed horribly, at one point ranking in the three hundreds among my competition while attempting to predict the weather in Chicago.

But when it came to calling the weather for two weeks in Pueblo, Colorado, I tried a different tack. Weather-wise, Pueblo is a tricky town—it lies just east of the Rockies, which means fast-developing mountain storms can undermine weather predictions. I performed a comprehensive analysis of Pueblo's atmosphere. Was the wind coming from the west or the south? Were there any pressure systems moving into the area? Where were the storms? Some forecasts called for Pueblo to expect winter-like temperatures and precipitation for mid-February. But I thought that the moisture would be wrung out of the storms well before they reached the southern Colorado town, or that a high-pressure system might move in—which would keep clouds away. I predicted mild conditions.

A couple weeks later I wanted to check my results. I needed access to a computer.

"Are you using your PC?" I asked when Rick answered the phone in his dorm. It was midnight on a Monday.

"What do you think?" he asked. "Yes. Come on up. But make it quick."

I hustled over to the elevator, and within two minutes I was sitting at Rick's desk.

"I was right, you know," I said, clicking on the contest Web site. "Springtime came early to Pueblo. Temporarily, anyway."

"How did you know that?" asked Rick between sips of Mountain Dew.

"I didn't just agree with what the model forecasts predicted. I actually performed some research. Bet you lunch at Wendy's tomorrow that I'm in the top fifty on this round," I said, clicking on another page to find my ranking. Rick and I loved Wendy's.

"What did you finish after getting the Chicago forecasts so wrong?" he replied. "Seven hundredth?"

"Three hundred something," I said.

"I'll take that bet," he replied.

I made the cut. If nothing else, all of my diligence and studying got me a free burger.

. . .

By mid-March I was itching to play meteorologist outside again. I wanted to apply some of my new knowledge and thinking to some real storm chasing. Instead, I had another lesson coming to me.

"What's in the backpack?" asked Aaron from the driver's seat of his car. Aaron was an unassuming and lanky fellow meteorology student from Maryland who played intramural basketball with me and wanted to storm-chase. I'd welcomed his interest, especially since Chuck had decided that he had no more time or tolerance for long and dicey storm-chasing excursions. I wasn't even through my freshman year and I'd already lost a chase partner.

"My math homework," I said to Aaron, throwing my book bag in the backseat. "I need to finish a problem set." I was determined to neither miss the chance to see a tornado nor blow off my school assignments. Aaron's car represented the first of what would become a long line of chase vehicles that would double as mobile study halls during my student career.

Our target was western Arkansas. The possibility of us intercepting a tornado was okay but not great—the CAPE was under 1,000, which meant that there might not be much upward lift in the atmosphere. Plus the SPC's convective outlook indicated only a slight risk for severe weather in the area. Tornadoes do materialize as early as March in the Great Plains, but not with great regularity. Some pieces of the meteorological puzzle often go missing.

Four hours into the journey, Aaron and I reached Arkansas. It was

the late afternoon. We encountered severe weather, too, and had no difficulty locating the huge rainstorm in a billowy, sooty supercell cloud. Aaron and I knew that the rain usually came out of the leading edge of the storm, and that the storms generally moved northeast. But no matter what direction we drove, the rain seemed to follow. What we didn't know at the time was that we were likely in a multicell thunderstorm—a cluster of thunderstorms that can feature several rain-filled downdrafts, several mesocyclones, and ultimately several tornadoes.

"Maybe we'll see Noah's Ark," said Aaron, his windshield wipers flying back and forth across the glass.

"Better that than stumbling across a tornado," I responded. "How do we get out of this thing?"

Aaron and I ultimately found our way out of the storm only to plunge in again, encountering more rain. The omnipresent downpour was completely disorienting, like being inside a gigantic drive-through car wash. We drove back that night having seen next to nothing.

"Do storm chasers often return home empty-handed?" Aaron asked as he parked the car.

Unfortunately, they did.

"They're called busts," I said, opening my passenger door. But I wasn't discouraged and told Aaron that he shouldn't be either. During my wintertime visits to the Map Room, several veteran storm chasers told me that no chase is made in vain. That's because each trip offers you a chance to look at the sky, watch the clouds, smell the moisture, and feel the wind. All of those experiences, I was told, add up. Learning to read the conditions when you're outside chasing, I was assured, is every bit as important as understanding the laws of thermodynamics or knowing the best forecasting Web sites.

So when I came up empty in one storm chase after another that spring, I reminded myself that the misfires were really all part of my chasing education—all part of chasing the dream that was intercepting

incredible tornadoes. By the time OU's finals rolled around in May, I'd storm-chased ten times that spring and seen one tornado. But I didn't lose faith. Then the day before my calculus exam, Rick called.

"Something's up," he said. "Tomorrow calls for exceptionally hot, sunny, and humid conditions. Windy too."

"Somewhere in Tornado Alley?" I asked.

"Yeah," he replied. "Right here."

. . .

The next day, I turned in my calculus exam before I'd finished. Who cared about derivatives and integrals when a potentially large tornado was brewing right outside the exam-room door? I kept thinking that this storm would be the payback for all of the spring's storm-predicting misfires. I also thought that the storm, after so many failed attempts, would spawn the tornado that I would chase to perfection: Along with three fellow chasers, I'd stay out of the rain and get close to the rotating winds. It would be an unforgettable event.

It was certainly unforgettable, for the entire state of Oklahoma and for me in particular. The horrific May 3, 1999, tornado outbreak forced me to ask myself, for the very first time, exactly why I chased.

"Switch on the radio," said Rick, looking up at the clouds through a side window of the car. "I don't see much happening yet."

"It's trying to get organized," said my friend Matt, who had one eye on the road as he navigated his tiny Jeep-style vehicle southwest out of Norman on Interstate 44. The other eye was tracking the clouds. A big, light gray supercell had already formed above some nearby hills. "It's gonna happen," he added.

"Follow this simple rule of thumb," advised an excited news-radio announcer over the car stereo as we blasted down the road underneath a portion of sky turning about seven shades of black. "Get as many walls between you and the outside as possible."

Well before we left our dorm—the team that day consisted of Rick, fellow meteorology students Matt and Harold, and me—the Storm Prediction Center had already hinted that a tornado could come down soon in the vicinity of a major population center like Oklahoma City, Norman, or Moore. At 11:15 A.M., the SPC had issued a moderate-risk forecast. But less than four hours later, the SPC upgraded the forecast to high risk. A high risk is issued only a few times a year, because, in the SPC's own words, it's "reserved for the most extreme events with the least forecast uncertainty."

What caused the meteorologists to sound the alarm was the arrival of a large, low-pressure "trough" in the Great Plains. Areas of low pressure are like giant sinks, drawing in the surrounding air. On May 3, hot air poured into the low-pressure area from the desert Southwest, while moist air surged north from the Gulf of Mexico. Then all that heat and moisture began to quickly rise, condense, and organize into monster supercell storms. All over the state.

Right about the same time that the Storm Prediction Center issued its solemn warning, Matt pulled the car off the road. But I wasn't about to take shelter. In fact, I got out of the car, on the shoulder of the highway, and tried to hurry Mother Nature along.

"Come on! Check out that rotation!" I bellowed to nobody in particular, absentmindedly walking alongside the speeding traffic. "Drop it! You know you want to!" I added, sounding much more like an amped-up teenager at a wrestling match than any kind of student of meteorology.

"Take cover now!" warned the radio announcer.

Then, almost on cue, one tornado formed, then another. The vortices were thin and white and several miles from us. Like tentative, giant spider legs, they poked at the green fields and hills that lay on the outskirts of Norman and the neighboring town of Moore.

"This is absolutely incredible," said Rick, who stood beside me.

"Check out those suckers," yelled Harold as cars flew by.

The two tornadoes soon roped out, or dissipated. But that was just the beginning. A rapidly rotating wall cloud exploded into existence right in front of us in a matter of fifteen minutes. Wall clouds are those knobs of dense condensation that form below the other clouds and near the strongest part of the storm's upwardly rotating winds. They're often precursors to tornadoes.

In short time a wide tornado formed.

"Look at that monster! It's vicious," said Matt. His voice wavered a bit. "Is it coming toward us?"

Matt sounded as though he might have seen enough. Rick and Harold were excited. I was going nuts.

"We've got to go," I announced, and Matt seemed relieved.

Then I added, "Go after that thing!"

So much for taking a calculated approach to stalking the tornadoes. Youthful exuberance had kicked in. I was nineteen and feeling immortal, I guess. I wanted to surge forward like the cavalry.

While we gave chase in our neck of the woods, tornadoes were touching down throughout southern Tornado Alley. In the history books, May 3, 1999, will be remembered for some of the most freakish tornadic weather in U.S. history. Before the storms receded, more than seventy tornadoes touched down over an area covering Oklahoma, Kansas, and Texas. Together the twisters caused over $1 billion in damage and gutted the Oklahoma town of Moore. Nearly fifty people died in the apocalyptic weather, and over eight hundred others were injured. The storms' destruction was so thorough that the Federal Emergency Management Agency and other government organizations would rethink where people should seek shelter from such severe conditions.

Gripping the steering wheel like a vise, Matt chased the tornado down one Oklahoma farm road after another. The rain came down hard, and then we saw snowball-size chunks of hail on the ground. I urged Matt to keep up the chase, and his car fishtailed on the muddy paths.

"Many reports of damage!" the radio blared.

But no sooner had that tornado in front of us dissipated than another one came into view, only a few miles in front of us and headed our way. It was a miserable, thick gray, and it moved toward us so quickly that it began sucking in the surrounding air with tremendous intensity. The convertible top on Matt's vehicle began to shiver and whistle. Tall, mature trees bent in the howling winds.

Matt's compact Jeep became impossible to handle. Water rose on the road. We saw a family hiding in the nook of an overpass and decided that joining them was our best chance to escape danger. We parked the car and ran.

Then the tornado ground straight in our direction. Thick tree branches snapped like breadsticks but made gunshot-style sounds that pierced the tornado's baritone howl. Mud flew everywhere. Air getting sucked into the tornado rushed through every seam in the overpass.

"Oh my God!" said Rick as the tornado closed in. I looked over and saw the honest fear in his face and unblinking eyes, and I realized that the chase was no longer a game. The adrenaline rush and the sensory overload were gone. In their wake was terror.

I knew we needed to get out of there. But I didn't want to leave. Fear *and* the thrill of getting so close had completely taken hold of me.

And then I looked back over at Rick, whose eyes were tearing. "It's going to hit us!" he yelled, watching the huge wedge move closer. "Oh my God!"

CHAPTER 2

IS THIS REALLY HAPPENING?

...

W atching the huge Oklahoma tornado maul a metal radio tower as it closed in on the overpass, I had one thought: "Is this really happening?" What's strange is that, in the wake of miraculously surviving the storm, I had plenty of reasons to keep asking myself that very same question.

No other state in Tornado Alley suffered Oklahoma's bitter fortune in the May 3 and 4, 1999, tornado outbreak. Over those two days, forty tornadoes touched down on Oklahoma soil. The tornado we faced from beneath that overpass turned out to be the meanest, most destructive funnel of the bunch. Ultimately, the tornado was classified as an F5, with wind speeds (measured via radar, approximately one hundred feet off the ground) as fast as 318 miles per hour. That's the highest wind speed ever recorded.

Of course, it could've been far worse for us. The tornado's fury ebbed and flowed, and the funnel had been even meaner before it approached the overpass. Then there was our insane good luck—the tornado turned left immediately before it would've engulfed Matt, Rick, Harold, and me.

The tornado had originated fifteen miles southeast of our location, at about six thirty P.M., and began life as an F3 with estimated wind speeds of 160 to 200 miles per hour.

This particular tornado, shortly after it touched down, grew and grew. Maybe fifteen minutes after it formed, the tornado intensified and expanded until it was three-quarters of a mile wide, and then plowed into the small community of Bridge Creek. There it annihilated even sturdy, frame-built homes, killing a three-week-old baby and the woman holding him, who were hiding under a staircase. The tornado peeled asphalt off the road and roofs from houses, dissected heavy machinery, and deposited torn-off airplane wings into distant fields.

But a tornado is an unpredictable beast. It's affected by changes in ambient winds, the intensity of its updraft, the movements and conditions of its parent thunderstorm, and friction from whatever enters into its path. For these reasons and more, there isn't a tornado scientist on the planet who can tell you with 100 percent certainty exactly what a tornado will do one moment to the next.

The F5 tornado's capriciousness saved us, and a few others too. As it traveled toward us, the funnel lifted one trailer off the ground, only to set it right back down. The family inside was fine. Another family lost all of the walnut shade trees in front of its house, but not even a single piece of the home's window trim was harmed. The mother and daughter who cowered inside one of the home's closets emerged unscathed. Their prayers had been answered.

Matt, Rick, Harold, and I felt so fortunate. Watching the tornado close in on me, its sides filled with the pink insulation of destroyed homes, as well as branches, car parts, and that warped radio tower, was surreal. The mass of cloud, wind, and moisture seemed so alive and full of swagger.

And then, I don't know. A hiccup in its suction of hot and moist air? A deeply rooted tree that wouldn't give way and yanked the tornado in a different direction? Whatever the reason for the funnel's abrupt left turn, watching it move away from us brought an almost out-of-body sense of relief.

Others who had also cowered under highway overpasses weren't so fortunate. At one point during its run, the tornado killed one person and injured approximately eleven others who had thought they'd found a safe haven by hiding underneath a highway. Like me, they'd assumed that a huge overpass might interfere with the flowing winds and create shelter from the storm.

We were all wrong. An overpass only forces tornadic winds to intensify, by as much as 25 percent, as they're forced to squeeze through the structure's relatively small gaps and crannies. Overpasses are also elevated, and when you climb up to hide in their supporting structures you're elevated, too. Since the ground causes friction that slows a tornado's winds, climbing up into an overpass puts you in a path of greater fury. Worst of all, overpasses leave tornado victims exposed to flying debris, or all the vegetation and man-made materials being swept up, chewed up, and hurled around by the storm. On May 3, those unfortunate folks ducking underneath overpasses, winds pounding them at an estimated two-hundred-plus miles per hour, suffered horrific injuries—dismemberment, shattered bones, and impalement. One person who died was later found under about eight feet of debris, and in the wake of her death, government agencies and the media have gone on a widespread campaign to warn people about the dangers of climbing underneath overpasses during tornadoes.

After leaving our overpass behind, the tornado headed northeast, paralleling Interstate 44, as if it were going to Oklahoma City for dinner. It would definitely have company: May 3, 1999, was a Monday night, and around seven P.M. plenty of Oklahomans were home.

The storm did scrape south-central Oklahoma City, crushing an apartment complex across the street from Westmoore High School. But then the tornado steered more east than north, which was fortunate news for the half million people of the state capital. However, Moore, a forty-thousand-person suburb just south of Oklahoma City, wasn't so fortunate. According to later radar reports, the tornado reached some of its peak velocities while in Moore.

It swept commercial buildings off their foundations the way one cleans crumbs off a table. The tornado invaded Regency Park, one of Moore's most concentrated residential neighborhoods, and left a wide stripe of scarred earth behind. It consumed homes and spat out debris in yellow, blue, and tan—ribbons of roof insulation, shards of bathroom tile, and six-foot splinters of hardwood floor raining from the sky. Cars that had been parked in Regency Park were flipped over and at rest on their tops, as if they were dogs lying on their backs in surrender.

Maybe ten minutes after the tornado turned away, we left the overpass where we'd been hiding. Driving in Matt's car, we followed the tornado's damage path as best we could and quickly found chaos in western Moore. An eighteen-wheel semi tossed into the side of a destroyed building, electrical wires down and crisscrossing the roads, disoriented horses roaming around on one street. The fencing that had contained them, I guessed, was long gone.

Rick, Matt, Harold, and I jumped out of the car to try to help members of the National Guard—who'd been at the ready in anticipation of such a catastrophe—direct traffic. Tiny bits of debris hung like snowflakes in the evening sky. We smelled natural gas and knew that a single spark could cause a huge explosion. It was a scary scene, and soon we retreated back to campus. We knew we couldn't contribute very much. We needed to get out of the way.

Rick and I sat in front of his television that night, fortunate to have electricity when 145,000 others in the state were left to huddle around candles and radios. We were also lucky to have shelter. The tornado hadn't crossed into Norman. OU had to postpone some of its exams, but you could hardly call the logistical problem a tragedy.

The TV images were unreal: bloodied survivors being pulled from the wreckage and a soot-covered baby who'd come away alive, bleating like a lamb. Numbed cops who told reporters that they were disoriented. Entire neighborhoods were reduced to what looked like slag heaps, and the policemen struggled to figure out what street was where. The citizens of Moore were clearly overwhelmed. Some were too shocked to speak. Others openly wept.

Rick and I were pretty quiet ourselves. We were frozen in the cool glow of that screen. How does one say the right thing when they're feeling such awe and sorrow?

"Is this really happening?" Rick said numbly. "The damage is just massive."

"Those poor people," I added. "What a slaughter. I can't believe I ran after that tornado," I said, clenching my fists. It was true. After the tornado spared us, my adrenaline kicked in, and I took off, in a dead sprint, in the tornado's wake. As if the tornado feared *me*. I'd almost gotten me and my friends killed by pushing to get closer and closer. I pushed us right into the path of an oncoming F5 tornado. Some storm chaser I was.

"How lucky were we?" Rick asked.

"How stupid were we?" I asked. "How stupid was I?"

None of us wanted to see the destruction of people's property or homes, or to hear about injury and death. Nobody in our group headed out that day thinking that they were on a suicide mission. In my dreams, such a spectacular tornado would appear and rope out in the space of an empty landscape, and do little or no damage to anyone's property. No lives would be threatened, much less lost. But seeing the aftermath of a tornado blasting a town gave me pause. Could I really stomach this inevitable part of the pursuit? Playing the oboe sure had its positives.

But Rick and I kept watching. We were absolutely riveted by the destruction. And that's when another thought occurred to me. As dark as it sounds, I couldn't stop watching, because I wanted to see what the weather was capable of doing. Of course I felt no joy. But I was gripped by the tornado's power. I was dumbfounded and impressed by what a tornado could do.

Was I alone in having such conflicted feelings? There were people throughout our dorm—throughout the nation—who were glued to their TVs. We were all drawn to the rare, intense drama that a natural disaster delivers: spectacle, tragedy, and heroics. Within hours, camera crews and star reporters from the nation's biggest media outlets would arrive in central Oklahoma. They'd come seeking all the incredible stories and film footage they could find, including the tales that I had from the overpass and the videotape that was inside of my camera.

. . .

I'd brought along a video camera on May 3. I wanted to remember the occasion, and I also thought it'd be fun to share what I had hoped would be a harmless but huge adventure with my friends. I had no idea that, come May 4, what I recorded would change my life.

The night before, after finally turning off the news, I'd shown my video footage to other students in my dorm. Word quickly got around that it was outrageous.

Scott Currens, another student who lived nearby, was an experienced storm chaser who had enjoyed some success actually selling tornado footage to news and media outlets. Back in 1999, there were maybe a few dozen people in the entire country earning significant money selling storm videos, out of a population of perhaps hundreds of chasers nationwide. Those numbers would ultimately balloon. But when I was a college freshman I didn't know who any of these people were, save for a few OU students and teachers who chased as well as several longtime storm-chasing videographers, like Tim Marshall and Jeff Piotrowski, whose clips I'd been watching on weather shows and news channels since childhood. I certainly didn't know there was a storm chaser *community*.

Early on the morning of May 4, Scott called me in my room to ask if I'd be interested in selling my video. Sure, I said. I was amused at the notion that anyone would consider buying my raw footage.

Not long after, Scott was at my door, accompanied by a big-boned, fast-talking producer for *Real TV*, which at the time was a syndicated video-clips television show that frequently featured extreme moments captured by amateur videographers.

The producer barely offered his hand to shake before launching in.

"I hear you got close to that killer tornado," he said, wrinkling his nose. My room's odor had immediately registered with him. "Can I see it?"

"Of course," I said, in disbelief that a television producer was actually in my dorm room.

"You know, we were really close," I added, trying to generate a little excitement.

I played back the early part of the chase, when Rick, Matt, Harold, and I stood next to the highway and witnessed two skinny tornadoes touching the distant ground. I noticed that I shouted a lot on the film and practically beat my chest. I was really excited.

"This is boring," said the producer.

What's worse than a surprise audition is a surprise audition that goes poorly.

"Yeah, uh, yeah," I said, trying to think of a smart response. "We're yelling because, you know, we're meteorologists. These are incredible storms."

He shrugged. "Anything else?"

I fast-forwarded the tape. The producer looked around my dorm. It was messy. Cleaning had remained a low priority for the duration of the school year—much lower than storm chasing, studying, or listening to a good song nine times in a row.

I played the video clip from our time spent under the overpass. There was Matt's vehicle, and the trees towering above it, all getting buffeted by the winds. There was the mud and the clumps of grass getting hurled through the air. There were the broken branches darting every which way. You could hear Rick yelling, "Oh my God!" in the background. There was the huge, dark, ominous tornado coming toward us through the trees.

"Okay," said the producer. "This works. How much?"

How much . . . money? I couldn't believe it. My homemade film was going to appear on national television? First I'd almost lost my life in the storm, then I'd been sobered by its heinous destructive forces, and now someone wanted to pay me money for my video? What was next? My family and friends back in Michigan would flip. They'd also be freaked out when they saw the video and my close call with that tornado.

We settled on $500, which I thought was a lot of money. Little did I know that the producer had just paid several thousand dollars for someone else's inferior footage of the same tornado.

Soon after Scott and the producer left, my phone rang. It was Scott.

"Listen," he said. "Sell your footage again."

"Again?" I asked.

Scott explained that plenty of other opportunities existed: video-clips programs similar to *Real TV,* standard television news outlets, and television production companies that make documentaries and other specials on weather.

"Right now, since this tornado is such big news," he said, "go to the news channels."

Scott gave me the lay of the land—how I should hightail it over to the news networks' satellite trucks, which were all camped out in Moore near the wreckage that used to be the city's Regency Park area. Someone there would decide if my material was worth using.

My head was spinning. Go from truck door to truck door pitching my video wares? Wasn't I already taking advantage of other people's misfortune? Wasn't this wrong? But I carried on. Matt gave me a ride. When I arrived in Moore, I felt increasingly uneasy.

The multiple satellite trucks were hard to miss. Aside from all the emergency vehicles, the monstrous, flat-paneled, multidish trucks, parked in a row in front of Moore's First Baptist Church, were the only things in the area that weren't mangled or reduced to rubble.

The church had suffered extensive damage. The big cross and sign that were once held aloft by a post were now hanging upside down, and the sign was completely twisted. A two-by-four was creepily embedded in one of the church's walls. Nearby were the destroyed homes of Regency Park, which didn't look like homes at all. They looked like the result of a giant demolition effort made to raze old buildings in exchange for new ones. The troubling thing was, there had been no plans to plow under this neighborhood.

Inside those satellite trucks, however, there was no time for reflection. The vehicles were beehives: studios on wheels full of people manning workstations that were lined with screens, buttons, and dials.

"I'll give you a hundred dollars for it," said a producer for ABC after watching my footage taken from beneath the overpass. I didn't bother suggesting that he watch the rest of the tape. The terror-filled overpass scene seemed to be what the media wanted.

I nodded absently. I was very much feeling the weight of the chain of overwhelming events. After I signed some paperwork, I turned to go.

"Wait," he said. "Don't you want to know who else is interested?"

I was confused. Hadn't I just sold my footage to this guy? To ABC?

He explained that he'd uploaded my video via satellite so that competing stations could simultaneously view my footage. Contractually speaking, I could still sell more footage. The producer was doing me a favor by shopping my video around in some sort of virtual media bazaar.

Soon the phone rang inside the truck. The ABC producer had a brief conversation with whoever was on the other end of the line.

May 4 was about to get even weirder.

"CNN wants the footage," said the producer. "They also want an interview," he added. "Better hustle over there."

• • •

Who in the world cared what a nineteen-year-old college freshman thought about the weather? Oklahoma and its tornadoes were unquestionably the moment's top news story. But CNN could have asked any number of veteran meteorologists, environmental scientists, or even chirpy weather personalities to feed America more information about what had just come down out of the Tornado Alley sky. Why, in the immediate wake of a huge natural disaster, give airtime to a kid with some video that he was lucky to shoot and who had a mere nine months of basic meteorology under his belt?

Credit for my first brush with fame goes to a strange mix of ingredients: warmer weather, one politician, one product, a convergence of media forces, and a bunch of outlandish athletes. In other words, everything from an oddball car to some crazy sky surfers helped me to land in front of the CNN cameras.

Back in 1999, before the F5 tornado appeared within the borders of Oklahoma and the viewfinder of my video camera, America already had a growing preoccupation with the weather. One big reason was Al Gore. In 1992, when he was still a United States senator from Tennessee, Gore wrote a book titled *Earth in the Balance: Ecology and the Human Spirit*. Gore may not have coined the term "global warming" or been the first to describe its potentially huge effects on both the weather and the planet, but the book popularized the concept that our increasingly warm weather was foreboding.

"The real danger from global warming is not that the temperature will go up a few degrees," Gore wrote a decade before global warming became the hot-button issue it is today. "It is that the whole global climate system is likely to be thrown out of whack." Even before he was elected vice president in late 1992, Gore's *Earth in the Balance* became a national bestseller.

The book also gave weight to the words of other scientists and climatologists who had made hyperbolic predictions associated with global warming. A professor from the Massachusetts Institute of Technology claimed that global warming could someday cause storms to produce 50 percent more kinetic energy, and thus generate hurricane winds that could exceed 220 miles per hour. One of NASA's star scientists warned that global warming might cause ferocious drought. Other researchers connected global warming to an occasional, notable heating of the Pacific Ocean called El Niño and wondered if horrific flooding was just around the corner. The theories and rhetoric haven't immediately proven true, but ever since Hurricane Katrina harnessed its demonic energy from hot ocean waters before striking the Gulf Coast in 2005, and killed nearly two thousand people when it struck, scientists have been obsessed with the possibility that our warmer environs are creating unprecedented meteorological catastrophes.

Businesses, of course, have long since seen opportunities in global warming, and the arguable hood ornament of the consumer-product trend can be traced back to 1997, when Toyota calculated that there would be an emerging market for drivers who wanted to spew less heat-trapping exhaust into the atmosphere. That year, the huge Japanese car company debuted its first gas-electric hybrid car.

Around the same time that Toyota unveiled the Prius, the media was championing weather as if it were a celebrity. If you missed a daily fore-cast in *USA Today,* with its full-color page dedicated to the weather, you could tune in to the Weather Channel. By the late 1990s, the network was delivering much more than weather updates to commuters worried about rush-hour conditions, or obtuse satellite imagery understood only by weather geeks like Rick and me.

Instead, the Weather Channel remade itself into a man-versus-nature network. The station created what it called an "emotional connection" with its viewership by moving its army of meteorologists out of the TV studio and under the clouds. The worse the weather, seemingly the better the opportunity: Jim Cantore, the station's highest-profile weatherman, has been called the "Angel of Death" because he shows up in cities and towns right before a weather disaster strikes. But as the years went by, Cantore and his network only became more popular. After struggling to survive in the early 1980s, by the year 2001 the Weather Channel appeared in eighty million U.S. households. Today that number is approximately one hundred million.

Twister, meanwhile, had made tornadoes seductive. Some of the savviest minds in entertainment—including Michael Crichton (writer), Steven Spielberg (executive producer), and Jan de Bont (director)—shaped the film's tornadoes for the silver screen, creating snarling, blood-sniffing funnels that only became more intriguing as Helen Hunt and her costar Bill Paxton crept ever closer to the storms' flanks. The movie was nominated for two Oscars in 1996 (for best sound and for visual effects) and grossed nearly $500 million worldwide. But nearly every moviegoer walked out of the theater thinking the same thing: No real-life storm chaser would ever really stick his nose into a tornado.

Sometimes truth is stranger than Hollywood. The 1990s also gave rise to a new type of celebrity known as extreme athletes. Extreme athletes attempted feats that most people thought were insane or impossible. They skydived on miniature surfboards and then performed aerobatics before opening their parachutes. They launched bicycles out of halfpipes, spinning them wildly before coming back to earth. They bungeejumped, snowboarded, and rocketed down paved roads on wheeled luges. By the mid-1990s, ESPN's X Games gave extreme athletes their very own Olympics. Over and over, the gold medal winners' unthinkable performances left national TV audiences wondering, *How can anyone top that?*

As I walked toward CNN's satellite truck on May 4, 1999, tracing a small part of the F5 tornado's unbelievable damage path, I wasn't aware of all the elements coming together to make my upcoming interview a reality. Really, I was thinking only about how nervous I was. In my mind there was a huge difference between my past media experience— forecasting the weather in front of a little video camera for the other students at my west Michigan high school—and talking tornadoes on live national television. I was a meteorology geek—albeit an expressive one—who worried that I'd fumble my words, start sweating buckets, and make a fool out of myself.

But the kid who knocked on that CNN truck door unknowingly hit a nexus of American interests. He was crazy about the weather. He yearned to get close enough to see a tornado's every ripple and shade. And like the over-the-top, gonzo athletes of the day, he pursued his passion with seemingly reckless abandon.

Millions of people were about to meet Reed Timmer, who would accidentally become America's first extreme storm chaser.

• • •

I'd already been through a whole lot in the last twenty-four hours, and now I was wondering exactly how to carry myself in front of a huge television audience. I had no clue. In the CNN "studio," which was nothing more than a television camera, some lights, a couple of chairs, and Moore's destruction serving as a backdrop, I sat alongside Martin Savidge, one of the network's easy-talking top reporters.

CNN rolled short clips of my video in the seconds leading up to my interview with Savidge. Through an earphone that a producer had placed in my ear, I could hear the sound bites. There were our crazed moments under the overpass, with the tornado bearing down on us. I heard myself taunting Mother Nature, begging her to drop a tornado down to earth.

In a reverential tone, Savidge then asked me if it was hard to get as close as we did to the tornado.

I decided that I should sound tough and nonchalant.

"You know, we almost wiped out several times," I said casually. "My life flashed before me."

Savidge asked me if I'd take such crazy chances again.

"It was all worth it to see the wrath of Mother Nature," I replied with a nod. "I mean, Mother Nature was going *medieval* on us."

Seconds later, the bright lights behind the TV camera shut off. But before I had time to digest what Savidge had asked me—or how I'd replied—I was swarmed. NBC's national news wanted an interview. So did a Fox affiliate. And MSNBC. I made the rounds, from one satellite truck to another.

"I've been dreaming about seeing an F5 since I was four years old," I told MSNBC.

"Hard to believe something as beautiful as this could kill so many people," I said to a local Fox affiliate.

Hours after I'd arrived, I was ready to leave that bizarre scene and retreat to my dorm. I thought that was that, my fifteen minutes of fame. But later that day, a call came to my room from Los Angeles. On the phone was a producer for *Leeza*, an NBC daytime talk show hosted by someone named Leeza Gibbons. Could I come to Los Angeles tomorrow to tape a show? I asked the producer if I could call her right back.

Gibbons was a Hollywood reporter, and, to be honest, her show wasn't very substantive. But I decided not to overthink the situation and go for it.

In 1999, I was just a kid who wanted to go to California. I'd never been. I called Rick.

"The producer wants us both," I said. "We'd leave tomorrow morning."

"I'll pass," said Rick.

"Free flights and hotel," I replied. "Picked up by a limo."

"I need to study," said Rick.

I had to prepare for the same exam as him—the final for Physics 2514. We were both pulling A's in the class. I figured that I'd study on the red-eye flights. After all, I'd gotten A's in all my other classes, in part by studying as a passenger on storm chases extending from Arkansas to Texas. I was a hard worker, and I knew how to focus. I could fit everything in.

Gibbons had two other storm chasers as guests alongside me, and they spoke about the act of chasing a tornado in humble tones.

Still not knowing much about the culture of storm chasing, or how I fit into it, I maintained my John Wayne persona. Looking back, I can only ask myself, *What was I thinking?*

"You know, at one point I thought this might be the end," I said during the taping. The comment made one of the other chasers flinch.

At least the limousine tour of Beverly Hills went seamlessly.

. . .

My bags were packed for summer break in Michigan when I received some feedback on my media splash. It was a brief, harsh review of my few moments spent on CNN.

"Reed Timmer should be taken to the woodshed for this," wrote the author, who was someone I didn't know.

I read the note on Rick's computer. A friend had forwarded it to me. The message had made its way around select storm-chasing circles.

I reread it a few times and then asked Rick to read it.

He shook his head. "Doesn't sound like a fan," he said.

I turned away from the monitor. "It's a joke, isn't it?" I asked. "It's sort of funny. I know I had kind of unleashed during the interview and said some crazy things when we were out there chasing. But who would take me so seriously? And who is this guy? Why does he care?"

More people, I'd discover, cared about my appearances than I'd anticipated. Many more people. My brush with fame after the Moore, Oklahoma, F5 tornado launched my first interaction with the storm-chasing community, which I'd discover could be an image-conscious bunch. In fact, I'd find that some of the community's more outspoken members thought there was a specific protocol to storm chasing and rules of conduct. The "woodshed" note was the first indication that I wasn't following protocols or rules.

Like I said before, back in 1999 I didn't know a formalized storm-chasing community existed. I'd been living in Oklahoma for nine months, busy trying to ace my classes and get underneath the Tornado Alley sky at every opportunity. I thought any brotherhood of storm chasers amounted to a group of individuals like me that I occasionally ran into on the roads of the Great Plains, when a bunch of storm chasers would gather on the same shoulder to look at cloud formations before going their separate ways. There were also those few other storm chasers who occasionally landed their video footage on documentaries, news, or the Weather Channel, as well as my fellow chasers at OU.

In time I'd learn that I'd seen only the tip of the storm-chaser iceberg. There was a real community out there, made up of scientists, intellectuals, weather nuts, nature lovers, cutthroat businesspeople, photographers/videographers, tour guides, and thrill seekers. Storm chasers had their own newsletter, heroes, scientific discoveries, picnics, and decades-long history. Among all of those types, the person who recommended that I should be "taken to the woodshed" obviously didn't appreciate my telling CNN that Mother Nature was going, well, *medieval*.

Undoubtedly, the e-mail made me self-conscious and a little embarrassed of my on-screen performances. When I watch some of that tape years later, I'm very aware that my comments could've been perceived as insensitive. Folks had lost their homes, businesses, and in some cases friends and family. Dozens of people died in the May 1999 two-day tornado outbreak.

Still seated in front of Rick's computer, I decided to write a response to the person whom I had offended. I thought about composing an apology—how I'd just begun storm chasing and was still learning my way. Or I could've said that I'd had my moment in the spotlight, and the public would never hear from me again. But I decided that I didn't want to say those things. It was my choice to shadow the F5 so closely. As for my media appearances, they were awkward and somewhat inappropriate. But they weren't mean-spirited. I gave myself a break for being young and new to the adventures of chasing.

I decided to keep the response simple and upbeat.

"I'd like to avoid the woodshed," I typed. "I'd rather be out storm chasing." I sent the e-mail.

Soon I got a response: "Know who you're talking to before reversing the woodshed statement."

The comment didn't make much sense, although I think I got the gist of it: Behave yourself.

I refused to get caught up in trying to act the way others thought I should. As a boy I'd been comfortable as a science nerd, even though the football players at my high school threatened to stuff me into a locker. Listening to different music than other kids had never mattered to me either. In college I'd thought about pledging a fraternity until I realized that my senior "brothers" might tell me what to do. No, thanks. In a nutshell, whether we're talking about exploring the Michigan woods or the Great Plains skies, I'd much rather lead than follow.

So I wasn't going to pour a lot of effort into continuing a dialogue with this particular storm chaser. I pushed Rick's chair away from the desk without typing another response. I wanted my huge passion for the weather to take me wherever it wanted to go.

CHAPTER 3

EXPLORE THE
POSSIBILITIES

. . .

*T*he fall semester of my sophomore year at OU had barely begun when the phone rang. A producer from *Leeza* was on the other end of the line. He asked if I chased hurricanes.

I didn't say no. But not only had I never chased a hurricane, I knew next to nothing about chasing hurricanes. The storms—really, they're storm *systems*—were hundreds of miles wide and often struck coastlines with amazing ferocity. Where do you position yourself? How close can you get? How long does the storm last?

Before I could say much of anything, the producer posed another question: Along with another chaser, would I fly out to the Atlantic seaboard to intercept Hurricane Floyd? The show would pay our expenses. If we captured great video footage, he said, he might dedicate a lengthy program segment to the chase.

The producer had one more question: How soon could we leave? The storm was projected to hit land as early as September 15, which was the very next day.

I had been tracking Floyd's progress on the Weather Channel and the Internet. Meteorologists predicted that when Floyd made landfall in North Carolina, it might be classified as a Category 4 hurricane, meaning it could deliver sustained winds of over 131 miles per hour on what's called the Saffir-Simpson Hurricane Wind Scale. The five-category scale, which was developed in 1969 by a Florida-based structural engineer and wind-damage expert named Herbert Saffir (and was later expanded on by Robert Simpson, a former director of the National Hurricane Center), advanced hurricane assessment because it linked a storm system's force and energy specifically with the level of damage it could generate. Before the scale's existence, hurricanes were only characterized as "major" or "minor."

The Saffir-Simpson scale neatly pinpoints a storm's intensity, from a Category 1 (featuring winds of 74 to 95 miles per hour, which can down power lines or snap large tree branches) to a Category 5 (winds of over 155 miles per hour; will easily destroy frame-built homes). Today emergency agencies, insurers, weather experts, and people who live in hurricane zones all know the Saffir-Simpson scale intimately.

Being the weather nut I am, I was aware that a Category 4 hurricane's winds could wipe out power grids for months, uproot mature trees, and create a "storm surge," or storm-related tide, of eighteen feet—which was plenty big enough to overwhelm many a beachfront property. Hurricane Opal, which had bounced between Category 3 and 4 ratings and had winds gusting as high as 144 miles per hour, struck the western Florida panhandle in 1995. Opal washed out $3 billion worth of highway and beachfront homes and property, and killed nine people.

The TV producer said he was waiting, jolting me out of my racing thoughts. He wanted an answer.

The fact that I knew little about chasing hurricanes made the invitation all the more tempting. I thought I'd be a fool to turn down a Hollywood offer to subsidize my storm-chasing education. So at that point I made the choice that I've consistently made in life: to explore the possibilities. Ever since I was a kid, I'd plunged headlong into crazy adventures or ideas that piqued my interest—like catching live raccoons when I was eleven. Along with one of my sisters, I had the bright idea to dig a hole so that I could safely capture the clawed animals. My sister and I eventually dug a nine-foot hole in the ground and called it a trap. But all we caught was some grief from our mother. The project turned our back-yard into a hazard zone.

"We'll go," I said to the *Leeza* show producer, and then wondered how I'd convince Rick to join me.

At this point, Rick and I lived together, but he wasn't home when I accepted the offer. For our sophomore year, we'd moved into a modest four-bedroom residence in a student section of town with two other guys. It was a decent enough place, but the landlord would one day end up asking me and Rick to vacate the premises. One reason? A wild post-physics-exam celebration where we put holes in the walls and nearly burned down the house with flaming class notes. But that fireworks show was still months away. Another one, involving incredible wind, was just around the corner.

"You have that look in your eye," said Rick, walking through the front door about midday. "I was on the SPC earlier. I didn't see any tornadoes brewing."

"A producer from *Leeza* wants us to intercept Hurricane Floyd," I said, standing in the kitchen.

"What?" Rick said, furrowing his brow. "A hurricane? Reed, that's supposed to make landfall in North Carolina tomorrow," he said, setting down his book bag. "With huge winds."

"We'll rent a car and line up shelter," I said, stretching my arms lazily upward as I spoke, like I had all the logistics nailed down. I wasn't wor-ried. I was excited. "And yes, the storm will be huge. That's why we're going," I added. "The show will pay for everything."

I expected Rick to dig in his heels. The trip would be a haul. A four-hour flight to Charlotte, followed by a two hundred-mile drive east to Wilmington. Then we'd have to find a place to stay and decide how to catch the best moments of the hurricane on film. Plus we were barely into the school year, and Rick was already complaining about all the math and science woven into our new meteorology courses. I thought he'd object, saying school was difficult enough without missing days' worth of classes to see Floyd.

In retrospect, the journey seemed like a crazy, modern-meteorology *Adventures of Huckleberry Finn* redux. Which nowadays makes me all the more surprised that I successfully sold the trip to Rick.

"The conditions will be incredible," I said. "The storm will be explosive." Then I crossed my arms. "Why did you leave home to come to school if not to take chances? Don't you want to experience this?"

Rick slowly nodded. "Let's do it," he said. "It'll be an adventure."

• • •

North Carolinians were particularly worried about Floyd. It was following closely on the heels of Hurricane Dennis, a weaker storm system that nonetheless had soaked the state with heavy rains only weeks earlier. Floyd had the potential to slam the coastline with high winds and then drench North Carolina again.

Not that there's such a thing as a waterless hurricane. Hurricanes are swirling storms that develop and gather strength exclusively over oceans, and they go by different names in different parts of the world: They're typhoons in the western North Pacific; tropical cyclones in the Indian Ocean and western South Pacific; and hurricanes in the North Atlantic, the Caribbean Sea, the Gulf of Mexico, and the eastern North Pacific where it borders the United States. The storm systems mostly develop during the summer and fall, which occur at opposite times of year in the earth's two hemispheres. The height of hurricane season in North America is generally August and September, although it officially runs from June 1 to November 30.

Hurricanes are just like tornadoes in that they're rotating storms fueled by the ascension of warm, moist air. But hurricanes receive a lot

of their fuel from warm oceans instead of pipelines of warm shearing air, like the low-level jet stream that helps spark tornadoes in the Great Plains.

Hurricanes often start as a cluster of thunderstorms at sea called "tropical disturbances" that are blown together around low-pressure areas (wind occurs when air molecules are naturally pushed from high-pressure areas, where the density of molecules is great, toward low-density, low-pressure areas).

You know the thunderstorm drill: Hot air is less dense than cold and therefore rises. This air, which carries vapors sourced from the warm (specifically, 80 degrees Fahrenheit or greater) ocean waters below, cools as it rises higher into the atmosphere, and via condensation the vapor turns to droplets that organize into towering cumulonimbus clouds, producing heavy, wind-driven rain. Meanwhile that process of condensation itself releases heat, which generates more upward lift in the thunderstorms. More upward lift means the storm pulls even more warm ocean vapor off the water's surface. As long as they're positioned over warm ocean water, the storms can continue to fuel themselves even while dumping as much as ten inches of rain per hour.

As these storms get stronger and release more heat, they in turn act to intensify the initial low-pressure area that they all congeal around. The bases of these strengthening storms also behave like mini-vacuums, sucking up increasing amounts of heat and moisture from the ocean. These dynamics attract wind, too. As the low-pressure area inside the cluster of storms continues to strengthen, fierce winds blow toward its center from all directions.

The winds, however, don't hit the cluster of thunderstorms straight on. They bend, or rather the earth rotates under them as they blow, which in the northern hemisphere means that the winds, for all intents and purposes, bend right (in the southern hemisphere they bend left; winds directly over the equator don't bend at all). The faster the winds blow the more they are bent by the Earth's rotation. This curvature is called the Coriolis force (named after the nineteenth-century French scientist Gustave-Gaspard Coriolis), and it helps to initiate the rotation of the storms in a counterclockwise motion—sort of like what happens if you spin a playground merry-go-round to the right.

But conditions for a hurricane aren't fully ripe yet. Remember the low pressure area at the center of the cluster of storms that brought them together in the first place? As the winds get closer to this low-pressure center they blow faster, and the intensifying Coriolis force bends them farther to the right. But at the same time, the strengthening low-pressure area actually pulls the right-moving winds back to the left. That is, the low-pressure area pulls the incoming winds in the other direction, although not enough to do anything other than force the winds to hug the cluster of rotating thunderstorms and encourage their counterclock-wise circulation. The low-pressure area in the middle of the storm remains calm and, if conditions are perfect, can develop into a cloud-free area that resembles a doughnut hole. It's called the eye.

If an eye forms at the center of the now rapidly rotating cluster storms, a hurricane has likely formed, too.

However, before this storm system can be called a hurricane, it has to exceed lesser classifications for "cyclonic" storms that generally form in the tropics: A tropical depression has maximum wind speeds of thirty-eight miles per hour, and a tropical storm has wind speeds of thirty-nine to seventy-three miles per hour.

A hurricane's wind speeds exceed seventy-four miles per hour, and on September 14, when Rick and I arrived in North Carolina late in the night, Hurricane Floyd had already reached the Bahamas and was approaching Category 5 status on the Saffir-Simpson scale. It had a text-book cloud-free eye. Its winds were howling at nearly 156 miles per hour.

All over the Charlotte airport, television monitors were broadcasting news of the storm. Floyd was approximately four hundred miles wide, or about 25 percent bigger than the average hurricane (although hurricane size fluctuates greatly). It was the fourth hurricane spawned that season—a season that, before it was over, would notch a record five Category 4 hurricanes. After the 1999 season concluded, the phenomenon would move scientists to start aggressively asking if there might be any connection between global warming and the occurrence or intensification of hurricanes. When the same metric was achieved six years later (in 2005, the year Hurricane Katrina struck), the questions and conversations linking severe weather and global warming only became louder.

But as we eyed the glass TV screens and waited for our luggage to arrive, Rick and I were consumed with the storm at hand. The monitors kept showing satellite images, which made Hurricane Floyd look like a giant, counterclockwise-moving buzz saw. And we were headed straight for it.

. . .

I tried to downplay our inauspicious start.

"No luck, but it's not the end of the world. We'll figure out something," I said to Rick after going from one rental-car kiosk to the next. Rick had been waiting for me on an airport bench. Neither of us was twenty-five years old, which meant we were too young to rent a car. We hadn't thought that through before traveling, although to be fair, we'd only had a couple hours to prepare for the trip and make our flight.

Welcome to seat-of-the-pants hurricane chasing.

In the wee hours of the morning, we finally found a cab to take us the two hundred miles toward Wilmington and the state's eastern seaboard. The journey was anxiety inducing and expensive. My continuous promises to give the cabbie a big tip weren't enough to keep him from becoming visibly twitchy the whole way down Interstate 74. We were the only car headed east, and the highway in the other direction was wall-to-wall traffic. A gigantic, mandatory coastline evacuation was forcing a wave of humanity to travel west.

"Stop here," I said to the driver in front of a small Wilmington hotel with a parking lot full of cars. I paid him three hundred dollars. Inside the hotel, the lobby was brimming with folks looking for somewhere to ride out the storm.

Rick dozed off in a lobby chair and left me to secure a room. I stood in a long line leading to the front desk and struck up a conversation with a very nice, tall African-American man standing in front of me. Within a few minutes I got out of the huge line to tell Rick the great news.

"I found us the perfect place to watch the storm," I said, my loud voice waking him. I gently jostled his shoulder to make sure his eyes stayed open. "We'll get maximum wind gusts. There won't be a lot of land to get in the way."

Rick blinked slowly. His brown eyes were bloodshot.

"We're not staying in the hotel?" he said, coming to and looking confused.

We walked back over to the long line of people waiting to check in. I made introductions.

"Rick, this is Ernest. Ernest, Rick," I said.

They shook hands.

"Rick, I told Ernest about our videotaping and how there might be a television show made out of our filming of Hurricane Floyd.

"Ernest offered to let us stay in his home near the water to ride out the storm," I added. "We can film and look after Ernest's house at the same time."

The bags under Rick's eyes scrunched up as he glared at me.

"It's safe, right, Ernest?" I said to him.

"You should be okay," he said slowly, scratching his head. "The place is raised off the ground. There's plenty of food. Go hungry at my house and there's something wrong with you."

Rick's shoulders slumped. He looked exhausted and resigned, and said nothing. He'd seen this kind of manic energy from me before. I was

just as giddy when we were en route to intercepting the F5 Moore, Oklahoma, tornado. Now, just months later, Rick was following me into the teeth of another huge storm.

Ernest lived in a single-wide trailer, in a stark mobile-home park that was situated only a mile or so from the coast. It was also a mandatory evacuation zone. When we arrived in his pickup truck, the place looked deserted save for Ernest's wife and son, who were packing old suitcases and watching the news on a small television. The local anchorman was warning people in trailer parks to evacuate. Ernest showed us around. The trailer home was tidy. There were a few family pictures on the walls and a plastic table in front of a worn, soft-cushioned couch. The refrigerator was bare except for bologna, milk, and some old mustard.

Within minutes, Ernest's family piled into their truck to retreat to the hotel.

"I'll come back for you tomorrow. Soon as I can," he said, getting situated in the driver's seat. "Right after the storm passes."

Rick and I watched Ernest pull away. The day's light began to fade. Strong gusts from the outer bands of the hurricane's circling winds were arriving out of the north, which likely meant we wouldn't experience Floyd's biggest punch.

Hurricanes generally blow stronger on one side than the other, courtesy of the speed of the storm's movement. In other words, if the eye of a make-believe hurricane featuring hundred-mile-per-hour rotating winds moves toward the beach at a speed of twenty miles per hour, the side of the storm in line with the twenty-mile-per-hour forward motion (generally the hurricane's right side, relative to the direction that it's traveling) would deliver hundred-and-twenty-mile-per-hour winds; meanwhile the opposite side would deliver eighty-mile-per-hour winds. Hurricane Floyd wasn't make-believe, and it ultimately would reach landfall riding on a twenty-four-mile-per-hour current headed northeast. One side of the hurricane, therefore, would be blowing forty-eight miles per hour harder than the other. Because we were likely on the storm's left side relative to its direction of travel, we'd be in *somewhat* calmer conditions.

There would still be plenty of action. I thought Rick and I had a great chance of capturing impressive video footage. Being so close to the coast and its warm Gulf Stream water, I knew that Floyd could enjoy plenty of ocean-based fuel right up to its landfall. And Rick and I had the equivalent of front-row seats on the meteorological roller coaster.

But as the winds picked up in the lonesome trailer park, there was a voice sounding off inside my head. Were we storm chasers or sitting ducks? Excited as I was, I hadn't totally forgotten about the terror and sorrow associated with the F5 tornado we'd narrowly escaped under that overpass. I'd vowed never to put my friends or myself in such a dangerous situation again, and yet here I was, chasing a Category 4 hurricane on a whim, in a mobile home, dragging Rick along with me. Ever since we'd arrived at the trailer, he'd gone nearly silent. I think he was more than tired. I think he was mad, and scared too. I also felt plenty of fear, but for me the fear always ran neck and neck with excitement. Nonetheless, the voice kept asking me if this was all really worth risking our lives.

I didn't have a solid answer. I didn't yet know what really compelled me to chase down storms. I didn't know when I should chase. Or when I shouldn't.

In my hasty decision to become a hurricane chaser, I didn't take time to listen to reason. I'd later learn that one of the first rules of hurricane chasing is to have an exit plan. Rick and I didn't have that exit plan. We didn't have transportation. We didn't have cell phones (we didn't even own them) or even a portable weather radio. We were truly on our own.

. . .

The North Carolina sky rapidly filled with the low-lying, vaguely feathery, dark stratus clouds that are the ominous calling card of many hurricanes. These clouds may frequently show a nearly uniform and featureless base,

but because they move so rapidly you can definitely tell that something is going on up there. It's just that you can't see the hurricane's structure, or the occasional tornado that can drop down when a hurricane's edge reaches land, and the ragged portions of the storm system's outer rotating winds generate enough friction with the ground to create a funnel.

The North Carolina air was extremely humid, and the strong wind tasted salty, courtesy of the ocean water being sucked up by Floyd. Temperatures hovered around the seventies. Rick and I took some video of the nearby mature live oak trees that were swaying dramatically, and our clothes were quickly soaked through. Soon we went inside.

We ate a few slices of bologna and watched Ernest's tiny television. A weather update appeared, and Rick adjusted the rabbit-ears antenna to minimize the snow on the screen.

The newscaster announced that Floyd could reach the North Carolina shore as a Category 4 hurricane. Rick finally spoke up.

"Sustained winds exceeding a hundred and thirty-one miles per hour," he said, staring blankly out the window, reciting Saffir-Simpson scale stats from memory. Rick finished eating and lit a cigarette. He took a long, anxious drag.

"You know that most mobile homes are destroyed by a Category 4," he said with a resigned calm. "Even if this place makes it through the wind, it could be shredded by debris."

I mumbled something about the storm probably losing steam.

Rick just stared at me.

"I'm sure we'll be fine," I said. "The newscasters always give the worst possible scenarios."

Our hopes of capturing great video, however, were doomed. The TV meteorologists were now consistently predicting that the storm would make landfall in the middle of the night. Shooting good footage would be all but impossible in the dark, and just offering the producers of *Leeza* a good story probably wouldn't fly. It had been my video, and not my interviewing skills, that had landed me media coverage after the F5 tore through Oklahoma. But all of the TV stuff was secondary to me anyway. No matter what, I'd still get to face down Hurricane Floyd.

"I'm lying down," said Rick. He stood up from the small kitchen table and walked across the dimly lit trailer to one of the beds. Rick put out his cigarette and pulled a thin, narrow mattress off a box spring. He inched the mattress over to the couch. Then he lay down on the couch and pulled the flimsy mattress over him like a blanket.

"What are you doing?" I asked.

"At least it's something," he said. "We're totally screwed if the walls fall in."

"What will you do under there?" I said, looking at the lumpy mattress with Rick underneath it.

"I'm exhausted, Reed," he said. "I'm going to sleep."

Sleep? My mind raced at night when I *wasn't* sitting in a single-wide trailer in an abandoned mobile-home park that was in the path of a major hurricane. As a child I was, as I've said, always super-energized. At night my engine kept running, too, and I'd had a hard time going to sleep ever since I was a baby. At one point my mom took me to the pediatrician and asked him why I didn't rest more than six hours a day. The doctor said not to worry, that my brain was developing faster than my body. There was no way to know if that's really true, but the next thing the doctor said my mother would certainly agree with: Your kid is wired differently.

About ten P.M. the power cut out in the single wide. Without the noise of the television, the wind's roar was more pronounced. Rain now dumped on the weak trailer's windows and roof, sounding more like it was pouring out of a bucket than falling in a series of drops.

I finally shimmied under a mattress, too, but I doubted that I would fall asleep. For a while I did what I never do, which is to say I caught my breath. I reflected on the situation. Despite the raging conditions outside, and the dangers Rick and I faced, I marveled at the science occurring above me—the elegant organization of the spiraled rain bands ripping around the eye of the storm. I considered how these amazing but rare occurrences in nature have such extraordinary impacts on huge populations of people. And then, finally, I fell into a fitful sleep.

Hurricane Floyd hit the North Carolina shore about two thirty A.M., and it knocked hard on the trailer door. For better or worse, Rick and I were positioned directly under the storm's eyewall, which is the dense wall of thunderstorms encircling the eye, and the fiercest part of the storm. The eyewall is where all of the winds blowing toward the hurricane converge and where incredible amounts of air travel straight upward, which generates more energy inside the eyewall's thunderstorms that in turn creates more rain, heat, and wind.

Down on the ground, the hurricane was no longer buffeting Ernest's single-wide trailer. It was squeezing it. I came to, and the rain sounded pressurized, like it was shooting out of a fire hose and etching the trailer's flimsy paneling. The wind sounded like a freight train, except that it occasionally surged like no freight train ever could. Ernest's home shifted back and forth considerably in the gusts, and I thought it was only a matter of time before the hurricane pried its fingers underneath the whole structure and flipped us over. There was little relief even when the wind backed off. The house still shuddered, and the water in Ernest's aquarium moved around. Plus I knew it was only a matter of time before the howling began anew.

"Rick! Rick! Are you awake?" I yelled from underneath my mattress. I was no longer enjoying myself.

"What's going on?" Rick said groggily. I could barely hear him. Then he came to, near me somewhere. The mobile home was pitch-black. "Are you okay?"

"This has to be the full force of the storm," I said in a raised voice. "What else could it be?"

Suddenly glass shattered loudly in the back of the single-wide. Did the wind break the window? Debris? I couldn't see anything and didn't want to get up to look. What if I got struck by a stray tree limb? I heard a seemingly endless number of tree branches outside generate loud snaps as they broke off of trunks. I clung to the mattress and felt the floor vibrate underneath me. The roof groaned.

"Is it going to peel off?" Rick said from underneath his mattress in a big, terrified voice. "Please, hold together!"

Along with blowing rain, warm, moist air streamed in through the trailer's broken window, and soon the mattress above me and the carpeted floor beneath me had the unmistakable feel of clammy sponges. The roof didn't give way, but Rick and I were dripping wet nonetheless.

Cowering under the mattresses, we were silent, buzzing with pure adrenaline for hours. We listened to the storm rage around us. Only when the wind began to subside did we believe that the hurricane might be on its way. Somehow we dozed, and when Rick and I finally came to around dawn, the storm had passed. Or was it just the calm before the rest of the storm?

"Are we in the eye?" said Rick, rising stiffly and looking out one of the mobile home's few intact windows.

There was blue sky above us. But the unfathomably calm eye of a hurricane can be up to forty miles wide, and since hurricanes might move at only twenty miles per hour, unsuspecting victims can be lulled into thinking that the worst is over for hours. What they don't know is that you can be sitting in the eye of the storm, when—boom!—winds can almost instantaneously elevate from breezes to over 130 miles per hour.

Rick's soaked black T-shirt stuck to his chest. His brown hair pressed against his scalp. Meanwhile the wet baseball cap that I'd worn all night was causing a blister to rise on my forehead.

Rick and I looked around. Ernest's house was a disaster. There was broken glass everywhere, and papers and other items were strewn about.

Pictures had fallen off the walls, and enough leaves were inside to make one think that someone had used a leaf blower to force them *into* the trailer. Which isn't too far from the truth. Surfaces felt wet to the touch. But the walls were still vertical. We ventured outside.

Other mobile homes were much worse off. One trailer's roof was gone, and the remaining house looked like a two-bedroom convertible. Another home's walls had cratered. Lots of trees had fallen, including one that shaved off the kitchen of someone's double-wide.

The hurricane had left huge puddles and forced down electrical wires throughout the trailer park. Rick and I retreated to Ernest's trailer and ate bologna for breakfast. We dozed off again, too, and while the storm never reappeared, Ernest finally did, pulling up in his truck that afternoon.

"You guys made it!" he said with a gleeful chuckle. "The house! It is still here!"

"Some night, Ernest," I said, at a loss to say much. "I felt like it would never end."

Ernest looked around his place and seemed unconcerned by the chaos.

"Do you know anything about the hurricane?" he said.

We said that we didn't.

He told us what happened. Before reaching land, Floyd had run into a patch of dry air that caused the eye to lose its form. Even a temporarily misshapen eye can cause a spinning hurricane to go off-kilter and trigger a weakening of the entire storm system. That happened with Floyd.

The hiccup in the weather machinery might have saved our lives: Hurricane Floyd reached land as a Category 2 hurricane, with sustained winds measuring up to 110 miles per hour. Such wind speeds are still enormously forceful. But they were moderate enough that Ernest's home—and its house sitters—survived.

Ernest gave us a brief tour of the area. The storm surge, which is the wall of water that builds as a hurricane sweeps across the ocean surface, was ten feet high, and that caused considerable damage to the coastline. We also saw lots of wind damage, and some areas were under two or three feet of water.

But the worst damage was to come after Rick and I retreated home a day later. Like most hurricanes, Floyd was sapped of its power after reaching land and losing its warm-water energy source. Yet as it moved northward through the state, Floyd was absorbed by a low-pressure trough that was already cruising across the northeastern United States. The trough drew all the moisture out of the dying hurricane and caused incredible amounts of rain to pour down. Between hurricanes Floyd and Dennis, parts of the Carolinas received about forty inches of rain within a couple of weeks' time. The deluge caused catastrophic flooding. The storm caused an estimated $6 billion in damages. Nearly sixty deaths were attributed to Floyd's floods.

In the wake of the disaster, North Carolina took unprecedented steps to prevent such devastation from occurring again. The state allocated tens of millions of dollars to comprehensively map its floodplains. It secured hundreds of millions of disaster dollars to buy out homeowners and farmers living in low-lying areas and encouraged them to get to higher land. Sure, the damage was characterized as freakish, a "five-hundred-year flood." Nonetheless, the hope was that North Carolina would literally lift its metaphoric pant legs out of the water and never lose another 4,100 homes to such a deluge again.

Rick and I were lucky to escape North Carolina without so much as a snapped shoelace. But Floyd had its lasting effects on us.

"I'm not sure that I'm up for more of that kind of thing," Rick announced to me soon after we returned from North Carolina. We were sitting around the kitchen table at our place in Norman. "Between the F5 and Floyd?" he added. "I've seen a lot."

"They don't all have to be that intense. It was a learning experience,"

I said. "Next time we'll be prepared. Bring more supplies, have an exit strategy. We'll know to do it differently."

Years later I would chase a devastating hurricane again, and I would do it much differently. I'd pack enormous amounts of food and drinking water. I'd bring waterproof clothing, a chain saw, and other survival equipment. Basically, I'd prepare for Armageddon, and be glad I did.

Floyd, however, still made me smile. I was terrified by that beastly storm, but I was energized by it too. I'm not just talking about the adrenaline rush, either, although the pure excitement of the chase unquestionably held tremendous appeal for me. There was something more, something that I felt in that brief respite when I first pulled the mattress over my head in Ernest's single-wide: contentment. Even though Rick and I were in a tiny trailer, and we were soaked, exhausted, and sometimes terrified, I was still right where I wanted to be. Storm chasing fed me in a way that my classes, going to OU football games, and great friends and family did not. My friendship with Rick didn't wash away with Floyd. But things were different after that trip. He would never chase truly epic storms again.

My smile only grew at that kitchen table as I thought about the past two days.

Rick smiled too.

"I know that look," he said.

"What?" I asked, shrugging my shoulders. "What are you talking about?"

"I can appreciate your passion," he said. "For me, that was a once-in-a-lifetime experience."

"I'd head out for another one tomorrow," I replied.

• • •

Indeed, the experience of Hurricane Floyd spoke to me. Over the next couple of years, my priorities began to shift. I became less interested in shooting hoops with my friends and drinking beers with my house-mates, and increasingly drawn to meteorology and storm chasing. I embarked upon many outrageous or long-shot weather-related adventures. My appetite for storms had nothing to do with landing in front of the microphones of *Leeza* or CNN, although I always brought along a video camera. I sought out severe weather in Tornado Alley—and well beyond—because for many reasons the sky brought me incredible satisfaction. It was science, adventure, and freedom all rolled into one.

One night when I was back at my mom's house in Michigan on summer break, my old friend Chris Chittick called, asking if I wanted to hang out.

I had a better idea.

"Want to storm-chase?" I replied.

The SPC had issued a high-risk convective outlook for severe weather over a good part of Nebraska, which meant the chances of storms occurring in the area were quite good. Such sobering forecasts came infrequently.

It didn't matter to me that there was a gigantic hurdle for both of us: We were about a thirteen-hour drive from where I believed that the supercell thunderstorms—those super-tall cloud structures with rising and rotating winds in their guts—would develop. Plus, Chris and I had to be back to Michigan in thirty hours for our summer maintenance jobs at a local Grand Rapids golf club. Our boss was ridiculously strict.

But Chris, forever wearing his happy-go-lucky smile, was soon at the front door of my mom's house. We loaded up my little sedan, which, like most of the cars I've ever owned, resembled my college dorm room: It was a mess, and not just the interior, either. The shock absorbers were shot, the muffler was rotten, and the engine had already logged 170,000 miles. But cars, like my bedrooms, were never priorities for me. Talking tornadoes all day in the Map Room, for instance, seemed much more attractive than getting an oil change.

On the long trip to Nebraska, at least the car delivered. Chris and I never let up on the gas, taking turns at the car's steering wheel and living on 7-Eleven hot dogs, fast-food French fries, Coke, and Mountain Dew for the next thirty hours. We arrived in Kearney, Nebraska, in the early afternoon and drove up and down country roads for a while. But we only saw cloudless skies—in *chaser-ese*, it was one of those regretful "blue-sky busts." What's known as the "cap"—a layer of warm, stabilizing air that regularly sets up approximately five thousand feet into the atmosphere—wouldn't break apart the way that it generally must for warm, moist air to sufficiently rise and create thunderstorms. Chris and I turned around, drove all night, and returned to Michigan just in time to start work the next morning.

Not long afterward, Chris embarked on another road trip on my behalf, although this time he didn't think storm chasing would be involved. It was.

In October 2000, Chris drove from Michigan with three buddies to join me for a big OU football game. Oklahoma's Sooners were facing their rival Nebraska Cornhuskers. That year the Cornhuskers were ranked number one in the nation in college football. Oklahoma was ranked number three.

The night before the game, I camped out in a line in front of the stadium to get great seats. I'd painted my body *and* my car Sooner crimson, or at least something close. The game was incredible: OU came back from 14 points down in the first quarter to crush the Cornhuskers, 31–14. Afterward was mayhem: students hugging and dancing all over the field and pulling down the stadium goalposts. Chris was psyched to party the night away. I had somewhere else to be.

"What?" said Chris, beer in hand, as he leaned over to hear me above the mayhem going on all around us on the field.

"I said, do you want to come storm chasing with me?" I yelled into his ear.

He looked around at all the college kids celebrating. Norman would go wild that night.

"Now?" Chris asked.

Upon hearing promising reports of high-level wind shear in the southwest (wind shear is, again, what helps rising, rotating winds form inside a supercell), that same afternoon I left to storm-chase in the Texas panhandle. I hoped that Chris wasn't offended—my leaving had nothing to do with him. *I'd just rather chase than celebrate,* I thought while looking at Chris wave good-bye to me through my car's rearview mirror.

Indeed, all the stuff of college—the fraternity parties, eating nachos at the Mont, intramural basketball games (the name of my team, of course, was the Weather Channel)—also began to lose some of its luster as I hit the books hard. It felt better to study, to practically climb into the clouds and understand them. Whatever I was missing in the social scene, I came to think, could be experienced another time.

I was doing pretty well then, studying until the wee hours in my house or in a basement lounge on campus. I'd grind through texts filled with scientific esoterica like Newtonian particle mechanics and the dynamics of rotating planets, strangely enjoying every minute. Meanwhile, my class—the School of Meteorology's class of 2002—seemingly shrank each semester. Statistically, I believe that only about 25 percent of OU freshmen entering the school graduate in four years with a meteorology degree. I swore we were losing twenty or so kids per semester, and the complaints from those who dropped out were often the same: too much math, too much science, too much work.

. . .

During the second semester of my junior year, OU lost me too. But only temporarily.

I'd often wondered what the weather was like—what life was like— in other parts of the world. I'd never been out of the country but was

eager for a chance. In the spring of 2001 I became only one of two exchange students from OU's School of Meteorology to successfully apply to Britain's University of Reading, which is forty miles west of London in southern England. I'd spend the first seven months of 2001 studying in the UK.

When it comes to meteorology studies, the University of Reading is Europe's top school. The professors there have performed leading work in what's called synoptic scale meteorology, or atmospheric conditions spanning many hundreds if not thousands of miles. It was a much broader look at weather—say, conditions that would affect all of Europe and beyond—than what I was used to in Oklahoma. OU focused on mesoscale meteorology, which is the study of smaller-scale weather systems, or those ranging from a few to a few hundred miles.

The semester abroad opened my eyes to weather away from the United States, and not just the Scotland fog. I became curious about severe weather occurring all over the world: Australian dust storms, Indian monsoons, and Argentinean tornadoes. I was taught that climate conditions from one pole to the other could perhaps tell me something about the state of the planet. I vowed that someday I'd spend more time researching weather around the globe by experiencing it firsthand.

The semester abroad also opened my eyes to what I was missing back home. Just so you know, England's tornadoes are crappy little funnels wrapped in rain.

One day while I was in England I called Rick to catch up. He told me that there was a supercell thunderstorm suspended right above our house in Norman. I missed that spectacle more than just about anything else.

• • •

When I think about it, it's no accident that I'm drawn to something that looks like a funnel. The classic tornado shape is a metaphor for my upbringing. The wide part of the funnel represents the array of hobbies and interests that I pursued as a child. And the narrow part—the tornado-type spout at the bottom—says a lot about the way I pursued the ones I focused on: with incredible—you might call it alien—amounts of focus. Before I left home for college, I had become a very intense teenager. And I was ready to obsess over just one thing.

I like to remind my family that I was born in Grand Rapids, Michigan, during an outbreak of severe weather. It was a snowy March night in 1980, and I came into the world at 11:17 P.M. That's the time when evening TV news programs train their cameras on the meteorologists.

I was curious about weather from an early age. Western Michigan has lots of thunderstorms and lightning, and severe weather quickly intrigued me. Why did the sky make those cool exploding noises and sometimes light up at night? When I was four, my dad was pulling my older sister, Cortney, and me down the sidewalk in a little wagon when the tornado sirens sounded. My mom ushered us, along with my little sister, Dayna, down to the basement. I could hardly wait for the tornado to come our way. Unfortunately (to my young mind, anyway), the warning was a false alarm.

But that's the last time I can remember my mother, who was the driving force in my childhood after my parents divorced in 1991, ever wanting the three Timmer children to sit still. My mom comes from a long line of go-getters—her father (a mechanical engineer) flew bomber missions during World War II, her great-grandfather homesteaded in Nebraska, and somewhere in the family lineage a relative fought in the American Revolution. My mom's chosen field is science, and she studied biology, environmental science, and geology in college, has a master's degree (as do her six siblings), and still teaches middle school science in Ada, the semirural suburb southeast of Grand Rapids where I grew up. My mom wanted her children to achieve in life, too.

Our house didn't have video games. Instead, the family entertain-

ment center was a wooded area outside our back door, which was crawling with insects and small reptiles. Every day, year-round, my mom would send us outside, and my sisters and I would spend hours in those woods. I frequently had a butterfly net in one hand and a clear, perforated, plastic case to carry my captured prey in the other. The insects intrigued me. Of course I thought they were cool to look at. I also liked that they were unpredictable and hard to find. Spotting an insect didn't mean I could catch it. I had to learn to hunt it down.

I was only six or seven when my mother handed me my first bug book, and when I quickly read it cover to cover, she bought me another, and then another. Even though I was little, and often restless, I could focus my attention on those books. Nobody in my family knows exactly where the trait came from—even my mom doesn't have my intensity. But she was still thrilled to feed my desire to learn.

"We'll get you every book ever written on the subject," she'd say, and the next thing I knew I'd have an Audubon field guide and three others to go with it.

After a while, the books weren't enough. I began to draw bugs, and not just wings, legs, and a body. I drew all the parts, and labeled them too: head, thorax, abdomen, and so on. When that didn't satisfy me anymore I caught the bugs and dutifully mounted them in glass cases so that I could admire their characteristics for years to come.

I became just as absorbed in the chases. Like my mom, who herself loved to garden in the backyard when she wasn't cooking or teaching, I was graced with plenty of energy. I'd drag Dayna, who was four years younger than me, on nature walks that went on for miles. Sometimes I'd forget to stop. I wasn't trying to wear my little sister out—we were very close, as she was a science nut too. (Today Dayna is a nuclear pharmacist; she works with select radioactive materials that are used in medicines.) I was just focused on the mission. I loved feeling the rush of adrenaline when I climbed high into the trees to reach tent-caterpillar nests and cicadas, and when I walked through tall grass to snatch up slithering snakes with my bare hands.

"You worry me sick," my mother would say upon our return from adventuring in the dark. She'd be standing in the backyard with her hands on her hips and look at the snake slithering around in my plastic case. "You'll pick up anything."

I mostly tolerated school. The work itself was okay, although I never quite understood why I was always being told what to do: I was going to read whether or not someone stood over me. But being a bookworm had its downsides, and I was teased a lot. I was the classic preoccupied geek— oversize glasses, small for my age, and dominant in science class—but that was okay with me.

Indeed, the Science Olympiad was my event and what I loved most about school. The Science Olympiad is a national network of contests that tests the science-oriented knowledge of individual students as well as middle and high school teams at regional, state, and national events. The challenges were perfect for an intense kid like me, because while I liked playing sports I wasn't big or physical enough to make headway on the school squads. Some kids had dads who taught them to play baseball, but my dad and mom had endured an acrimonious separation, and my sisters and I wouldn't really connect with my father until we were adults. Instead I had a mom who coached me in science tournaments.

The Science Olympiad gave me another opportunity to wield my science obsession. I competed in multiple subjects, including chemistry and biology, and amassed dozens of medals and awards.

My top year was 1996. I decided to become a tree expert, stuffing my head during all-night cram sessions with obscure knowledge about American Sycamores, Slippery Elms, and live oaks. Even my Science Olympiad buddies thought I was nuts—a high schooler pulling all-nighters to remember a bunch of trees? But I loved the material, as well as challenging

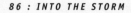

myself to see how much I could absorb. That year I became a Science Olympiad national champion in tree identification, and also used my deep knowledge of science to help earn myself Eagle Scout honors as a Boy Scout. I practiced the oboe daily, too. Yeah, pretty cool, right? Crazy, too.

And then there was the weather.

As I have said, it had always intrigued me. I ran outside every time thunder roared, lightning struck, or snow began to fall, and my older sister, Cortney, and I were addicted to the Weather Channel, which was the one television station our mom consistently let us watch. We'd picked our favorite meteorologists and gained an understanding of Doppler radar (a giant, weather-predicting antenna that sends out radio waves, which bounce back differently depending on the conditions that reflect them). But even into my high school years, I didn't really obsess over the weather the way I did the science stuff. It was too hard to track—weather changed every day, sometimes each hour. It couldn't be preserved behind glass for future study.

Then one early winter day in my senior year of high school, a huge storm rolled into western Michigan—rain, hail, and fierce winds. I had an idea. I was in the house, preparing to go outside, when I spotted the old family video camera. It was a dinosaur device that didn't get a lot of use. I grabbed it after putting on my jacket and went into our front yard.

I recorded everything I saw—forty-five-mile-per-hour winds howling through the trees, black clouds surging across the sky, and rain and hail pummeling the roof of our house.

I'm sure if someone had been watching me they would've shaken their head. Videotaping a downpour? What was that kid doing? After a while the camera stopped working.

I didn't travel very far, but I consider this my first storm chase.

From that point on, weather grabbed more and more of my attention. I loved bugs and trees, but the weather was more visceral and chaotic. It had more energy than I did.

Cortney and I wrote the Weather Channel nonstop until we received an invitation for our family to tour the network's Atlanta, Georgia, headquarters. I sent a note to Tim Marshall, who back then was about the only storm chaser I'd heard of, because his videos appeared on the Weather Channel. I asked him for tricks of the trade. Weather even helped me become more popular in high school: I began to deliver daily forecasts on the intraschool TV network. I swapped glasses for contact lenses and wore Hawaiian shirts in front of the camera.

During my senior year I also got my first car, which was an old clunker, of course. I remember driving it to go on dates, play basketball with my friends, and commute to my internship at the National Weather Service's Grand Rapids office, where I recorded regional weather observations for southwest Lower Michigan.

But the best part about having my own car was that I could storm-chase, albeit only a little bit like *tornado* chaser Tim Marshall. During late 1997 and early 1998, I'd often tell my mom that I would be back in a while and then drive twenty miles south. I had no idea what I was doing. Still, I wanted to intercept a storm.

Western Michigan often experiences lake-effect snowstorms. Lake-effect snow can fall wherever cold air travels across relatively warm bodies of water, which are exactly the conditions that can be found during the late fall and early winter in the Great Lakes region. From approximately November to January, the Great Lakes haven't yet frozen, but cold Arctic air has begun to surge south and east across the United States.

I'd drive south and watch the storms roll in. The frigid wind would blow out of the west over Lake Michigan, where the lowest layers of air warm up while sweeping moisture off the lake. Then the heated air would begin to rise and cool, and the added moisture inside of that air would condense, which caused the rapid formation of storm clouds.

The snowstorms can begin over Lake Michigan, but they intensify when they slow down after reaching the lake's eastern shore. That's when

convergence—or the phenomenon of the clouds literally piling up—occurred. I'd watch in awe as the skies became a snowmaking machine. Everything—bushes, sidewalks, parked cars—would turn as white as if being smeared by a giant paint roller. Traffic would grind to a halt. Lake-effect snowstorms can dump an intense five inches or more of snow per hour. That's about as hard as snow comes down in any type of storm.

At first I convinced high school pals to join me in making the trip to see lake-effect storms. But they soon came to their senses. The driving conditions were absolutely treacherous. And I was quickly becoming too obsessed ever to retreat from a great storm.

I was in my *element*. I didn't care about what my friends thought or the traffic jams that were caused. That snow was so beautiful and such a meteorological miracle. It would fall so fast, not only muffling every sound outside but also quieting my mind, focusing my thoughts.

Years later, when my mom found out about those chases she'd say what she now frequently says about my storm chasing: "I don't want to hear all the details, Reed. I'd worry more than I already do."

But to my mind, the details of those early chases were great: I remember sometimes entering such heavy snowfall that I'd have to stick my head out the driver's-side window to see the road.

What I didn't realize in those cold moments was that I was grooming myself for the kind of Tornado Alley chaser that I'd become. Maybe I was still just a high school kid. But I was learning to stick my nose right into the storm.

CHAPTER 4

NATURAL HABITAT

...

I wanted Aaron to steer. I was driving my car east on U.S. Route 380 in north-central Texas, just outside of the tiny town of Throckmorton. Up ahead of us was a massive, meaty storm that looked like it was poised to extend a funnel toward earth. Before our eyes, I could see that the storm was consolidating. That was good. If it could sort out a couple of ingredients—like converting intense wind shear into a strong mesocyclone, or rapidly rotating and rising winds—we could be in for some incredible weather.

"Get ready to grab the wheel," I told Aaron, my friend and fellow meteorology student, threading my hand through the handle of my video camera. He looked at the speedometer. We were doing 110 miles per hour.

There were no other cars around, and I felt perfectly comfortable with Aaron reaching his long arms from the passenger seat to maintain our bearing on the gently curving road.

Whether or not Aaron, let alone the three storm chasers riding in the Lumina's backseat, was totally comfortable was another matter. The date was April 7, 2002, and I was in my final semester as an undergraduate meteorology student at OU. But in some ways I felt like I had when I was a high school senior.

Four years earlier in western Michigan, my friends had stopped accompanying me into those chaotic lake-effect storms. Too risky, they'd say. You never know when to give up, they'd complain.

Now, a college undergraduate career later, my energetic attitude toward intercepting tornadoes was yielding many of the same responses. People said I was too intense, that I wanted to get too close. But once a tornadic supercell was in my sights, there wasn't anything or anyone—including reluctant chase partners, grumbling adversaries, or girlfriends—that could slow me down. I had become a predator, and Tornado Alley was my natural habitat.

"I really want to get up to this thing," I said to Aaron as the Lumina screamed across a stretch of lonesome Texas land. My foot was heavy on the gas pedal, and my video camera was aimed at the front windshield and the supercell several miles beyond it.

I was shooting video for the memories, yes. But I was also capturing storm footage so that I could sell it to media outlets in order to support my storm chasing. Among the estimated hundreds or even thousands of storm chasers who then existed, there were several dozen or so of us who made some money doing what we loved to do. One hundred dollars here, two hundred dollars there, sometimes much more. But even thirty dollars would fill a gas tank. That meant I could drive another three hundred miles down the road to keep chasing. The competition to get the best footage was cutthroat and only deepened my obsession with chasing.

"We could be out here by ourselves!" I cheered, driving down the empty road, knowing that if a tornado dropped I might get exclusive footage. "You've got to be kidding me!"

Aaron, along with meteorology students and backseat passengers Adam, Wally, and Holly, were all laughing nervously. I'd asked my old friend Rick to come on the chase, but he'd politely declined. He'd left meteorology entirely to pursue a degree in botany.

"We're going to see some great stuff soon," I said, one eye squinting as I kept looking through the camera's viewfinder.

The storm had sorted itself out, and the sky unleashed. The tornado that emerged from the supercell quickly turned gargantuan—a half mile across and directly next to us in a field. The fast-moving storm churned up a huge dust cloud and changed colors, from black to white to dust brown, and then pink—the last color reflecting that of the surrounding sky. The tornado plowed across open fields, sending cows running and (thankfully) avoiding crops, barns, and humanity with seemingly as much intention as the F5 in Moore, Oklahoma, from 1999 had in seeking out people and their property. Aaron, Adam, Wally, Holly, and I had front-row seats for the tornado. Nearly every other chaser missed it.

"Holy cow!" said Holly, her eyes fixed on the storm.

"We are seeing a monster tornado," I shouted. "A monster! She's a beast! Listen to the roar!"

"Oh my God," said Adam, his mouth wide open.

When the tornado roped out—dissipated—we all breathed sighs of tremendous satisfaction. For every time that I intercepted a tornado, I figured, I'd embark on ten chases where I'd see nothing.

But this day in North Texas would turn out to be something special.

"I don't think we're done yet," I said, glancing at the sky and then turning the car north onto a farm road.

As the tornado had died, I'd spotted another clear slot in the storm. Storm scientists aren't exactly sure, but they believe that the clear slot is a seam in the supercell where warm air blows downward, wrapping around the mesocyclone and tightening its rotation to the point of producing a tornado. The downward rush of air is often dry but sometimes carries precipitation. It's known as the rear flank downdraft (RFD).

The clear slot—which I've observed nearly every time I've intercepted a tornado—is a beautiful sight: It's frequently a light-colored patch in the storm, even with rays of sun shining through, located just aft (southwest for most storms) of the gray, dense, and low-hanging wall cloud that spawns the tornado. The clear slot adds contrast to the sky, and texture and depth to the darkness.

We drove around for a while and saw nothing develop. But when we pulled over to get a fix on the situation, something strange happened. Warm wind whistled hard through the prairie grass all around us. Was it the RFD? Where was the rotation? Where was the funnel?

Aaron craned his neck out the car window and looked straight up.

"It's on top of us!" he yelled.

I looked up. The sight of clouded, rotating winds directly above us was bizarre and incredible—a giant mass that looked like a darkened, spinning cinnamon bun.

"We're okay," I said, getting out of the car and pointing my camera at the spectacle. "We're fine."

Holly gave a squeamish chuckle.

"Dude, we've got to get the heck out of here," said Wally.

"It's coming right at us," said Aaron with clenched teeth.

"What does it look like behind?" I said, sitting back down in the driver's seat. I glanced over my shoulder before throwing the vehicle into reverse. The spot we vacated was soon filled with swirling winds.

· · ·

How did five wide-eyed OU storm chasers find themselves among the few people to witness Tornado Alley's most dramatic action on that spring day? April 7, 2002 was a Sunday, which meant that hundreds of chasers across the Great Plains likely had time to go to the SPC Web site, check dew points, study radar reflectivity, and monitor the low-level jet, if only by looking out their kitchen windows. Earlier on April 7 Aaron and I had taken such steps ourselves, and the impressive wind shear data alone—indicating that wind would blow across the Texas region from different speeds and directions at different altitudes, and could possibly help generate a mesocyclone—left us insane with anticipation. But like only the most obsessive tornado hunters, I wanted to exploit every possible resource to help me find where this magical weather might appear.

On April 7 the key to our conquest was actually hundreds of miles due north of our position. Joel Taylor, a tall and quiet OU meteorology student whom I'd chased with previously, couldn't make the trip to North Texas. He was stuck in his Norman apartment. But Joel loved to chase, and I knew he'd be tracking the very same weather patterns on his computer that we were driving underneath. I thought his observations could be helpful. Joel agreed to support this chase by being a remote set of eyes and playing the role of a "nowcaster."

Back before storm chasers had mobile Internet access, the most determined among us would engineer various ways to receive highly detailed, up-to-the-minute weather updates on the road. One way was to stay in contact with someone who could closely monitor the chase-day weather on a computer—the nowcaster.

Storm chasers also figured out ways to receive data updates on their own. They'd pull up in front of motels across the Great Plains, walk into a lobby with a laptop computer, and ask for a few minutes' worth of Internet access.

And before we all had laptops? We'd hit public libraries. The libraries—no matter how modest—always had Internet access, and within a few years of becoming a storm chaser my wallet bulged with library cards from some of America's tiniest towns. I'm a member of public libraries in Scottsbluff, Nebraska; Woodward, Oklahoma; and Russell, Kansas, among many others. Along the way, I quickly learned one key to these pit stops: Arrive before school lets out. You don't want to waste precious chasing minutes waiting for the kids to tear themselves off the keyboards.

On April 7, we used one of my chase partners' cell phones to receive nowcasts from Joel. Back in 2002 I didn't yet have my own cell phone and didn't yet realize how cellular technology would eventually revolutionize storm chasing.

"What do you see?" I said over the phone, looking up into the Texas sky about an hour before we intercepted the first Throckmorton tornado.

"Where you are? The odds don't look good," said Joel. I could hear him tapping on his computer's keyboard as he bounced from one weather Web site to another. "A lot of red and yellow coming together," he said, and I knew Joel was looking at radar reflectivity. The red and yellow regions on his screen indicated intense precipitation. "Squall line," he added.

Joel confirmed what I feared I saw in a gray and rainy sky. A squall line is a series of thunderstorms that are literally all lined up. While that setup might sound optimal—multiple storms mean several chances for a tornado to touch down—the opposite is true. The thunderstorms all compete with one another for the surrounding atmosphere's available warm air, which is the required fuel for tornadic conditions. The storms end up starving each other. Squall line storms can generate huge straight-line (nonrotational) winds and impressive rainstorms. But generally they don't produce tornadoes.

"What we do now?" I said over the phone, staring up at the sky. I'd parked on the shoulder of a two-lane road outside of Aspermont, Texas. The windows were fogging in the crowded car. Everyone else was quiet and wondering if we would see anything besides rain.

"Looking," said Joel, and I heard more keyboarding over the phone line. "There may be something to your east. Could be interesting."

Joel described what caught his attention. Relative to the squall line, it was just a small splotch of red on the radar screen. The radar wasn't picking up any precipitation nearby the red area either. This was all potentially good news. "Plus there's a hook," he said, his voice lifting with excitement. "You should think about going east, and fast," he said.

Joel saw a rogue supercell thunderstorm (also known as a renegade cell) that had developed out ahead of the eastward-migrating squall line. We both knew that because the storm stood alone—as the radar had indicated—there was the chance that the lone storm could fuel up on the surrounding warm air needed to help create a tornado. But the action would have to happen before the advancing squall line potentially overtook that lone storm.

The "hook" that Joel described was a telltale hook-shaped appendage that trailed on the southwest corner of the storm and is a standard trait of a tornado-producing supercell. Called a hook echo, it indicates that precipitation from the storm is wrapping around the mesocyclone, which is an indication that the storm is rotating. A tornado might not be far behind.

"The rogue cell is your best opportunity," he said. "It's maybe forty miles from your position. Fly east."

I fired up the car, and Aaron looked at me.

"What did he say?" he asked.

"Let's move. East," I replied.

I told Aaron, Wally, Adam, and Holly about what Joel had seen on the Web. We all agreed to chase the rogue supercell, knowing that the decision was a gamble. The odds were against our seeing a tornado come out of one of the storms in the squall line. Meanwhile we could deploy east only to have the rogue storm with the "hook" fall apart before we arrived or get rapidly absorbed into the moving squall line. We'd also have to contend with some sketchy driving conditions. Between that lone storm and us were the squall line's seventy-mile-per-hour winds and potentially intense rainfall. I could tell that my chase partners were uneasy with me behind the wheel.

Soon we were under siege in the storms' heavy precipitation. "Will this get a lot worse?" asked Holly from the backseat, the anxiousness obvious in her voice. I barely heard her over the pounding rain and constant swipes of the windshield wipers. "Can you see where you're going?"

The rain was coming down in varying degrees of downpour, and no, I couldn't see much, which is why I kept the Lumina's speed under eighty miles per hour through the storm. The road was largely straight and empty, and I felt like I was in control. Nonetheless, I'll admit that the fierce wind and rain weren't the only forces influencing my driving. My obsession with intercepting the storm kept me from going a much safer sixty.

By the time I could peel my eyes off the road to check on Holly in the rearview mirror, we were on the eastern side of the squall line and out of the storm. We were surging toward Throckmorton. When I looked again through the windshield, I saw the rogue supercell in front of us. The dark cloud looked like it was about to produce a once-in-a-lifetime tornado.

"There it is!" said Aaron, pointing to the thunderstorm. That's when I pressed the Lumina's accelerator to the floor, reached for my video camera, and closed in on the supercell.

. . .

I'm hardly the first person to be laser-locked onto tornadoes. But shortly after the April 2002 Throckmorton chase, I learned once and for all that the huge enthusiasm for tornadoes that I share with other storm chasers isn't enough to unite us. My hard-charging, predatory style for intercepting storms is very different from the approaches taken by some influential chasers who came before me. I'd argue that my fanatical methods represent an evolution in storm chasing. Some of my peers, however, think otherwise. They see my extreme ways and changes to storm chasing in general as steps in the wrong direction.

Chasing didn't always have a right and wrong way of doing things. In the beginning, there were no guidelines, probably because there was only one storm chaser.

When he started chasing, David Hoadley, a polite and understated former government worker whom many consider to be the grandfather of storm chasing, didn't have a signature "style." Hoadley, who had been drawn to tornadoes ever since he was a teenager, had a single, elusive objective: to spot *any* tornado. He began chasing in eastern North Dakota in 1956, when there were no modern weather-detection technologies, and there was no interstate highway system. In fact, chasing on North Dakota's bug-infested back roads occasionally left Hoadley struggling to see out of his Oldsmobile's windshield. He saw only two tornadoes in his first six years as a chaser.

Hoadley—and a few others who soon joined the quest with him—chased in obscurity for approximately two decades. Luckily, Hoadley's average got better. He intercepted plenty of tornadoes all over Tornado Alley in those twenty years. But independent of storm chasing's very loosely affiliated pioneers, who generally saw their outdoor pastime as just that, a pastime, emerged other individuals with additional interest in tornadoes. They were researchers and government employees.

Like the hobbyists, the early tornado-chasing data geeks were also in awe of what the earth's atmosphere could produce. In addition to their fascination with tornadoes, the researchers wanted to learn what they could about how tornadoes worked in the name of science and safety. Among other things, they were interested in keeping Americans better protected from the insane wrath of such storms.

The researchers and government employees of the 1950s and '60s performed sporadic fieldwork, capturing film of a tornado here and attempting an intercept via airplane there. Around the same time, the federal government began to build infrastructure aimed at addressing severe weather, first by creating the Severe Local Storms Unit in the nation's capital and then, in 1964, by establishing the National Severe Storms Laboratory. The NSSL was created in Norman and worked in conjunction with what is now the fifty-year-old University of Oklahoma School of Meteorology. One of the NSSL's missions was to better understand and therefore forecast severe weather.

The University of Oklahoma/NSSL Tornado Intercept Project was launched in 1972 and represented the first structured program to storm-chase in the name of science and research. TIP, as it was called, employed OU meteorology students to intercept Great Plains storms. As part of their duties, the students filmed and photographed tornadoes, which led to a dramatically increased understanding of the supercell storm structures that often produce tornadic conditions.

TIP also paved the way for further research. In the 1980s, storm-chasing scientists deployed probes ahead of tornadoes with the hopes that the measuring equipment inside of the probes would be swept into the rotating winds and provide valuable data. In the 1990s and into the new millennium, the government-sponsored VORTEX chase projects have sent scientists to chase with the hope of improved understanding of both how tornadoes develop and how to better forecast their occurrences. By definition, a vortex is any mass of whirling fluid or air. In terms of the project, VORTEX stands for Verification of the Origins of Rotation in Tornadoes Experiment.

The VORTEX efforts in particular have been admirable, and the data captured by the projects has been staggering. In 1994 and 1995, the original VORTEX chase project dispatched about a dozen instrumented vehicles, as well as a truck carrying a Doppler radar dish and two Doppler-radar-equipped airplanes, to collect data on tornadoes intercepted in north-central Texas. In 2009 and 2010, VORTEX2 dispatched approximately forty vehicles, many of them similarly equipped but with substantially more advanced technologies, across the Great Plains.

The projects generated millions of data points. Radio waves sent from Doppler radar antennas within a few miles of storms provided scientists with high-resolution pictures of the many winds rushing in and out of supercell thunderstorms and even inside the tornadoes themselves, as well as images of the cloud structures and movement of precipitation. Such pinpoint data can't be captured by distant, stationary

Doppler radar units and is helping scientists creep closer to answering an age-old question: Why do some supercell thunderstorms produce tornadoes while others do not?

But over the last twenty or so years, the *pursuit* of tornadoes has also become its own science. While no governing body officially oversees storm chasing, the research community that represents some of chasing's old guard has attempted to codify the act of storm chasing about the same way that scientists codify data. This group became increasingly outspoken once *Twister* hit the big screen in 1996, and with good reason: *Twister* motivated thousands of people who didn't know anything about storm chasing to consider running down tornadoes.

Nonetheless, there are also plenty of storm chasers who don't adhere to the accepted way of doing things, and I count myself among them. I've always been the type to figure things out for myself. That doesn't mean I don't take into account that what I do is sometimes perceived as very dangerous.

After my hyperbolic media appearances following the 1999 chase of that killer Oklahoma F5, I poked around on the Web, looking for what kind of logic was behind someone writing that I needed to be "taken to the woodshed" for my behavior.

I found some answers, from a legendary storm chaser who was known of and respected by many of his peers. According to Dr. Charles Doswell, a highly decorated, sixty-five-year-old OU research scientist and a one-time research chaser in the university's original Tornado Intercept Project, there's a right way and a wrong way to storm-chase.

I'd only heard of Dr. Doswell, who is a storm-chasing "celebrity" in that he often speaks at severe weather symposiums and is regularly quoted by like-minded chasers in various forums. But I knew nothing of Doswell's actual chasing commandments. On his Web site, he'd written extensively about the dos and don'ts of storm chasing: Do pull completely off the road before getting out of your car. Don't punch the core, or drive through the thunderstorm's heavy precipitation in search of a tornado. Avoid driving close to rotating wall clouds. Be mindful of how you publicly celebrate tornadoes. Cheer inappropriately at a beautiful tornado, Doswell claimed, and one person could tarnish the entire storm-chasing community's image.

Even today, Doswell, who's immediately recognizable courtesy of a big cowboy hat and a tall build, protests that storm-chasing might be changing, and for the worse. Because of the media's influence on storm chasers, Doswell is concerned that the pursuit of tornadoes is increasingly about adrenaline instead of science or the appreciation of meteorology. He is concerned that a chaser could soon get killed, or that a chaser speeding in his car to a chase could kill an innocent bystander standing by the side of the road. He worries that, should storm chasing's image become too tarnished, law enforcement officers and emergency services workers could become wary and distrustful of chasers. Such people potentially have the power to redirect chasers from following storms down public roads.

If I'd known in my undergrad days what I know now, I'd have to say that Doswell's concerns have always been, in a sense, prophetic. Storm chasing *has* changed, a lot. Today's storm chasers are a hugely varied population including scientists, weather enthusiasts, nature lovers, and adrenaline junkies. They're all ages (although still, much to the chagrin of many of them, primarily male), and they're motivated by the clouds, or the desire to road-trip, or the storm-chasing footage that they see on the Internet or television, or the need to socialize. After all, some people just love to stand together on the side of a lonely country road, look at a supercell on the horizon, and talk about the weather.

But I'd also argue that the vast majority of today's storm chasers, who likely number in the several thousands (though no hard data is available), respect storm chasing. Most storm chasers don't drive close to the storms or want to sell manic videos to media outlets. They're mindful of law enforcement and emergency management and are interested in helping *save* lives: Via the Internet, a storm chaser can submit real-time reports of weather developments in the field, and National Weather Service meteorologists have access to this kind of information. Such storm-chaser dispatches provide input for the meteorologists' forecasts.

So while I think that Chuck Doswell and other more conservative or traditional storm chasers are well-intentioned, I have to say that they seem afraid of the unknown. Not every new chaser will walk in lockstep with chasing's old guard, which knows its meteorology thoroughly, never ventures too close to the storms, and always parks its storm-chasing cars just so, deep onto the shoulders and well away from the flow of traffic. But that doesn't mean that someone who accidentally parks their chase car crooked or doesn't completely understand the clouds above them is bad, or dangerous, or doesn't deserve a view of the storm. Maybe one day that same beginner chaser will be a meteorologist with a PhD who figures out why some thunderstorms produce tornadoes and others don't. As long as they are cognizant of their surroundings and the people around them, then they should be able to pursue this hobby they love.

Sure, not every single storm chaser nowadays has good intentions. There have been isolated clashes with police officers, emergency managers, and even tornadoes. I've seen storm chasers shooting video of people mourning their destroyed homes and property, and I'd always rather that those chasers put down their cameras: They're capturing someone else's huge misfortune, and at the very least tornado victims deserve respect and privacy.

My personal storm-chasing philosophy is simple: Chase within *my* limits. That said, the closer I get to a storm, the more I'll see, the more I might learn, and the more satisfied I am.

• • •

Admittedly, in my undergrad years at OU, I'd gone against some prudent suggestions from Doswell's list. On CNN and *Leeza* in particular, I'd characterized myself as nothing short of a storm-chasing renegade, doing whatever I had to do to witness and capture Mother Nature's incredible violence. I was no model storm chaser, at least according to those in Doswell's camp.

After that appearance and in the years that followed, the fallout for my apparent bad-boy reputation was subtle. Other OU meteorology students regularly turned down my invitations to chase together. When I skipped classes to chase, a couple of my professors made cracks—"We all know where Reed is today," they'd say aloud—despite the fact that they also knew I'd always get my work done. As for Doswell, I only saw him occasionally in the Map Room and at school. I eventually met him, but I never got to know him. When our eyes did meet? The veteran meteorologist looked right through me.

Often the quiet ostracism didn't bother me. Between storm chasing, my schoolwork, and my obsession with tracking weather activity across the nation and around the globe, there weren't enough hours in the day to find a girlfriend, let alone worry what a select group of storm chasers thought of my tactics.

But occasionally the criticism stung. I'd be storm-chasing alone, or studying late at night in some basement lounge, and wonder why I was being singled out.

For years, the legendary chaser David Hoadley produced a modest publication for the storm chaser community called Storm Track. The newsletter always included one of Hoadley's "Funnel Funnies," which were hilarious, single-panel cartoons that gently mocked storm chasers for their many apparent faults: how they drove too fast, drove dangerously close to the storms, celebrated a little too loudly at the sight of an incredible tornado, and so on. Yet Hoadley, who still chases today, receives only praise from the fraternity of old-guard and research-minded storm chasers. Even Doswell, whom I think is an amazing scientist and has an impressive résumé, admitted on his Web site that he was occasionally guilty of "bending the rules." I didn't get the same latitude.

In those quiet moments behind the wheel or in front of my books, I decided that my problem was sincerity. I storm-chased like I studied, or played the oboe, or listened to the same Tom Petty songs repeatedly. That is, I did everything with genuine, bordering-on-extreme passion. Could I be an obsessed storm chaser and still be mindful of others? I thought so. I'd never become so absorbed in the heat of a storm chase that I'd caused an accident, and I'd always voiced honest concern and dismay when I watched a tornado swallow a building whole. I never tried to hawk footage of people in anguish in a storm's aftermath. I stayed out of the way of emergency workers and offered to help when I could. Shortly after appearing on CNN, I knew that I'd come across as young and naïve—embarrassingly so. But multiply my loud voice by my deep love for explosive weather times my inability to cap my emotions? The product is a storm chaser who probably comes across as more than a little over-the-top.

Shortly after the April 2002 intercept in Throckmorton, Texas, my style did nothing save widen the rift between the old-school storm chasers and me.

On our way home from that successful mission, I'd stopped at the offices of the ABC television affiliate in the Lone Star State's Wichita Falls to show the local news crew the incredible footage that I'd taken earlier in the day. The tornado *had* been a beast.

By the time I'd intercepted that storm outside of Throckmorton, I'd sold my video footage through the years to networks including ABC, CBS, NBC, Fox, and the Weather Channel.

The folks in Wichita Falls were so impressed with the material that they beamed it to the producers at the network's *Good Morning America* program. I quickly got the thumbs-up—the huge show wanted to air my footage and was willing to pay me a healthy $2,000. ABC also wanted me to appear on *Good Morning America* the very next day, to discuss the chase and the storm.

When we left Wichita Falls, everyone in the car cheered. Two thousand bucks! That was enough to fund plenty more chases.

"Are you nervous about going on national TV?" Aaron asked as he drove back toward Norman. I was sitting in the front passenger seat. The five of us were all tired and dirty after the daylong trip. It was almost midnight.

"A little," I said, twiddling a pen between my fingers. "But I'm more worried about getting these *meso* equations done by tomorrow."

On and off throughout the day, I'd been working on equations for my mesoscale meteorology class. The class was ridiculously math-heavy, and the problems I was wrestling with on my round-trip journey to Throckmorton addressed slantwise convective instability, an esoteric concept concerning the buoyancy of air rising off a sloped surface. As Aaron and I spoke, I was generating an equation that was already a half-page long.

The cell phone we'd been sharing all day in the car rang. The call was from a producer at *Good Morning America*. She wanted to conduct a preinterview before my appearance the next day with ABC's Diane Sawyer. The producer wanted all the details of the intercept.

I explained how we thought a storm was going to fire in one part of North Texas and then watched the chances for a tornado to emerge from that storm rapidly deteriorate. Based on the recommendation of a friend watching the satellite imagery back in Norman, I said, we'd made a quick and calculated decision to blast east and get under a different storm cell. We'd outfoxed a lot of the competition, I told her. I was quite proud.

Then the producer asked how fast we'd driven to reach our new target area in time to intercept the tornado.

"About a hundred miles per hour, but please don't mention that on the air," I said, a red flag waving inside my head. Why worsen my relationship with the community's more conservative storm chasers? I knew Diane Sawyer wouldn't give me a chance to explain that we were breaking the law while traveling down an empty road.

The next morning I was staring into the television camera at the studios of KOCO, Oklahoma City's ABC affiliate. Diane Sawyer introduced me on live national TV.

"Yesterday in Northern Texas," said Sawyer, "storm chaser Reed Timmer drove one hundred miles per hour to catch up to a tornado . . ."

I don't remember much more about the interview. All I could think about was how the storm-chasing world would accuse me of being an outlaw. There goes that Reed Timmer again, shooting off his mouth, breaking storm chasing's code of ethics, and misrepresenting the entire community on national television.

For several days afterward, I received e-mails from storm chasers and messages from online chasing forums filled with anger. I got abuse from every angle: You're reckless! Where's your integrity? Do you know how bad you made us look? Cops will hate us! Everyone in the meteorology department is talking about you! I'm terrified to be anywhere close to your vehicle! Where's your honesty?

My honesty? Out in the open, for everyone to see. I loved storm chasing—I lived for it. I crossed every T to improve my chances at intercepting a tornado and forced myself to do homework in chase cars until I was cross-eyed so I understood fully what I was seeing in the sky. Sure, I had driven too fast and confessed to the crime. But certainly I'm not the only one who ever drove fast in pursuit of a storm, and I had been on a totally desolate road.

I also decided that I wasn't going to worry about changing who I was or how I chased. In the days following my appearance on *Good Morning America*, life carried on as usual—which is to say, nobody said anything to my face about my fast driving or my media moment. Nobody spoke much to me at all.

...

OU might have hoped it was done with me. But I wasn't finished with OU, or the Great Plains.

In spring 2002, my dwindling undergraduate class—there were twenty or so of us left—was entering the homestretch of its senior year in the School of Meteorology. Some of my remaining classmates in the program figured they'd launch into forecasting careers, either working for the private sector in weather-dependent businesses like agriculture or energy, or for a government-run organization like the National Weather Service. Others wanted to stay in academia and pursue research-oriented work. A few hoped to land media jobs and become weather celebrities. As for me, I wanted to keep chasing tornadoes in Tornado Alley.

There were the obvious reasons. As a graduating senior, I was as excited at the thought of intercepting tornadoes of every size and shape— wedge, stovepipe, elephant trunk, rope, you name it—as the day four years earlier when I'd first arrived in Norman. But there was more. For those last four years, I'd also seen firsthand the devastation that severe weather creates. People hurt, homes dismantled, cars tossed. As much as tornadoes (and hurricanes) appealed to me, I knew that my sensibilities were aberrant. That kind of weather struck terror into the overwhelming majority of the population, and for good reason. If I was going to continue chasing, I should keep sponging up knowledge about the weather, too. Someday, I thought, I wanted to contribute to severe weather science. I wanted to be involved in helping mankind better understand tornadoes and be better prepared to get out of their way.

I wasn't quite sure how I was going to accomplish the latter goal, but I knew how to continue studying the weather. I could apply to graduate school.

Some of the most prestigious graduate-school programs in meteorology—like Penn State, Florida State, and OU—find places every year for only one out of every four or five applicants. Fortunately, I'd earned the right to apply to any of those institutions. I was on my way to graduating magna cum laude, and I'd never received anything less than a B in an OU class. My OU advisers told me that I might do well to get a different perspective on meteorology from another university faculty.

And yet I didn't want to leave Norman. I'd made a lot of great friends, and I knew there was no place I'd rather be than the Great Plains. I only applied to OU's graduate school, and later that spring I was accepted. Honestly, the first thing I did upon receiving my acceptance letter was fantasize about a flexible schedule that included storm chasing.

"Sleep late, eat lunch, and work. Or I guess in your case, work and chase," said my friend Don Giuliano, who was a year ahead of me and already pursuing his master's degree. He suggested that I could supplement my small grad-student stipend with some storm video sales.

If only it was that simple. As an incoming grad student in meteorology, I still had to land a demanding research assistant's job. Assisting a professor in his or her research is an essential part of being a graduate student at OU, and the obvious avenue for me would've been to take a research assistantship with one of the school's renowned tornado scientists. But none of them contacted me. I was never absolutely sure if or why the school's tornado research community blacklisted me, but I felt certain that they had. I ventured to guess that my outlandish statements to the media and intense chasing style had something to do with the silence.

However, my phone did ring before May graduation. I was invited to meet with a professor—Dr. Peter Lamb, a stern and highly esteemed OU climatologist from New Zealand—to discuss his needs for a research assistant. I'd heard the scuttlebutt about Lamb, how he gave six-hour exams, demanded students work overtime on research, and didn't support storm-chasing since it interfered with grad school.

"I understand that you do very good work, Reed. I'd be counting on you to keep that up," he told me in his thick Kiwi accent one afternoon that spring. "I've got funding for a climate project. We could both benefit from your participation."

The then fifty-four-year-old, gray-haired professor went on to explain how I'd be helping him create indices that linked North American climate and residential consumption of natural gas. Cutting-edge tornado science this wasn't, but what I didn't know then was that this obscure-sounding climate project would help shed light on the future of severe weather. Plus Dr. Lamb was highly respected in the meteorology community, and I knew by working with him that I'd become a better researcher and scientist.

As our initial meeting wound down, I told Dr. Lamb that I wanted to sign on. He didn't smile but he did nod and seemed satisfied. I prepared to leave his office, relieved to avoid the subject of tornadoes.

Then Dr. Lamb had one final thought.

"Oh, and Reed," he added, "we'll have to talk about storm chasing. We can't have any big distractions."

I swallowed hard. I needed this position. But I couldn't exactly tell Dr. Lamb not to worry.

• • •

The Norman I returned to in fall 2002 was far more welcoming than the one I'd left just weeks earlier. After graduation the previous spring, I'd embarked on two epic storm chases and come home batting less than zero, if that's possible. Not only were the long trips blue-sky busts, but I lost a car, too.

I'd journeyed that spring with another chaser to eastern Montana, where severe thunderstorms can develop in the high plains. Sure enough, the SPC that day reported a 15 percent chance of tornadoes in the area around the tiny outpost of Biddle, and soon after we arrived, we drove just south into northeast Wyoming and sat under an incredible supercell. The clouds were stacked like pancakes, and they were tinted a bluish gray. The spinning storm sat atop an open expanse of yellow prairie grass and against a crystal-blue backdrop. The scene couldn't have been prettier. All we needed was for the funnel to extend down, but that never happened. Moisture left the air, and I could see the mesocyclone—that rising, rotating column of wind—wither before my eyes. It was the most beautiful thunderstorm never to have delivered a tornado and was nearly worth the thirty-six hours of required driving in my old Chevy Lumina.

Something else died soon thereafter. I'd convinced an entire crew— my old buddies Rick and Joel, and my housemate Hal—to drive to an intercept target in southern Minnesota, near the town of Albert Lea. The computer modeling reported that the wind shear would be incredible. But the temperature inexplicably plummeted, at least outside. There was never a storm.

On the return trip, my car boiled over. Really, it had been a long time coming. You know me—back then, well before I became the proud and caring owner of my current vehicle (the custom-built tornado tank affectionately known as the Dominator, which I now drive all over the Great Plains), my head truly was in the clouds when it came to maintaining my cars and home. The Lumina had already been in a fender bender that had left it without headlights, and I had secured the hood with a roll of duct tape. I never serviced the engine again, for tens of thousands of miles. Around one A.M. on our return trip from Minnesota, smoke and stench poured out of the engine compartment 120 miles from home. We left the car by the side of the road. My chasing buddies were plenty mad. That summer was a bust all the way around.

But fall 2002 was different. I was so happy to see Niki and get back to Norman. For the first time since arriving as a college freshman, I had a relationship with someone in Oklahoma that wasn't connected to my studies or storm chasing.

Niki Darnaby was short and dark haired, with big brown eyes. She was my age—we were both twenty-two at the time—and from outside of Tulsa. Niki was an OU graduate and worked in a bank but was much more of a live wire than her job might suggest. She loved watching Comedy Central and laughed at my jokes, and we often in-line skated around Norman together. We'd started dating just before I'd left for the summer. In the fall our relationship fired up again. While our bond rapidly grew, she found my chasing life strange and mysterious. At first.

"So if bad weather is forecast for northeast Nebraska, how do you know exactly where to go?" she asked me one sunny morning over breakfast. "When do you decide what time you'll have to get out of bed to start driving? Who knows when a tornado will drop from the sky?"

I explained that pinpointing tornadic supercell thunderstorms involved skill, knowledge, experience, and luck.

"Your forecast helps you pinpoint where all the ingredients for a tornado come together," I explained. "You need to have unstable air, which means air that's different temperatures and that lifts in the sky. You have to have wind, and moisture too."

"If you have all those elements then you're guaranteed a tornado?" she asked, picking up her empty plate and mine and taking them to the sink.

"Then a tornado might happen," I said. "Conditions can fall apart—in just several minutes. You have to make quick decisions about which clouds in the sky might produce a tornado. Storms break up right in front of my eyes all the time."

"How great is seeing one?" she said.

"Every single one," I said, "feels like a once-in-a-lifetime opportunity."

She smiled. "How do you feel if you travel all that way and see nothing?" she said. "Like you've wasted all that time?"

"Never," I said. "I only want to chase more."

Niki got distracted with washing the dishes and didn't seem to dwell on my clearly intense cravings for severe weather. That side of my personality was yet to fully emerge.

That fall, Niki rarely saw the obsessive storm chaser in me, either. The skies were frustratingly quiet. Plus my graduate-school courses were hard. I regularly pulled all-nighters hammering through the physics and calculus involved in my atmospheric dynamics class. Dr. Lamb, I quickly discovered, was a perfectionist. The first work I gave him as a research assistant came back to me covered in red ink and requests for changes. Lamb critiqued my writing and thought my findings required more research. I had to revise material for him repeatedly. I didn't, however, resent him. Far from it. I knew that Dr. Lamb was grooming me to become a technical-writing machine, and forcing me to mind detail after detail. His demands would ultimately help me both as a scholar and an entrepreneur who was running a storm-chasing business.

Still, I needed more than a girlfriend and Dr. Lamb's challenges. I needed a great chase. But the 2003 spring season's early deployments had their misfires, none worse than when Joel's SUV hydroplaned on some wet Kansas roads with four chasers in the vehicle. We spun around twice at eighty miles per hour before he regained control.

"I'm so glad you're okay!" Niki said when I later called her from Joel's car on the cell phone I had finally acquired. I told her that the four of us were feeling lucky to be alive. "When are you coming home?" she added.

I returned that night but wasn't home for long. A massive opportunity came only days later: The SPC issued a rare high-risk outlook for May 15 for the Oklahoma and Texas panhandles. In other words, the likelihood of a tornado forming was high. Dew points were forecast to be in the sixties, and CAPE values—"convective available potential energy," which measures energy and is an indicator of how fast warm and moist air might rise—would rise to three thousand joules per kilogram. Those kinds of numbers suggested explosive severe-weather conditions.

Joel and I surged to the northwest corner of the Texas panhandle in the early afternoon. Above the bland and smelly landscape of cow farms, telephone poles, and flatlands was a huge, oval-shaped supercell thunderstorm with a rotating wall cloud at its base. All that we needed was for the cloud to spawn a tornado.

"It's getting its act together," I said, looking at the storm through the viewfinder of my video camera. "It'll be coming down pretty soon!"

The storm clouds produced a couple funnel clouds that didn't reach the ground. Those were just teasers. We waited and waited for the tornado to emerge. We both started to get antsy.

"I think we should head south," said Joel from behind the wheel, his glance darting between the sky and the empty road in front of us.

"Maybe this is still consolidating," I argued. "I don't want to miss anything here."

"We'll be better off to the south, Reed. On another storm," Joel said firmly. "This one is dying."

While we drove around under that incredible supercell, I gave Joel's suggestion some serious thought. I didn't always put stock in my chase partners' opinions, because most of them didn't chase as often as I did or have as thorough a meteorological background as me. Of course, there was also the part of me that didn't like listening to anyone else.

But I felt like I could trust Joel. He'd been a lifelong weather junkie like me, a good meteorology student, and a longtime dedicated storm chaser. As a college freshman, Joel had also chased the F5 that ripped through Moore, Oklahoma, in 1999. He loved to get close to the tornadoes, too—I'd experienced his fearlessness back in 2001, when we chased a storm that blasted through the Oklahoma town of Elk City. He'd also given me great advice as a nowcaster in spring 2002, when he correctly advised me to head east on my chase of the Throckmorton tornado.

I looked up again at the Texas sky and the monster supercell.

"You're right," I finally said. "This thing is dying."

Joel blasted south, and we punched through the core of another supercell east of Dalhart, Texas. Hail pounded the windshield and drummed the roof of the car for several minutes, and we didn't know what to expect on the other side of the precipitation. We could've run right into a tornado.

"Abandon mobile homes!" advised an announcer over the NOAA weather radio in Joel's truck.

Suddenly the hail let up, and just southwest of us was a massive, black, quarter-mile-wide wedge tornado.

"Look!" I yelled, pointing to the tornado a couple miles off. "It's rotating fast!"

The tornado scraped across the bare landscape.

"I'm getting great video," I said. "Let's get as close as possible!"

Joel gamely drove farther down the road.

"We're a hundred yards away," said Joel with a big smile on his face. "It's going to cross the road right in front of us."

Right then, my cell phone rang, and I glanced at the caller ID. It was Niki's phone number.

In a sign of decisions to come, I stuck the unanswered phone back in my pocket.

Nobody—not storm chasing's old guard, or a demanding professor, or even a sweet girlfriend—was going to divert my attention when there was a storm just ahead.

CHAPTER 5

LITTLE DECISIONS

. . .

W hat's the difference between intercepting a tornado and enduring a blue-sky bust? Selling a tornado video and throwing it on
the shelf? Returning from a storm chase triumphant or badly
shaken? Or, dare I say, lucky to be alive?

Very little.

As my obsession with storm chasing deepened, I increasingly realized that the smallest observations, decisions, timing gaps, and, of course,
bits of luck frequently played huge roles in whether or not I accomplished
what I always set out to do: find, marvel at, and better understand tornadoes.

Joel, for instance, had made the right call in the Texas panhandle in
May 2003. He came to the conclusion before I did that the mesocyclone
inside of the first storm wasn't gathering strength; the wall cloud beneath
that giant egg of a supercell suspended in the sky was rotating, but it
wasn't spinning with much fervor—which is always of concern to a
storm chaser. But I hadn't picked up on the detail. I thought the storm
was still gathering strength. We could've sat under that cloud for another
twenty minutes and come away from the whole chase with nothing. Joel
was smart to insist that we move on, based on intuition and a small indicator from the sky.

Now I wanted to return the favor.

A trough ejecting northeast out of the central Rocky Mountains was set to move high in the atmosphere over parts of Nebraska and South Dakota on June 24, 2003. A trough, like the name says, is an invisible trench in the sky, and because it's basically a giant pocket full of cold air, any warm air that's closer to the ground but near the trough has a tendency to rise with all the speed of a hot air balloon. If other conditions are right, the rising hot air will encourage the formation of clouds and even storms.

The conditions looked right—at least to me. Combined with a high dew point (more moisture means increased potential for the formation of storms), an incoming warm front (to further fuel the rise of warm air), and the promise of strong winds blowing in different directions at different elevations (causing any storms to ultimately twist and turn), conditions in the upper reaches of Tornado Alley seemed perfect for supercell thunderstorms. Storm chasers like to characterize such a potent vertical profile of the atmosphere as a "loaded-gun sounding": Every piece was in place for warm, moist air to gather enough energy to force a storm to explode into the stratosphere and produce severe weather.

"No," said Joel. I had invited him to chase with me over the phone, a couple days before all of the weather ingredients were supposed to come together.

"What do you mean, no?" I replied from my end. "You have to come. The setup is perfect. You may not encounter conditions like this ever again."

"The cap will be too strong," he said, referring to the layer of relatively hot air just above the ground that sometimes refuses to break apart and kills the development of thunderstorms by acting like a lid on their growth. "It'll be a blue-sky bust."

"The storms will blast skyward," I responded. "They'll break the cap."

"Bust," he said.

A mile-wide F5 tornado nearing peak intensity southwest of Moore, OK, on May 3, 1999. Note the incredibly smooth, cylindrical wall cloud above the wedge tornado. Since then, I haven't witnessed such a perfect supercell/tornado structure.

My storm-chasing partners and I watching in disbelief on June 24, 2003 as a violent F4 tornado roars into Manchester, SD, destroying a large house right in front of us.

This was the tornado I had been waiting for my entire life—slow moving, near enough to roads that we could get very close, and beautifully back-lit over open farmland. Sadly, this F4 tornado would not be "ideal" long after this photo, when the half-mile-wide wedge took dead aim at the small farming town of Manchester, SD.

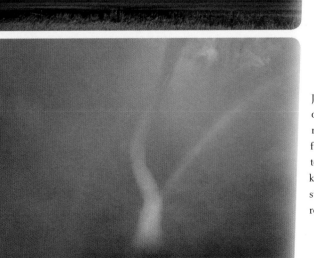

Just when we thought this tornado couldn't be more photogenic, a rainbow formed in front of the funnel. A "rope" in this photo, the tornado refused to dissipate and kept oscillating from a thicker stove-pipe/elephant trunk to a thin rope.

A small, photogenic rope tornado over Shannon County, SD, on June 6, 2007.

A classic "elephant trunk" tornado in northwest Oklahoma on April 26, 2009.

A strong tornado causing extensive damage to a farmhouse just east of Elk City, OK, on October 9, 2001. Joel and his family are friends with the residents of this house, who thankfully escaped the wrath of this F3 tornado. The white plume at the base of the tornado appears to be insulation and other minced-up debris from the home.

Reed shooting the Elk City, OK, tornado as it crosses the road only a quarter-mile to the north with insane inflow winds to our backs. This tornado would soon intensify into an F3 just to the east. This was the first successful storm chase I had with Joel, and the beginning of a long and occasionally unstable storm-chasing partnership.

A beautiful shelf cloud surging across Tornado Alley farmland ahead of a powerful squall line.

A high-contrast tornado from a cyclic supercell in Briscoe County, TX, on March 28, 2007. This was a great start to the best storm-chasing season I've ever had.

A beautiful tornado slowly dissipating in extreme northwest Oklahoma on May 4, 2007, just minutes after our near direct hit from this same small but violent twister. The supercell that produced the tragic Greensburg, KS, F5 tornado that day can also be seen developing to the north and west at the time of this photo. Freshly fallen hail, baseball to softball size, can be seen in the grass.

The Dominator geared up for its first storm season in early spring 2009, behind my house in Norman, OK.

The contents of the three-hundred-pound tornado probe pictured from above. Housed inside the polycarbonate bubble is the data logger, which stores wind speed and direction data at one-second intervals, an HD camcorder, and a power supply.

The Dominator preparing to intercept a developing tornado in north-central South Dakota in 2010. The vertical radar designed to measure the updraft winds inside a tornado is mounted on the back-right portion of the roof.

The TornadoVideos.net team (Joel Taylor, Reed Timmer, and Chris Chittick) standing behind the Dominator with incredible mammatus overhead.

Reed documenting the storm surge as Hurricane Ike was about to make landfall on September 13, 2008 in Galveston, TX. Reed is standing next to the 1900 Galveston Island hurricane memorial statue.

"Explosive," I argued.

"Cap," said Joel.

That was the difference, and one of us was going to be sorry that he got the one detail about his forecast wrong.

Actually, I would have been sorrier than Joel.

The year prior, Joel and I had graduated together from OU with our bachelor of science degrees in meteorology. But while he loved storm chasing and studying the atmosphere, Joel wanted a stable income and was earning his real estate agent's license. Meanwhile I was still very happy to live the storm-chasing dream: While my "day job" was learning more about climate variability while working under Dr. Lamb, I still pursued tornadoes at every opportunity, in the process becoming both a smarter chaser and a keener observer of the sky. My modest graduate-student stipend and small injections of cash from selling storm video provided sufficient income to fuel my obsession. And at the time, that was, quite frankly, enough for me. Unlike many kids who just graduated from college, I didn't think much about the future. I was lost in cool and interesting science, as I always had been. Unfortunately, my preoccupations weren't terribly reassuring to members of my girlfriend's family.

"CAPE values will likely exceed five thousand joules per kilogram over much of the northern plains, Mr. Darnaby," I told Niki's dad the afternoon before leaving to chase. "It could be the storm I've waited for my entire life." Niki and I were over at her folks' house for a weekend trip to a lake, and her dad had asked me what my upcoming week looked like. As usual, what came out of my mouth both overwhelmed and concerned him. His eyes glazed over, and then his brow furrowed. As I gave him more esoteric meteorological details of the impending severe weather, I'm sure Mr. Darnaby wondered what his little girl was doing with such an odd guy with curious hobbies.

"I don't know that we'll ever witness another storm like this," I added.

I was also well aware of the fact that, from time to time, I overstated my case for a storm chase. Despite what I'd often proclaim, not every storm chase was life altering. I'll admit, I'm prone to hyperbole and over-optimism. I can't help it.

But what neither Mr. Darnaby nor I knew was that I was selling this particular storm chase short. The tornado that would come out of a South Dakota supercell on June 24 would be one of the most memorable in storm-chasing history, period. It would bring me more unexpected media attention and put—for me—a lot of unexpected money in my pocket. The tornado would also sober me, wiping the small town of Manchester right off the face of the planet.

On June 23, I left Norman for the open road with Jim Bishop and Stefan Zack in Jim's run-down car. Jim was another hard-core storm chaser I knew, and Stefan was a German exchange student whom I'd met through the OU School of Meteorology's graduate program. Stefan had chased before but had never been too close to the action. He insisted that he wanted to see every detail of a tornado. I shrugged my shoulders. Stefan was a nice guy. I told him to join us.

That evening we stopped to sleep at a motel in the tiny, northeast Nebraska town of O'Neill. Even to a scientist like me, the night sky seemed supernatural. Right at dusk, dark blue and black supercell thunderstorms began ominously firing upward all around us, as if they were the breath of dragons. The air was warm, breezy, and humid, and a steady line of clouds streamed northward on the low-level jet, like they were being marched into battle. Night fell and we were treated to a phenomenal light-ning show that illuminated the pastures and cornfields around town. The night before, the sky had jettisoned half-foot hailstones over parts of Nebraska. Jim, Stefan, and I could hardly wait for morning to come.

We weren't disappointed. At ten a.m., towering cumulonimbus clouds were already taking shape, although they weren't yet producing precipitation or lightning. The cap that Joel had bet on, which generally establishes itself at an altitude of about five thousand feet, was preventing the cloud towers from growing high enough into the atmosphere to mature into thunderstorms. But that was okay. The air was already gloriously unstable and storm-friendly; if the cap could remain intact for a while it would generate the buildup of even more heat and moisture. In a perfect weather-creating world, the atmosphere would turn into a powder keg, with pent-up storms finally exploding upward by some time in the afternoon, packing so much energy that they'd smash the cap and stretch into colossal, fifty-thousand-foot supercells.

"That's a breakable cap," said Jim, looking over my shoulder at temperatures in the atmosphere that I'd called up on the computer monitor inside of O'Neill's public library. We were double-checking the forecasts and weather observations on a National Center for Atmospheric Research (NCAR) Web site. Then I clicked onto the SPC site. It reported a 15 percent probability of tornadoes that day in parts of Nebraska and South Dakota. On-screen, parts of those states were "hatched," or shaded on the map, indicating that they were areas with potential for strong tornadoes.

"Stick around here or head north?" said Jim, crossing his arms. Nebraska's "setup," or the weather one might expect to encounter, included a dryline. A dryline is created when there is hot, dry air blowing from the west/southwest and warm, moist air blowing from the south/southeast. Where the hot air pushes into the warm and moist air, the moist air gets thrust skyward. The beauty of a dryline is that the long, north-south contact area between the hot air and warm, moist air can also provide a long line of isolated supercell thunderstorms as well as great visibility.

But South Dakota's setup looked intriguing too. A warm front was moving through, and warm fronts invite clashing winds that create the wind shear needed to produce tornadoes. The dew points were already impressively high, resulting in those astronomical CAPE values that I'd gone on and on about to Niki's father. If the wind kicked in, and if the warm front developed without its semitypical cloud cover, eastern South

Dakota could turn into a tornado-making machine. Thunderstorms could shoot up like weeds. Still, those were big ifs.

Did we want to gamble? Drive into South Dakota, and if the warm front didn't cooperate, the trip could be a bust. But the best possible scenario in that state would be insane, and like I said, I'm a glass-is-half-full kind of guy.

Unlike many storm chasers that day, we gambled on South Dakota. We followed U.S. Highway 281 north out of Nebraska, driving for a couple hours through the rolling and green, beautiful Missouri River Valley. Shortly before crossing Interstate 90, Jim switched over to a network of much smaller roads. Driving north past the tiny town of Mitchell before dinnertime, Jim, Stefan, and I began to believe that leaving Nebraska was the right decision.

"Oh yeah! There's a lot of definition on the left side," said Jim, who from behind the wheel stole quick glances at an orange-tinted supercell just to the north. It looked well-defined and robust, like a cloud that had been working out in the gym.

"Those updrafts are rock hard!" Jim barked.

I was sitting in the front passenger seat, staring at the sight far north of us. Right before my eyes, orange-tinted supercells were coming together on the horizon and shooting into the sky. Every ten or fifteen minutes a new supercell sprang to life. These weren't sprouting like weeds. The scene was much more surreal than that. The fast-forming storms were more like instantly formed giant redwoods. One minute there'd be nothing, and then several minutes later, there'd be a forest of thunderstorms. Or a metropolis full of skyscrapers, depending on your imagination.

Jim pressed hard on the accelerator. After a while the supercells loomed much larger.

"We've got a funnel forming," said Jim, and I looked west. There was a tornado flickering about underneath a massive, unruly supercell.

"Nice cone!" said Jim. "Beautiful cone!"

The backlit tornado, which was shaped like a perfectly tapered sugar cone (minus the ice cream), was five or so miles from us.

"Can we go west?" said Stefan. "Can we get closer?"

Jim zigzagged on small roads until the backlit, blue-black tornado was perhaps a half mile away. It behaved like an unruly bull, blasting haphazardly through an open field and kicking up a huge dust cloud. Crystalline blue sky sat just off the tornado's shoulder. I captured some stunning footage.

"Amazing!" yelled Stefan in his thick German accent.

We watched the tornado rope out perhaps fifteen minutes after it formed, and then another wall cloud dropped out of the bottom of the same supercell. The atmospheric conditions were superb.

The wall cloud was to our northeast and moving away from us, and we wanted to be ahead of it. But to get there we had to drive through the rain and hail that was wrapping itself around that new wall cloud. For a moment all was mayhem, with windshield wipers moving at full tilt and still not clearing the screen. Then the hail, not too big but loud, turned the car roof into a snare drum.

When we punched east through this wrapping precipitation (remember, chasers call it the "hook"), we emerged into clear blue sky. It's as if a curtain went up: that huge wall cloud we'd wanted to get out ahead of was now just south of us and rotating extremely close to the ground. Storm chasers identify these kinds of wall clouds as "ground scrapers," because they're usually only hundreds of feet up in the air. The dark gray wall cloud was spinning faster than I'd ever seen a wall cloud spin. Inside of that beast rising winds were rotating very rapidly. I'd have bet every last cent I had that a tornado was coming.

And I'd have won the bet.

The three of us watched numerous small vortices come from the wall cloud and touch down, dancing around one another before disappearing into thin air.

They were just the opening act. The South Dakota sky then rolled out the real show: a half-mile-wide wedge tornado—wider than it was tall—that planted itself in the green South Dakota grasslands. Because the light of the sun was squarely behind it, the tornado was gray, even bordering on brown. Its outline was traced in sun-ray orange. The tornado was perhaps a thousand yards from us and churned in an open field. It didn't move much in any direction, as if it were content just to enjoy the dying day's lingering warmth, and just sit in neutral and rev its enormous engine. The question was if and when the tornado would drop into gear.

Jim and I were dumbfounded by the fast-developing tornado's size and might. I was glad it wasn't near any structures.

"I am in heaven," said Jim.

"Look at this meteorological beauty," I replied, staring at the tornado through the viewfinder of my video camera. The moment was sheer ecstasy for me, too—the payoff for all of my intense research and determination. The victory of my gamble on the storm, the reward for our deciding to head north to South Dakota instead of deeper into Nebraska.

But Stefan suddenly felt differently about the whole experience. Like he wanted to be anywhere but Manchester, South Dakota.

"Go! Go! Go!" he said from the backseat, and I turned around to look at him. His eyes were darting around. His hands were trembling.

What happened to this guy? I thought. Just minutes earlier he'd been so excited.

Jim and I were baffled.

"We're well north of it, Stefan," I said, trying to reassure him. "It won't kill you. The car can drive faster than that tornado can move. Trust me."

"I need you to respect me, Reed," said Stefan, his voice wavering. "Please. Go east."

I'd come to South Dakota for this exact moment. I wasn't willing to abandon the chase because Stefan had abruptly lost his nerve.

"We're safe right now," I assured him, holding up both hands. Stefan sat back and took a couple of deep breaths.

We got out of the car and watched the tornado for several minutes. The blowing air, filled with the odors of tornado-chopped vegetation, smelled like the air inside a forest, as if there were trees all around us. Wind was bending the surrounding tall grass. And the tornado sounded a lot like a jet airplane.

"Listen to the roar!" I said.

Soon, however, something odd happened. The tornado began moving, practically like it *was* a jet airplane, unexpectedly turning to the north and toward us.

"Get in the car! Get in the car!" I screamed, and we all piled into Jim's old beater, which had been idling.

But I didn't want to leave the scene just yet. I wanted the tornado to come closer. The video camera, of course, was running, as it almost always was when I witnessed a tornado on the ground. This was a rare opportunity to look at every crease and tendency in that oncoming beast so that I could better appreciate it. And it was about feeling that tornado's energy, that hyperfocused tornadic might that I could totally relate to.

"Now put it in reverse, and hold it there," I said to Jim while filming from behind the windshield. "Hold it," I said. "Hold it, hold it in reverse."

Jim had one foot on the brake pedal and one hand on the steering wheel. He was waiting on my word.

"Go, go, go!" begged Stefan.

"We're okay now," I said, interrupting. "But get ready to move."

"Go, go!" pleaded Stefan.

The moment was incredible, and I was shooting some of the most dramatic storm footage I'd ever taken. The tornado was closing in on the power lines that were probably just a hundred feet from our car and the empty road. My viewfinder filled with the tornado's darkness. The widest part of the tornado's wedge was now rotating above us.

"Please go back, go back," said Stefan. "Reed!" he screamed.

Then I saw nothing through the viewfinder but black wind.

"Back up! Back up!" I yelled, and Jim blasted down the two-lane road in reverse. "Keep going!"

I kept watching, kept feeling the storm's energy, kept the camera rolling. All I could hear was Stefan's anxious breathing, the whine of the car's transmission, and the howl of the storm. As Jim drove in reverse at high speed, a home suddenly appeared in my viewfinder. It was the only thing standing between the tornado and us.

· · ·

The roof, as is usually the case when a big tornado strikes a house square, was the first to go. Credit the Bernoulli effect, named after the eighteenth-century Dutch-Swiss mathematician Daniel Bernoulli. Bernoulli was a master of fluid mechanics, and one of his discoveries ("Bernoulli's principle") helps explain why fluid, when flowing horizontally over a given object's top surface faster than it flows over its bottom surface, creates a pressure difference—there's lower pressure on the top surface than the bottom surface. This pressure difference creates a lifting force. The Bernoulli effect thus explains why aircraft wings lift airplanes off the ground (air, if you will, is a "fluid"). It also explains why, when air from a tornado rushes over a home's roof, the roof rises like a wing. Then, if the tornado is strong enough, that roof is swept away.

The Manchester tornado then threw its second punch. Without the roof in place, the walls of any home are far less rigid—and sure enough, the home's second-story walls collapsed.

Tornado Alley has building codes specific to preventing tornado damage, but those codes focus on the building of concrete and/or steel-reinforced "safe rooms" within or underneath a home. (Fabricating entire homes to withstand tornadoes is generally seen as cost-prohibitive; even in Tornado Alley, the chances of any one home being directly hit by a tornado are, by some estimates, well below 0.1 percent.) In Oklahoma alone, an estimated six thousand "safe rooms" have been created in the last decade, many of them with federal monies set aside for such provisions in the wake of the horrific destruction caused by the May 3, 1999, F5 tornado.

Then the tornado engulfed the remainder of the structure, and soon the rotating air was filled with debris from the destroyed home. The pieces appeared about as fine as confetti.

I'd captured footage of similar destruction a few times before, and it always made me uneasy. Filming a tornado while it destroys a home, picks up livestock, or sweeps away a car is wrenching because you know that the victims of this destruction are suffering terrible misfortunes. Lives are being altered, if not lost, right before my electronic eye.

But I keep filming. I'm a scientist and a researcher, and engineers and scientists have long learned a lot about severe weather phenomena through reviewing the damage that it creates (recall that Herbert Saffir, who created the Saffir-Simpson Hurricane Wind Scale, was an engineer specializing in wind damage). I watch tornado videos over and over to learn more about tornadoes, wherever they may go.

But soon after the Manchester tornado unleashed itself on that house, I had to help an unexpected victim of our chase. Stefan endured a complete breakdown.

After the tornado destroyed that Manchester home, we veered away from the storm. We were able to stop driving in reverse, pull over, and get out of the car to watch and film the tornado as it surged away.

When I briefly took my eye off the viewfinder, I noticed that Stefan was behind Jim's car. He was dry heaving and shaking uncontrollably. I ran over to him.

"What's the matter?" I said. "What happened?"

Stefan was doubled over and slowly straightened himself. "It's coming back at us," he said, pointing to a small, harmless rain shaft remaining in the nearby sky.

"No, Stefan, the tornado has passed. It's gone," I said, gingerly placing my arm over his shoulder. "Everything will be all right."

Jim had walked away from the car but was now sprinting back.

"Three new tornadoes on the ground, and they're heading east. This is the storm that won't end," he said excitedly.

My eyes met Jim's, and I gave him a look as if to say, "Cool it." Jim looked at Stefan.

"You'll be okay, Stefan," said Jim. "I can't believe there are tornadoes on the ground and we're not chasing them."

"No, no," said Stefan. Sweat built on his forehead and began dripping down his face. He then began to cry.

I looked at Jim and shook my head. I understood Jim's response all too well. Jim loved tornadoes the way that I love tornadoes. They're rare enough that, once one is in your sights, you'll do anything to stay in contact. In those moments, nothing else matters.

Almost nothing, that is. Stefan was a wreck, and he clearly couldn't handle any more drama. The chase was over.

I sat Stefan in the car's backseat and got in next to him. His whole body shook. He would later explain that he'd suffered from panic attacks before, but that the act of escaping a tornado had brought on the biggest attack he'd ever endured. Stefan worried that he would have a heart attack.

"I want to go to the hospital," he said in Jim's car, and I bear-hugged him to try to calm him down. I wasn't having much luck.

The act of escaping a tornado is stressful, I thought to myself before I released Stefan. I could feel his heart, which was pounding like a bass drum. While I can't say that escaping a tornado was part of my daily ritual, for me something like that was reasonably within the realm of what might happen during a storm chase. But then I thought about how scary escaping such a meteorological monster really is.

Should I have been more cautious before inviting Stefan? I wondered to myself as he took some deep breaths in the seat next to me. He looked pale and terrible.

I thought that I should've warned Stefan of what could happen—what's possible—during a storm chase. Maybe I should've asked him more questions before I invited him along. Saying yes to him seemed like such a little decision, but bringing along Stefan changed everything. For me, Jim, the chase—but mostly for him.

Escaping a tornado, I thought again. *What kind of a person thinks of doing that?* Stefan's breakdown reminded me that I lived in a parallel universe to most people. A very foreign parallel universe. I needed to consider this when I brought people on a chase. Or when I talked to them in their living rooms.

Jim climbed behind the steering wheel and we drove through the tiny community of Manchester. Not only was there no hospital, there was no nothing. The town's half-dozen homes had been demolished. Outlying farms were annihilated. Huge trees were stripped of their leaves, and their thick trunks had been snapped in two. All in all, this was one of the worst damage paths I'd ever seen, ranking right up there with the destruction I encountered after the F5 tornado that destroyed Moore, Oklahoma, in 1999.

Later we'd learn that the nearby South Dakota town of Woonsocket had been badly damaged by a different tornado from that same weather system, and that the Manchester tornado was an F4, which means its winds were rotating at speeds of up to 260 miles per hour. *National Geographic* magazine later featured the storm in a story and ran photos of airborne telephone poles, shattered beams of wood, and a coat hanger embedded deep in a tree trunk.

The miraculous news out of the Manchester storm was that nobody was killed or seriously hurt. Jim and I, as well as several other storm chasers around the area (only later would I discover that a few others had chased the storm), did what we could to help by consistently calling the local National Weather Service forecast office to update the forecasters on the location and apparent severity of the tornadoes. In general, the forecasters' radar technology can detect wind rotation only on a larger scale than tornado winds and usually only track a storm's behavior as it happens thousands of feet up in the air.

Of course, acting as the weatherman's eyes on the ground was nothing new. For decades, "storm spotters"—members of an all-volunteer, loosely knit network across the nation that the National Weather Service rather optimistically claims is nearly 300,000 strong—have watched the weather and called in their observations to government forecasters. Some earlier storm chasers had called in their observations too, via ham (amateur) radio. The chasers' inputs complemented those of the spotters, because while storm spotters provide observations from an assigned location, a storm chaser's location changes with the storm.

But calling in weather conditions was new to *me*—and later on in my career, I'd establish a feature on my own Web site that I believe will someday allow severe-weather notification to make a huge advance, significantly adding time to government-issued tornado warnings. And the technology for that innovation would evolve out of the very thing that I carried around in my hand all day while we chased the Manchester tornado: that cell phone I finally purchased.

As Jim and I, along with a ghost white Stefan, drove west out of Manchester the night of the tornado outbreak, that very cell phone began to ring.

• • •

"Can you please hold on a second?" I told a producer at ABC over my cell phone while Jim drove east on Interstate 90 toward Sioux Falls. I put the producer on hold as I clicked over to the incoming caller. It was a producer from NBC. No sooner had I hung up with both of them than a producer from CNN called.

This was crazy. For years, the grueling process of selling severe

weather video was something that I'd endured because I knew it helped support my storm-chasing habit. And I'd obsessed over doing a good job selling videos because, well, if I was going to do anything, I was going to obsess over the process. But never before had I experienced a bunch of networks simultaneously banging down my door to do business. Then again, it's not every day that sixty-seven tornadoes touch down in South Dakota alone, and the event that day in 2003 became known locally as "Tornado Tuesday."

Back in those days, the weather-media business definitely wasn't crowded and frequently wasn't lucrative—as in it had never been very lucrative for me. But it was highly competitive, certainly among the handful of hustling videographers and photographers I knew who were involved, guys like Doug Kiesling, Simon Brewer, Jim Leonard, Warren Faidley, and Roger Hill. The group seemed to enjoy varying amounts of success. Faidley—a journalist and still photographer—was always appearing on national TV, and I recall him having a pretty sweet chase vehicle. Kiesling, whose company is called Breaking News Video Network, had a staff of people to work for him. Meanwhile I drove a string of beater cars, occasionally lived on my credit cards, and had a company of one. What am I saying? I didn't have a company at all.

But because I couldn't imagine doing anything else, during any moments of doubt I would always convince myself to stick with the business. Those were good decisions. My videos would someday springboard me onto a national platform where I could regularly raise awareness about severe weather and tornadoes to a national television audience.

In the early years of my video sales, I learned to carve out work for myself by being scrappy. For one thing, I was very proactive. All the television news outlets want the footage first, and they want it fast. After every successful tornado intercept, I'd insist that my chase partners stop at the first pay phone we could find. My agenda wasn't always popular with my storm-chasing pals, who usually wanted to eat, sleep, or drive home at the end of a long day of following storms. I wanted to do those things, too. But I didn't want to leave a window of opportunity for my competition.

I'd pour the quarters into pay phones. Initially I had only a few media contacts. However, my list of television producers consistently grew. I became familiar with people at small network affiliate stations across Tornado Alley and at the major networks too, from ABC to the Weather Channel to Univision, a huge Spanish-language television network based in Miami.

Negotiating underneath the sky, I'd sometimes be slammed by rain or wind from the same supercell that had spawned the tornado that I'd just filmed. I'd try to land an honest deal. If the producer wanted to pay me $250 and he'd paid me $300 previously, I'd remind him and try to receive what I thought was fair.

I learned that my competition frequently used the term "exclusive" in their dealings, and I felt that I should too. I'd sell CBS a weeklong exclusive on some video so that I wasn't restricted from subsequently selling to the cable networks or reality show programs later. Or even to ABC or NBC.

In fact, as Jim, Stefan, and I closed in on Sioux Falls after the Manchester tornado, I used the word "exclusive" a lot during my cell phone conversations. I believed that I had special footage of an incredible tornado.

I played a little more hardball, too, pitting one network against another. I kept thinking that even a little more money meant more chasing.

"CBS only wants a one-week exclusive," I told a producer at NBC.

Then I spoke to a producer at ABC, who told me that she wanted a ten-day exclusive.

"Why would I take that offer when CBS will take a shorter exclusive?" I said, looking back over my shoulder at Stefan. He was asleep.

"Just give us first crack," begged the producer from ABC. "I'm dying to see the footage."

We walked through the doors of the ABC affiliate in Sioux Falls and were immediately directed to the satellite truck. The producers in the truck were mesmerized. The Manchester outbreak was unbelievable—every vision of a tornado rolled into one storm, and we had seen it all. At different times during the chase, the tornado was black, backlit by the sun; white, front-lit by the sun; tapered like a skinny elephant trunk; and wider than it was tall—a classic wedge.

Minutes later I was on the satellite truck's phone with the ABC national network producer in New York.

"This part where you're backing up is really hairy," she said. "You really hang in there for these things."

At that very minute, Roger Hill burst into the satellite truck. He was a prolific chaser from Colorado and one of my direct competitors.

"You guys have got to see this," he said, holding up a video camera.

But Roger's shoulders slumped when he noticed me. Soon I alone landed the network's business.

Jim, Stefan, and I left the affiliate's offices feeling celebratory. ABC had agreed to pay us $5,000 for a ten-day network exclusive, and I could still sell my footage to cable stations.

"I'm feeling better," Stefan said over beers a little while later in a downtown Sioux Falls bar.

The next day we drove back to Norman by way of eastern Nebraska. We stopped so that I could appear in front of the camera for an interview with CNN's Anderson Cooper. He introduced me with this line: ". . . Timmer is literally the eye of the storm. He chases tornadoes down and takes pictures of them."

"What's it like," said Cooper, while my footage of us racing backward away from the oncoming Manchester tornado ran on the screen, "being that close?"

Again I was on national television, and again my appearance and daredevil footage would create a furor among more conservative storm chasers. They complained about my aggressive chase tactics and subsequent media moment extensively on some of the storm-chasing community's Internet message boards. Those who wrote in called me names like "Need Glimmer" and accused me of only showing up for the "big" storms so that I could pull off stunts like backing away from an oncoming tornado for money and fame.

If only I could predict when the "big" storms would materialize, I thought to myself upon reading the messages a few days after appearing on CNN. I didn't respond, because I began to think there was little chance of changing the minds of my detractors. They were right about one thing: I didn't chase like them. But was my style wrong? Stefan's breakdown had certainly confirmed for me that what I did wasn't for everyone.

I also thought that my critics were jealous. Back then there were hundreds of passionate storm chasers trolling the roads of Tornado Alley, and while the overwhelming majority of them didn't earn money or recognition for chasing, some of them wished that they did. I knew this to be true. My occasional moments in the spotlight, and the far more infrequent significant paydays, were not part of some master plan. They were by-products of my passion. Really, it didn't matter to me whether the chase vehicle was going forward or in reverse. What I cared about was the chase itself.

Soon after returning home from South Dakota, I spoke to producers at other television networks about my footage from the Manchester tornado. Ultimately I agreed to deals with the Weather Channel, Univision, and the syndicated television show *Inside Edition*.

I tallied up all the sales from the one tornado chase, and the total was over $20,000. I would share it with Stefan and Jim, but that was still huge for me. Upon first learning the size of my windfall, I still had only one thought: *more fuel for the chase-vehicle tank.*

• • •

Of course, I could've told my many detractors to take another look at the potential depth of a storm chaser's obsession. "Why don't you go ask another passionate storm chaser in Tornado Alley how he makes decisions?" I could have said.

Take a guy like Simon Brewer.

Only weeks before the massive Manchester tornado, I had embarked on a chase that left me frustrated and white as a ghost. On that very same day, Simon Brewer had enjoyed a fantastic chase, although he paid a price too. Simon is a longtime tornado nut and a friendly rival of mine. Between us, May 8, 2003, was a crazy tale of two chasers.

• • •

Simon woke up on that Thursday in May convinced that he wasn't going to chase. An OU undergraduate meteorology student at the time, Simon had a final in atmospheric dynamics the next day. He'd gotten the week off from work—the counter at Kentucky Fried Chicken—to concentrate on school. OU hadn't been a smooth experience for Simon. The then twenty-two-year-old native of Dayton, Ohio, needed the day to study.

I woke up that same day with a different plan. Joel and I, along with three other chasers, deployed first thing that morning for the town of Emporia in east-central Kansas. The setup was a classic dryline: hot, dry air blowing from the west/southwest, and warm, moist air blowing from the south/southeast.

It killed Simon that he couldn't chase that day. He knew of the potential tornado outbreak I was pursuing, as did many other chasers. Like a lot of storm chasers, Simon had grown up fascinated by the weather. When he was a kid, and his mom took him and his two older brothers to the library, Simon's brothers would sit down with storybooks and volumes from the Hardy Boys series. But Simon was always over in the nonfiction aisle. He wanted to look at books about volcanoes, oceans, and the weather.

When it came time to attend college, Simon had to choose between the meteorology programs at Saint Louis University in Missouri and the University of Oklahoma. The Saint Louis program was more nurturing, OU more of a place designed to weed out those who couldn't make the grade. Only the studious and determined survived. Simon was tempted by SLU's softer touch, but OU was smack-dab in the middle of Tornado Alley. Simon was an athlete, too—a tall and lean high school runner with big quads who was fast and strong enough to land a spot on a college team. Simon settled on OU; he believed that he could compete in both cross-country and track, study, and squeeze in some storm chasing. He had to earn money, too.

While Simon sat down to organize class notes in his Norman house—he shared a rental with some other OU runners—Joel, the three others, and I were already on the road in Joel's white Explorer. It was early in the season, and we were eager to see tornadoes. We made it the 260 miles to Emporia before noon, and nothing was happening quite yet. It was early in the day.

So we made a small tweak to the plans. We decided to go even farther north, heading the eighty miles past I-70 toward Manhattan in search of what's called the triple point. The triple point is, technically, where three atmospheric boundaries meet. On May 8, the triple point we pursued was where the two major elements of the dryline—incoming warm and moist air from one direction, and hot dry air from another—would intersect with cold air from the north. A warm front also extended east from the dryline/cold front intersection, which would only add to the day's combustible conditions.

Around the same time that morning, Simon was cracking the books when he decided to sneak a peek at the online weather forecasting models. Just a quick peek. He went to the College of DuPage's data-heavy Web site. He wasn't big on logging in to the Storm Prediction Center for another forecast perspective, where the maps were straightforward and simple, the statistics and data easily digestible.

Simon was old-school—he generally liked to create hand-drawn weather maps before he chased, and was obsessed with analyzing the bigger picture satellite images that show clouds, troughs, and jet streaks (very fast winds embedded in the jet stream that can trigger storm development). "Old school" forecasting is an hours-long process performed with a pencil and "surface map," where one carefully draws out a target region's wind flow, temperature, and dew points, among many other bits of meteorological data and input. The forecaster hopes to uncover trends and nuances in order to find the best place to chase—which might be totally different than what the SPC recommends. Before the Internet and computer-modeling Web sites were available, plenty of storm chasers would produce their own maps with pen and pencil, and today some folks still find these hand-drawn analyses helpful and fun. I'm not one of those people. I don't have the patience for drawing out my own maps when they can be generated by computer, and I'll always make the argument that I can generally create a solid forecast in my head, based on data collected from many modeling Web sites. *Plus* I'm open to consulting other opinions such as the SPC outlooks, while Simon utterly refuses. Sometimes I think that his stubbornness costs him tornadoes.

But today, Simon was supposed to study. No forecasts. Then the Web site that he accessed indicated high CAPE and huge wind shear right in the Oklahoma City area—just thirty minutes from Simon's house. In addition, temperatures high in the atmosphere indicated that the cap over the Oklahoma City metro area might break up.

Simon had to make a decision: chase the storm forming virtually right outside his window, or study for the next day's exam?

Meanwhile Joel and I arrived at our destination, where we'd expected triple-point fireworks and a more favorable environment for strong tornadoes than farther south in Oklahoma. We were wrong. The cold air had surged farther south and the dryline had literally avoided the cold air by shifting farther east. The dryline was perhaps fifty miles ahead of us and continuing east. Meanwhile we were in fog and cold air, and caught by surprise as the cold air surged south faster than we'd expected. Time to make a quick decision: Do we make a desperate deployment east to try to catch the dryline and potentially some thunderstorms, or do we stick with the triple point forecast and hope the fog burns off?

The first thing Simon said to himself: He needed to pass dynamics. He'd already been at OU for four years, and graduation for him wasn't anywhere in sight. After arriving at Oklahoma, storm chasing ultimately invaded Simon's schedule. He'd quit competing in cross-country and track and skipped plenty of classes. When his boss wanted to make Simon a manager at KFC, Simon declined. That was too much responsibility. He only tolerated the job to begin with because it gave him the money and a flexible enough schedule to chase.

And when Simon did chase, he wasn't interested in getting home in time for dinner, like plenty of casual chasers who had wives, kids, dogs, and jobs. He was always too busy to attend an annual storm-chaser picnic outside of Oklahoma City in Piedmont and never stopped to chat when chasers gathered on roadsides in vehicles loaded with radio equipment and antennas. Instead, Simon looked more like a grunge-rock version of a chaser, with a flannel shirt, unshaven face, and an old red van.

Simon sold video, like I did, and was fairly successful. But he worked with only a few clients, because he didn't care to deal with the dozen or so that I now regularly called. Plus, if someone didn't offer Simon at least $200, he would prepare to stop negotiating. Faxing paperwork back and forth into the wee hours of the morning wasn't worth it to him, even though he needed the cash.

Joel and I decided to get out of the fog and chase the storms to our

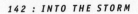

east. It was either that or endure a blue-sky bust. Joel pushed down the accelerator as we flew across Highway 24 toward Topeka.

Meanwhile Simon convinced himself that he might pass the exam without studying, and soon he was in his van, trying to figure out where the Oklahoma City storm would come down, heading east on Interstate 40 and getting pummeled with baseball-size hail. He knew that a tornado could be right behind the precipitation and held his breath—it was rush hour, and the highway was packed with scared drivers who had slowed to a crawl and didn't know what to expect next. Simon worried that the tornado would roll right over the traffic jam.

But when the hailstorm abated and Simon looked up, what he saw instead was a train of clouds, moving east to west. That wasn't a normal procession—usually the air flows the other way. These clouds, however, were the storm's inflow band—the moist air that the storm system was sucking down for fuel.

Simon finally fought his way out of the traffic and reached the southeast portion of town, where he was very close to I-240 and a huge General Motors SUV plant. Now the sky was overcast and the color of dingy bathwater. The murkiness and haze could've been the result of the fires currently raging in Mexico, with their smoke drifting northward. The wind was howling.

Joel and I and the three others in his SUV figured that we were within fighting distance of some storms because the highway surface was now wet from earlier rain. We believed that this was precipitation trailing a thunderstorm. Joel pressed down even harder on the gas. Suddenly his vehicle began to slide right.

Simon kept looking west, over a series of grassy knolls. The radio announcer had just warned of a "tornado emergency," which is the National Weather Service's dire warning of significant, widespread damage due to a violent tornado. Simon also heard that the tornado was headed northeast, which meant he was likely in a great position for the intercept. He was feeling better and better about his decision. Then a dark stain appeared on the western ridgeline of the grassy hills—a stovepipe-style tornado that evolved into a huge and messy wedge as it crept across the slopes. It was a half mile wide and dark with debris, as the storm had already chewed through several hotels and restaurants.

Joel turned the steering wheel left to counter the big vehicle's slide, and for a minute he seemed to have saved the five of us from a terrible accident. But then the car began skidding toward the median. Joel sawed at the wheel again, yet it was too late. Down the four-lane highway, the Explorer entered into a tornado-style counterclockwise spin. I remember thinking, as we were careening toward the ditch on the side of the road, *This is going to hurt.*

Simon hopped out of his van to film the Oklahoma City tornado and patiently waited for it to square up to him, due north. The tornado's rotation wasn't going to engulf him. But Simon was surprised by the strength of the surrounding downdraft winds being pushed outside of the tornado. The winds began to pummel him, first like a heavyweight boxer and then like they wanted to blow Simon into the next county. He stood closer to his van, but as the tornado traveled within a hundred yards of Simon, his van started to shake.

Simon backed away from the van only to be pelted by debris—the roofing shingles, insulation, and wood that the tornado had probably carried since the last county. That's when he decided to turn his back on the tornado and run.

Simon tanked the next day's dynamics exam and wouldn't graduate from OU anytime soon. But he did film what was an F4 tornado as it plowed past him through the GM factory and beyond. He then sold the video footage.

Miraculously, the Explorer pulled out of the two-revolution, across-four-lane spin. Although we were all shaken, we were more disappointed

because we would miss all fifty-four of the tornadoes that came down that May 2003 day in Tornado Alley. Joel's hands shook violently as he tried to grip the wheel after pulling out of the spin, and he was hyperventilating. We all knew we had just dodged a bullet.

Should Simon Brewer have done anything differently that day? He caught the storm and captured the footage but put his academics on the back burner and paid the price. We nearly flipped our vehicle and missed the storms completely. I should've set up a tripod and a camera at home, since the tornado Simon intercepted only missed my apartment by a few miles when it first touched down! Such is the nature of storm chasing.

You choose who, if any of us, made the wrong decisions.

• • •

I consider myself an optimist even when I'm inside a spinning truck, but after earning quite a bit of money from the Manchester, South Dakota, video, I'll confess that I wondered if I'd ever do it again. I didn't pretend to imagine that another Manchester-type F4 would drop down in front of me anytime soon. But I contemplated another idea that might fund an entire chase season.

When I wasn't chasing, or spending time with my girlfriend, I put in plenty of hours in my graduate-student office, working, studying, and daydreaming about big weather with my OU meteorology friends. They always lamented the fact that we couldn't be graduate students forever. Our peers who were already grinding away at real jobs liked to remind all of us that our day would come. They said that we'd ultimately land in a cubicle somewhere, putting in the hours under some tough boss.

I'd throw out the occasional suggestion for permanently avoiding a nine-to-five existence.

"Why don't we all run a weather consulting firm? We could each take turns overseeing the business," I thought aloud to fellow grad students

Don Giuliano and John Esterheld one late afternoon in the spring of 2003. We were in room 1510 of Sarkeys, a graduate-student office that I shared with Don, John, and a couple other guys. The fifteenth-floor office had a fantastic view of storms that came from the south. "Between us, I bet we could create forecasts for any company that relies on the weather. If we all had a slice of the business," I added, "we could each generate some income and all have free time during the days."

"We all know where a certain someone would be on his free days, don't we?" said Don, looking over some wind shear research on his desk. He didn't have to look up. John and I both knew that Don was referring to me. "Three people need to earn three salaries, and they would each have to work hard," he continued. "I don't know. Maybe the answer is academia."

If working for Dr. Lamb was any indication, I was not convinced that I was cut out for a life in academics despite my love for science and research. Lamb was very exacting, and his demands were tough on me. At that moment I was working on an involved report for him that concerned Pacific sea surface temperature anomaly patterns. Lamb wanted to know more about the relationships between Pacific SST anomaly patterns like El Niño—which is characterized by notably warm temperatures in the equatorial Pacific—and energy usage in the United States. I didn't mind the subject matter, and actually enjoyed studying climate variability. But I'd already written the report twice. Another revision was due back to him the next day.

"I'm going home to tank up on caffeine, eat, and push through these changes," I said, packing up my papers. "See you guys tomorrow."

I was only telling a half-truth. Late that evening, I met with my friend Dean Schoenick. Dean and I had gone to meteorology school together, joined forces on some storm chases, and tossed a few back in the same bowling league. Dean also developed Web sites for a living, and figured out how to drive traffic to those sites.

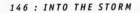

"It's not exciting," Dean told me. "But it's a living."

I briefly entertained the idea of launching a freelance business doing what Dean did. Then I had a better idea: a Web site of my own. I envisioned a site that allowed me to sell some of my wild storm-chasing videos on DVD. I'd already tried to make some money selling such DVDs in the storm-chasing community by posting notices on online message boards. That hadn't been a huge success. I wondered if there was a way to reach a wider audience and mass market my videos—I thought other weather nuts, and maybe some people who would see what I did as interesting, brave, or outlandish, would buy my wares.

I'd posed my ideas to Dean. His eyes got big.

"Put some clips of your videos online—enough to tempt someone to want to buy a DVD," he said. "Give the customer a taste, and then the option to buy more of the same."

I thought about Dean's suggestion. There were already weather Web sites on the Internet. But most of them didn't feature video "teasers," or samples. In 2003, the thinking among storm chasers was that the more people who could see your hard-earned video for free, the less reason anyone would have to buy it.

Dean thought the opposite was true. In spring 2003, he convinced me to create a Web site that played clips of my chases in order to promote my DVDs.

I was too broke to hire someone to do the design work, and Dean was a Web site designing machine, so we formed a partnership to split the DVD income and designed the Web site ourselves. (Dean taught me how to use design and editing software and I pulled a few all-nighters to learn how to write in HTML.) After a week of slogging through, I had a basic Web site ready to go. Dean performed some analysis of search terms used to find storm videos and the smart money was on calling the site something obvious: www.tornadovideos.net.

The Web site was primitive—it was only 2003 and the Internet was still rapidly evolving. Tornadovideos.net offered visitors only some sneak preview video and a way to buy my DVDs. It wasn't Amazon, but from the very beginning I considered it a success. Right away, I was selling $300 worth of DVDs every month. For me that was a gift, and it paid the rent.

The site also offered another way to generate income. Tornadovideos. net was a storefront that sold clips of my storm-chasing videos. Now producers at video clip shows like *World's Most Amazing Videos* or PBS's *Nova* could find my Web site via Google and download whatever footage they needed for a fee. I soon discovered that video of the May 3, 1999, F5 was just as shocking for audiences in 2003 as it was in 1999.

That spring, my footage from the Manchester, South Dakota, chase— the chase where Stefan had panicked—was the gift that kept on giving. Producers consistently asked for the same thing: the footage taken while our chase car was surging backward down the road away from the storm, as I was screaming, "Back up!" With every sale, I was making money— and learning more about what kind of storm chasing America wanted to see.

• • •

I didn't know what to do with the money in my pocket. Tornadovideos. net's immediate, positive cash flow was generating income for me that arrived like pennies from heaven. There would be $20 from a weather nut in Tennessee who had bought a DVD and $315 from the BBC for purchasing seven seconds' worth of footage. Nearly every day brought another purchase on my Web site at a time when I truly needed the money.

I'd never had much cash. Growing up, I was never wanting for anything, although I can't say that I asked for much. My mom was far more interested in giving me facts and knowledge than things. As a child, her parents had taken her on education-oriented family vacations. They'd travel to Mt. Vernon, Monticello, and battlefields from the Civil War, and when I grew up my mother frequently took my sisters and me to similar places. For holidays and birthdays, my mom showered us with books, art supplies, and butterfly nets instead of toys. My grandfather once gave my sisters a gift of live chickens, with the hopes that they'd learn to raise the birds.

Soon after the money from my Web site started flowing in, I decided to go on what seemed like a prudent spending spree. I bought some new electronic equipment for my business. I wanted high-end photography and video-editing equipment, the necessary accessories and lenses, and a powerful laptop computer. In the late spring of 2003, I invested $25,000 in the hardware. The amount far exceeded what I had in the bank, and I loaded up my credit cards with the purchases, confident that, in a short time, tornadovideos.net and my storm chases to come would generate the money to pay off my debts and then some.

I also had an urge to show Niki that I could be a breadwinner. When we first started dating, I didn't even have a car, and I often wore crappy T-shirts that I'd sometimes wear inside out when I didn't have time for laundry. Niki hadn't complained too loudly. She would do the driving and sometimes loaned me her car (although not for storm chasing). When I changed the look of my shirts by cutting off the sleeves, she tried to hold her tongue. We split the tabs on a lot of our dates. Now I wanted to show her my gratitude.

"I have a surprise for our one-year anniversary," I said one night in the summer of 2003. We were at a bar and grill in Moore, and when the waiter came with the check I grabbed it to pay the full amount. "I'm taking you away."

"Ooohh," she said, smiling. "Where are we going?"

A few weeks later, I took Niki to San Antonio for several days. We stayed in a nice hotel, toured the Alamo, ate great food, and strode along the River Walk, holding hands in the warm Texas evenings.

Life was great all through that summer. I had a strong relationship with my girlfriend, compelling schoolwork, and a little business courtesy of what I lived to do—chase the science and the fury of tornadoes. I was on a hot streak, right down to my stock investments.

Early in July, I'd received a tip from an investment outfit called Roller Coaster Stocks to invest in an oil and gas exploration company called Ivanhoe Energy.

Roller Coaster Stocks, I'd thought to myself. *That company is tailor-made for a guy like me.*

I knew nothing about investing or the stock market, but I went with the tip and purchased about $7,000 worth of Ivanhoe at about $1 per share. By fall, the stock was over $5 per share, on the announcement that Ivanhoe was launching a promising project in a gas-rich region of China. On one day in particular, I followed the stock closely, and it seemed to climb as fast as I could hit the "refresh" button on my Web browser.

Yes, my life was a lot like Ivanhoe's stock performance. Too bad the investments and my luck couldn't hold up forever.

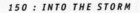

CHAPTER 6

BLOWN BACK

J oel sighed. Sighs were his way of communicating that a chase had gone bad without his having to say as much. I never enjoyed hearing those sighs, because they represented defeat and were no help in terms of getting closer to the tornadoes. I'd grown up in a household where the negatives were seldom articulated. Even today, my mom refuses to worry out loud about my strange line of work. "Oh, Reed, I'm not sure I want to see up close what you do," she says. "Best to let nothing stand in your way."

Unfortunately, back in 2004 I met obstacles. I'd hear sighs in stereo, and for months on end. They'd come from my longtime friend and storm-chasing partner Joel, other people in my life, and my own head, too. Just when I thought everything was going right, my tornado-centered existence was about to get unexpectedly tough.

"Kansas will be better," I said to Joel, keeping the conversation positive. "Southwest Kansas. It'll be better there."

Honestly, I was having a hard time remaining upbeat too. It was Tuesday, May 11. We were driving south on U.S. Highway 83, outside of Valentine, Nebraska, in my very used red pickup. We were both grimy and sleep deprived. Joel and I had been awake for most of the last thirty hours after making a late-afternoon decision a day earlier to deploy from

Norman to northwest Nebraska to chase a storm. But after driving 660 uninterrupted miles, we arrived in Cherry County only to see harmless, puffy, white clouds. The dew point in northern Nebraska didn't climb nearly as high as I'd hoped it would. The air was dry, which put the odds of us seeing a tornado at zero.

"Why did I listen to you?" Joel finally said, staring straight ahead, his hands barely moving the steering wheel as we drove down the arrow-straight road.

"You agreed that it was worth a try," I said, sipping some coffee. "And you know tomorrow's setup for southwest Kansas looks insane."

"That's an exaggeration," he said. "Besides, I have a meeting tomorrow in Norman. We're heading back."

"Joel—"

"Reed, I'm a forecaster, not a *wishcaster*," he said, interrupting. "I'm not breaking my commitments tomorrow in Oklahoma to chase a fantasy tornado."

"You're wrong about Kansas. Just like you were wrong about Manchester," I said.

"Okay, Reed, are we going to play that game?" he replied. "Just like you were wrong about Minnesota and that hell ride we took in your dying car?"

Joel was right—I'd made plenty of mistakes and bad chasing calls. We'd been friends and fellow chasers for years. But he used to be more accepting of the numerous busts that came along with the relatively few but incredibly gratifying successes. We both understood that failure was part of the game. Now he seemed to have less patience. Joel was becoming increasingly intolerant of my relentless enthusiasm, increasingly reluctant to go on long chases with me, and increasingly interested in building his real estate business. I felt like the encroaching responsibilities of adulthood were perhaps pulling Joel away from me, as well as the tornadoes. I understood—not everyone prioritizes the same way. And I admired how Joel was building his career.

But for better or worse, in the wake of my huge intercept the year before in Manchester, South Dakota—that incredible F4 tornado that I watched from a reversing chase vehicle—Joel and I were in unspoken agreement that I had the hot storm-chasing hand. For example, earlier in the spring of '04, I'd convinced Joel to come with me on what resulted in a successful chase in western Oklahoma—despite the fact that the SPC had put very narrow odds on a tornado occurring. Joel had been forced to admit that he was pleasantly surprised to see that tornado.

As we rolled south down Nebraska's Highway 83, we approached the town of Thedford and a fork in the road. I argued again that we should continue south toward southwest Kansas, and not southeast toward Oklahoma and home. I *knew* this was the right decision. And perhaps that was the first indication that dark clouds might be gathering on my own horizon. I had a little money in my pocket, and the distractions of going out and taking trips with Niki that went with it. Perhaps I had gotten a little cocky about my own ability to successfully intercept storms. Maybe Joel wasn't the only one losing his focus.

"I'm positive that southwest Kansas will explode tomorrow," I said. "High CAPE values, gulf air surging toward Oklahoma and Kansas, a dryline to the west. We're crazy to go home."

"Sometimes the smartest decision is to pass," said Joel, turning left onto Nebraska Highway 2, which led toward the town of Grand Island. From there we'd go south to Oklahoma.

We drove in silence for hundreds of miles. How could he skip such a potent setup? In my mind I could see the low-level jet intensifying, transporting warm, moist air from the Gulf of Mexico into the plains, where it would be launched skyward by the dry heat of the incoming westerlies behind a textbook dryline. Then the condensation would occur, and seemingly out of nowhere there'd be an expanding supercell thunderstorm, a cauliflower-shaped, fifty-thousand-foot cloud being torqued by opposing winds until it started spinning like a top. Then the tornado would come down, at first barely visible, almost like a phantom, as the upwardly rotating winds strengthened and felt their way to the ground. And once it was firmly established, the tornado would change shape and personality right before my very eyes. One minute it would be a skittish, long and thin drill bit; the next it'd be a curvy and crooked elephant's trunk that's happy in one place; and then suddenly it'd be a squat wedge chugging over the ground cover. Why wouldn't Joel want to check out the spectacle that I was so sure was coming?

Well, if he was going to be stubborn, so was I. I'd find someone else to chase with.

Joel left me at my house at six A.M. I was exhausted. But I would've made it back out to southwest Kansas that day on pride alone. Later that morning I called Dean Schoenick and asked if he was interested. Soon I was on the road with Dean and his girlfriend Ehle. We surged toward Attica, Kansas, 230 miles away. I dosed up on energy drinks and deemed myself ready to chase.

An hour after we'd left Norman, my phone rang. It was Joel. He'd reconsidered. He wanted to come. I said it was too late and that we weren't going back for him.

But this was one trip that Joel wouldn't regret missing. In retrospect, I wished that I'd stayed in Norman and slept the entire day of May 12, 2004. It wasn't the sky's fault—it did its job. Even tornadoes, however, couldn't prevent me from suffering through a living nightmare.

• • •

"Which one do we chase?" asked Dean, pulling over on the shoulder of a two-lane, paved road outside of tiny Attica, Kansas. The three of us got out of his black Isuzu Rodeo to take in our surroundings. Ken Cole,

Harold Peterson, and Harold's wife, Kelly—other friends and fellow storm chasers who followed us in another car—did the same.

All around us were green grassland and farm plots. Above us were not one but two insane cumulonimbus clouds, and both had the potential to produce tornadoes. They were only several miles apart, and each looked impressive, as they were both capped by giant anvil clouds: These are the horizontally expanding, relatively flat clouds above the storm's vertical column that are very good indicators of a storm's strength and full growth. Anvil clouds are the spillover of the storm's fast-rising, moist air that has now cooled and is spreading across the upper atmosphere. The most promising anvils are thick and hard edged—proof that the cumulonimbus cloud has plenty of moisture and a strong updraft, or upward movement of winds.

Both of these storms had notably crisp anvils, shining a brilliant white as they reflected the rays of the slowly setting sun. Having two such storms was an embarrassment of riches, and for a few minutes I struggled to commit to one. What to chase? Little did I know then that my indecision would literally turn our day's mission upside down.

"Let's go south," I finally said, squinting at the southern storm. Since the tropical gulf air was coming from the south, I also thought that the southern storm would be first in line for that wave of warm moisture. I sat down again in the front passenger seat, and as Dean drove us the several miles toward the southern storm, it began to rotate. Bingo! That meant the presence of a mesocyclone—the spinning updraft inside of the storm. I watched the steel-colored clouds turn in the sky, marveling at how their rotation made the storm seem like it suddenly had a heartbeat and a brain. The wall cloud—that appendage of thick condensation that sits lower than the rest of the storm and indicates the strongest area of the mesocyclone—had already formed too. It was a mean, dark gray, and spinning. When would the storm decide to drop a tornado? That's still one of the great unsolved mysteries of tornado science.

We pulled over again and got out of the SUV. Dean left the vehicle running.

"It's really consolidating now," I said, my new video camera aimed at the rotating wall cloud.

Ehle and Dean were beside me and looking up at the sky too. I didn't see Ken and Harold.

"It's trying to get organized," I added.

"Are we in a dangerous spot?" said Ehle in a worried tone, looking up at the sky and then looking around. "Could it come for us?"

I assured Ehle that we were well ahead of the storm and safe, and immediately flashed back to the memory of my friend Stefan panicking during our chase together in South Dakota. I sure hoped never to duplicate that experience.

The supercell's rotation was impressively quick—as if you were watching a video of it playing in fast-forward mode. But then one minute went by, then two, then five, and then ten.

I had a bad feeling in my gut. There was no tornado. Nobody knows exactly why tailor-made tornadic thunderstorms sometimes don't produce tornadoes.

Dean's weather radio was on inside the idling Rodeo, and I heard some frustrating news. A tornado was on the ground, north of Attica outside the town of Pratt. We were south of Attica! Had the southern storm been the wrong call? I made a split-second decision.

"Ehle, Dean, get in the car," I yelled. "Deploy north! The explosive weather is north of us! Tornado on the ground outside of Pratt on the northern storm!"

The move was a gamble. What if the storm we left behind suddenly produced a tornado? What if we didn't reach the other storm in time?

We got in the Rodeo and blasted north over a dense network of southern Kansas dirt roads. But this time my optimism didn't serve me well. The supercell was much farther away than I'd thought. After playing catch-up for thirty minutes, we finally came upon the northern storm. But the tornado was gone. The supercell evaporated right in front of us.

Dean pulled over again.

"Now what?" he asked.

I sat there for a second, thinking. This was crappy luck. Yesterday, there had been the blue-sky bust in Nebraska, and then the fight with Joel. Today, I was ping-ponging between storms and coming up empty. Plus I was very tired. I hadn't slept for two days.

My mobile phone rang. It was Ken.

"Are you guys seeing this?" he asked, his voice excited and his words coming out quickly. "What are we on?" I heard Ken asking Harold over the phone. "The fifth tornado?"

"What?" I shouted. "Where are you?" I asked, suddenly feeling queasy.

"We're south of Attica," said Ken. "Where are you?"

"We decided to go north. We thought that was the right play."

"You're missing out," said Ken. "I'm looking at the tornado right now. A huge cone. It's massive."

I hung up with Ken and looked at Dean and Ehle.

"We have to go back to the southern storm! Stat!" I said.

We were halfway to Ken and Harold's position when we reached the outskirts of Attica and encountered an intense damage path. We saw a house, bordered by vehicles with flashing lights, without a roof—a sad but sure indicator that a strong tornado had come through. Wood framing and insulation were in the nearby fields. The air was thick with humidity, and it had that telltale earthy smell of churned-up dirt. A fireman at the scene of the destroyed home waved us and other drivers past.

The damage path—a wide swath of dirt and mauled vegetation—led due east, although we couldn't see a tornado in that direction. But we could see a large, gray wall of precipitation against an otherwise blue sky. That moisture was likely the hook precipitation around the back of the storm. Truth is, there was a large stovepipe tornado just on the other side of the rain. Too bad we'd never catch up to it.

The shortest route to try to intercept the stovepipe was to drive ten miles east on a dirt farm road. It was another gamble: The storm's "hook precip" could have turned the dirt road into slick and gooey mud. We could get stuck. We'd also have to drive right through the precipitation—punch the core—in order to reach the tornado. As I've explained before, some chasers argue that punching the core is dangerous because you can go straight from a nearly blinding (and potentially damaging) rain-and-hail storm right into the tornado's circulating winds. But I've punched cores for years and have always found that the precipitation eases, and visibility markedly improves, before I ever encounter a tornado (I will warn you that taking a risk like this really does require a lot of experience and isn't for the amateur storm chaser).

"Let's go east," said Dean, nodding. "We'll be okay in the truck. It's a good bet that the tornado is just beyond the precipitation."

Dean's enthusiasm motivated me. I was tired, but I'd come too far in the last several days to miss everything.

"Let's go east," I said in agreement.

Dean carefully accelerated as he hit the first dirt road, and it was immediately obvious that the roads were soaked. When the SUV would occasionally lose traction, Dean would correct the skid to keep his vehicle straight.

We drove several miles, and the gray mass of cloud and storm ahead of us drew very close. Dean grew more confident, raising his vehicle's speed from twenty miles per hour to thirty-five.

"We're almost there," said Dean. I looked at the road surface. It was now a glistening muddy brown. The storm's heavy precipitation had rolled through just ahead of us.

I also looked up. The back side of the storm was beautiful. The hook of rain was a rich, dark blue, and well-defined—like a cloak wrapped around clouds. Above the hook precipitation, the vertical portion of the supercell was lit up bright white by the sun that was fading behind us. Above that was the anvil. It sent bolts of lightning crashing down to the bright green winter wheat fields that were all around. Bolts of lightning known as "anvil crawlers" shot within the anvil, too. They lit up the top of the storm like a Times Square billboard.

We entered into the outer reaches of the hail and rain, and I opened my window halfway and put my video camera's viewfinder up to my eye in anticipation of soon spotting the tornado. The truck's rear wheels slipped again, and the slip grew into a small skid. Dean turned the steering wheel to compensate for the SUV's slide, but it wasn't doing the trick. We weren't straightening out. By the time we were traveling at a diagonal down the mud-caked Kansas farm road, I knew that we wouldn't pull out of the fishtailing slide.

The next few seconds took forever. I lowered my video camera and saw the worry in Dean's eyes as the vehicle kept skidding to the left. I looked at the big ditches on either side of the road, and beyond them giant embankments. I saw hail hit the windshield.

But in reality we weren't moving slowly, and as the car approached the edge of the left side of the road, I knew we were in for a fall and a violent impact. I blinked and we were plunging into the ditch. We were all wearing our seat belts, and still the force of the vehicle's left front fender hitting the far wall of the ditch jolted all of us and sent everything in the car flying. My new still camera slammed against the dashboard, my new laptop computer dove to the vehicle's floor, and my new video camera went I don't know where. The SUV bounced off the far wall of the ditch and recoiled, landing on a steep slant and then tipping over onto the passenger-side doors before coming to a rest. Everything fell toward my side of the car, which quickly began to fill with murky water.

"Is everyone okay?" Dean asked. He was still strapped into his seat belt, which held him in place above me and out of the water.

"I think so," said Ehle. "Oh my gosh. That was scary."

"I'm all right. Pretty sure," I said.

We tried to gather ourselves for a couple of minutes, and then the cold water sobered me.

"Oh no!" I said, and struggled to undo my seat belt. The brown water was now above my door and continuing its rise. "My equipment!"

I leaned down while lifting my chin to keep my head out of the water and fully extended my right arm so that my right hand could feel under the water around my feet. The first thing I touched was the still camera. I pulled it out.

"Hold this," I said to Dean, and he took the waterlogged camera from me. Then I plunged my hand back into the water and grabbed my video camera. I went back a third time for my new laptop.

"It's all destroyed. Unbelievable!" I yelled.

Dean held my ruined gear and looked at the water in his truck. "Is this really happening?" he asked.

Ehle struggled to hold on to the interior handle of the left rear door, which was above her. I was now craning my body toward Dean to keep the rising water away. I wasn't having much luck keeping myself dry.

"What is that smell?" said Ehle.

"The water? It is foul," said Dean.

We began thinking about how we'd climb out when someone stepped from the dirt road onto the driver's door.

"How's everyone doing?" said a tall, thin man looking down into the truck. He was wearing a cowboy hat and well-worn blue jeans.

We all thought we were okay.

"Let's get you out of there," he said. "You're sitting in sewage runoff."

Ugh. We squirmed out of the vehicle as quickly as possible. The man leaned over and helped each of us climb out.

We all stepped off the truck and onto the road. The guy was a farmer, and we'd dumped Dean's vehicle into the ditch right in front of his property. He gave us some towels and used his tractor to eventually pull Dean's SUV out of the ditch, although not before it had been completely submerged in storm runoff. The truck was filled with mud. Dean looked like he wanted to cry.

"Can you come pick us up?" I asked Harold from my mobile phone, which was miraculously still functioning. I made a quick call to Niki, too, and told her what had happened.

"I'm so glad you're all right," she said. But I could hear the impatience in her voice. "I'm always worrying about you on these crazy chases," she added.

I wanted to crawl into a hole instead of a car for the four-hour return trip to Norman. Sitting in our wet and smelly clothes, Dean, Ehle, and I listened to Ken, Harold, and Kelly recount their stories of multiple tornado sightings. Some of the tornadoes were thin and translucent (which happens when the air underneath the storm is relatively dry). The most incredible tornado of the outbreak, they explained, dropped from a black wall cloud that was spinning very quickly and was set against a pink and blue sky. Before the tornado touched down it was beautifully symmetrical and rounded, and looked a lot like a child's spinning top. When it finally hit ground, they explained, the tornado elongated, taking on the silhouette of a stovepipe. Shafts of light poked through some gaps in the storm's upper clouds, and the tornado's color alternated between black and white as it moved in and out of the light. All totaled, the Attica outbreak consisted of about twelve tornadoes. We had seen none. Fortunately there were no fatalities.

The stovepipe sounded so gorgeous that it was hard for me to listen to the stories. As for Dean, he wasn't listening at all. He was crushed about losing his car. I felt terrible for him. My intensity had undermined our chase; I'd been so focused on seeing something that we ended up intercepting nothing. I'd also played a big role in our pursuing that storm down the muddy road.

When I arrived home, I peeled off my disgusting clothes and took a long, hot shower.

. . .

A week later I pulled out my credit card to buy another video camera, which cost me $2,500 that I didn't have. I didn't think twice about it. I needed the camera. As I watched the store clerk run my credit card, I thought about the realities of a life that was taking on more and more responsibility: There just went another withdrawal on my increasingly debt-ridden existence.

My financial fortunes had swung ridiculously fast. Hadn't it only been yesterday that tornadovideos.net went live and was met with a huge demand for footage? But my last intercept was now almost a year old, and I didn't have any new intense tornado video to offer as an encore. The fall 2003 chasing season had been frustratingly quiet. And I'd just spent the best day of the spring 2004 chase campaign in a south Kansas ditch.

A new lifestyle only made my financial situation worse. Niki wanted to move into a nicer apartment complex in Moore, which had a pool, tennis court, pond, and golf course. She suggested that I get a place in the same complex, as a next step in our maturing relationship.

"It's time that you graduate from the college pit," she said. "We can hang out more. It's not like we're married yet."

Yet, I thought to myself, and wondered where our relationship was headed. I liked Niki a lot. She had a lot of fire and a contagious laugh. I didn't want to lose her.

I also kept thinking that there was so much more to learn about the weather and tornadoes, and I was reluctant to slow down. There was no doubt—I still wanted to chase tornadoes in order to marvel at their spectacle, to be fed by their power and intensity. But after seeing tornadoes cause so much damage, I was becoming increasingly interested in understanding them and finding ways to protect people from becoming their victims. I asked myself questions: What influences a tornado's intensity? How can we better warn people when they're coming?

Unfortunately, the storm-chasing ranks are filled with guys who have relationship problems. Many a storm chaser has told me that his wife or girlfriend complained loudly that chasing required too much time, too much travel, and too much energy. Lots of storm chasers are bachelors or ex-husbands. Nonetheless, I decided to move into the same apartment complex as Niki and attempt to juggle the girlfriend, my finances, and the chasing. My old chasing partner Aaron would be my apartment-mate.

"Will you walk Roxie today?" Niki said to me in her apartment one Tuesday morning, a few weeks after the car crash in Attica.

She was dressed for work at the bank, and I was in an old T-shirt and jeans. I had begun to write my master's thesis, which focused on the development of indices that correlated U.S. seasonal temperatures with the nation's habits of consuming natural gas. As dry as that might sound, I found the topic very interesting, particularly as it related to climate research. Like many other scientists at this time, I was asking myself— and being asked by others—if climate was affecting the weather. Dr. Lamb noticed my enthusiasm for climate research too, and my solid work, and in the summer of 2004 he encouraged me to apply for a PhD in meteorology at OU. He wanted to be my adviser and had already secured a climate-related research project that I could sink my teeth into. This was a huge honor: Dr. Lamb is a director at OU's School of Meteorology and one of the university faculty's most highly regarded research professors. I gladly accepted the offer. Unfortunately, I'd also just agreed to take an intense and rigorous two-day test called the "PhD qualifier." The subject matter spanned much of what I'd learned at OU. Preparation required months.

"Sure, I'll walk the dog," I said to Niki, and bent over to pick up Roxie. She was a cream-colored Pomeranian that Niki and I had chosen together.

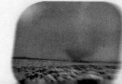

She was tiny, and cute enough. But I didn't much like the image of me taking Roxie out for walks on her little pink leash.

Niki came home that night and sat down to my home cooking—spaghetti.

"How's the thesis coming?" she asked. "Good day?"

"I hit a little hot streak," I said between bites. "I managed to write almost a thousand words."

I didn't tell Niki about all of my day's activities. I'd killed some time looking at the Storm Prediction Center and forecasting models on the National Center for Atmospheric Research's Web site. I also took a long look at my own Web site to see how I might generate more video sales. I needed money.

A couple days later, I had to put checks in the mail to pay down my maxed-out credit cards. I didn't have the funds to make the minimum payments, so I pawned a stereo that my mother had given me for Christmas. Handing the gift to a stranger was not a happy moment.

Later that day I took Roxie for a walk and opened the door for Niki after work. I said nothing about my trip to the pawnshop.

• • •

The storm system looked like it could ease my financial pain. On Saturday, June 12, 2004, a dryline structure was set to trace a path over the southern plains and to branch into a classic "double dryline" to the south over parts of Kansas and Oklahoma. A double dryline consists of two eastward-moving moisture boundaries, staggered and perhaps fifty miles apart, where hot air from the west clashes with warm and moist air from the south and even the east. In double-dryline conditions, if supercell thunderstorms don't thrive after forming at the first (western) dryline, there's always the opportunity for them to gain strength when they move across the second (eastern) dryline, where the moisture is considerably greater. The Storm Prediction Center put the probability of a tornado forming in southeast Kansas on June 12 at 15 percent.

"I'm not sure about the wind shear. But the CAPE, temperatures, and dew points all say tremendous instability. We'll be fine," Joel told me over the phone about forty-eight hours before the anticipated chase day. Neither of us brought up the blue-sky bust and ensuing argument of a month earlier. Joel didn't even give me grief about the SUV skidding off the road at Attica. I was happy he was enthusiastic about a chase.

"I'm in," he added.

Joel, Dean, and I left in Joel's car on the morning of the twelfth, on a four-hour drive up Interstate 35 to the target area around McPherson, Kansas. We decided to probe the single-dryline conditions around McPherson to see if any storms would fire to life. If they didn't, we'd immediately deploy south and position ourselves in the more moist conditions just east of what was the second dryline in the double-dryline setup. We hoped that the comprehensive strategy would allow us to intercept something.

East of McPherson we were greeted by a young but intense storm and pulled over to see if the supercell featured much rotation. Supercells can take anywhere from a few minutes to a few hours to "get organized" before they'll produce a tornado—assuming all the ingredients are in place.

"Look at the power of that updraft!" I said, watching the scud clouds get sucked rapidly into the storm. Scud clouds are small, low-hanging, ragged and wispy formations that are often found beneath cumulonimbus clouds. When they're in the vicinity of a powerful mesocyclone, or rotating updraft, like they were that day, the scud clouds get eaten by the storm for lunch.

The air underneath the storm smelled good—moist, like it came straight from the tropics. There was a wind in the air. Meanwhile a farmer just across the road from me seemed completely oblivious to the potential weather danger in front of him. He drove his harvester, busily scooping up the golden wheat in his fields.

Or did the farmer know something that I didn't?

My camera was running, the storm was getting organized, and then . . . nothing. Soon we could see the sun peeking through holes in the updraft, and we knew the storm was thinning and losing steam. It came apart rapidly.

I refused to be denied. We made a quick pit stop at the McPherson, Kansas, public library, called up the weather radar on the Web, and discovered that we had a viable Plan B. Southwest of Wichita and eighty miles from us, another isolated supercell had formed along the first dryline, and was headed east toward the second dryline and its deeper moisture.

We flew south down Interstate 135, and when we were just below Wichita and approaching the small town of Mulvane we made visual contact with an incredible supercell. You could just tell that the storm had crossed the second dryline and was feasting on the deeper moisture. Cool air and condensation were practically erupting out of the top of the storm the way lava fires out of a volcano. The mesocyclone was sucking in the warm and moist air, the supercell was growing taller, and the exhaust— in the form of that flat cloud atop the storm known as the anvil—was bright white and crisp.

We drove around Mulvane for a while with our necks craned, looking up out of the truck's windshield. The storm consolidated, and its lower portion took on the appearance of a big, black, hovering spaceship. Blue sky surrounded the lone supercell.

We pulled off the side of a lonely road south of town and hopped out of Joel's car in an area surrounded by open field.

"It's tightening up!" I shouted, looking straight up. We were positioned directly under the guts of the rotating mesocyclone. Above me a

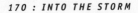

whole column of clouds was spinning like a wheel. "It's just about go time!"

A light gray tornado sprang to life about a mile south of our vantage point, and it kicked up dirt and dust. I waited for it to turn into more. But the tornado stalled. I felt teased.

And then I spotted a wall cloud that had formed in a different part of the storm, northeast of us. We got back in the SUV and drove in the same direction, stopping north of where we thought the wall cloud might spawn a tornado.

I got out of the car. "This could be the big one," I yelled, and suddenly Mulvane kicked into a severe-weather symphony. Tornado sirens came to life with a loud whine. Thunder boomed. Hail wrapped around the back of the mesocyclone and pounded Mulvane's metal-roofed structures.

Lightning shot down from all over the storm. Joel stayed in the vehicle. At six-foot-seven he's like a human lightning rod.

We repositioned ourselves farther east a couple more times, and then the tornado came down. It didn't look real: A shiny-smooth, white, perfectly straight tornado dropped from the wall cloud and landed just behind some trees, maybe two miles from us.

"Perfect cone," said Dean.

"Amazing!" I said to Joel while shooting from the front seat.

But tornados almost always have multiple personalities, and this one quickly went from photogenic to mean. Soon it became an uneven mass of spinning dust and dirt. It was like a kid throwing a tantrum. The tornado grabbed everything within its reach. Boulders. Fence posts. It yanked and pulled on trees until they came up, roots and all. Then everything was sent flying.

"What are those things getting lofted?" I said. I could see small cubes flying through my viewfinder.

Dean was next to me.

"They're hay bales," he said.

Hay bales typically weigh more than a thousand pounds, and even more when they're wet. The tornado was launching them with ease.

We repositioned ourselves farther east and the tornado seemed to intensify again, growing whiter, longer, and faster. It reflected the sun in just such a way that it shone as white as the pearly gates. Or maybe I should say white as a specter.

The tornado ducked behind another stand of trees. In an instant, an enormous amount of debris appeared. It was pretty, glittery, like confetti raining down at a New Year's party.

Then there were some bigger pieces, bigger than the hay bales and trees had looked. And then suddenly the rotation at the base of the tornado turned a murky white, as if it had run into something dense that it was liquefying.

"Oh my God," I said, looking through the viewfinder. "Not good."

The tornado was pulverizing a house. As fast as the eastward-moving storm had been traveling earlier, now it seemed to stop in place. The tornado suddenly seemed mean-spirited, like the bully that wouldn't get off the bloodied kid even though the fight had been decided.

Joel grabbed his cell phone to call in the calamity to the Mulvane fire department. But we could already hear and see the emergency vehicles, with their sirens screaming, coming from town. There were a lot of other moving vehicles, too, especially for such a small town. There were news trucks, and cars and vans with lots of accessory lights and multiple antennas on their roofs. Those tricked-out vehicles probably belonged to storm chasers; there's an entire subset of chasers who think that more equipment makes you a better chaser. Of course, years later, I'd have a tricked-out storm-chasing car too, although I will argue that it's different than anything else out there and is more about science than appearance.

Finally the tornado weakened and cycled through a breathtaking rope-out phase, turning a brighter white again while kicking up orange dirt all around it. We followed the long-lived storm well into dusk. I kept my camera on it for hours.

When it was nearly dark I pulled out my cell phone to call a few of the many players I now knew in the news media.

I tried a producer in Wichita.

"It's amazing footage. Just ridiculous," I told her. "The tornado is bright white. I know you're going to love it."

"Thanks, Reed, but I'll pass," she said. "I've got what I need."

I tried another producer in Kansas City.

"The tornadoes today were insane," I told him.

"Maybe next time," he said. "We're good."

I called producers I knew at local Fox affiliates and at the national networks. I called my contacts at Univision and the Weather Channel. Nobody wanted the footage.

"Why aren't you interested?" I asked a producer at CNN.

"We are interested," he said. "I should say, we were. A lot of storm chasers have been in touch with us about Mulvane. I've seen a lot of good footage."

I hung up with the producer and put my mobile phone in my pocket. Not one sale. I knew that I should've called earlier, but I'd waited as long as I had because I wanted to capture every last minute of the storm— every possible angle, every potential funnel. Had I been beaten at my own game?

Watching that Kansas supercell weaken, Joel and Dean noticed that I was extremely quiet. I was never quiet after a successful intercept.

"It's a Saturday, Reed," said Dean, leaning forward from the Explorer's backseat to cheer me up. "How many storm chasers were swarming around Mulvane today? Fifty? A hundred?"

"We also saw those camera teams from the local news stations," Joel interjected.

Joel was right. The local media had been out in force. Storm-chasing teams from the local stations take away a possible sale in terms of a local outlet and a national network. The local affiliates feed their footage to their national counterparts for free.

That day, part of me cared a lot that I didn't sell my incredible footage. I needed the money, and badly. Were the crowds at Mulvane a sign of things to come? Was the storm video business becoming more cutthroat and more crowded?

This was a rare day where I just didn't care to fight. I'd been so amazed by the storm's many personalities and moments that—destruction of the house aside—I enjoyed filming the storm just for me.

Too bad I didn't return home from that chase with any sales. But I did have lots of memories.

· · ·

Honestly: Was I really any sort of casualty of that Mulvane tornado? The answer, to be clear, is no. In the days, weeks, months, and even years after Mulvane, I was often reminded of true bad luck associated with that storm.

I knew some chasers who opted to drive around Mulvane right after the tornado struck. They couldn't believe what they saw: One of the homes in the tornado's path had literally disappeared. Gone. I'd later look at the intense photos of the damage and watch stories about the devastation on the news. Years into the future, I'd do my own reporting for television documentaries on the tornado's violent impact on this particular house.

For me, there was a sum effect of repeatedly revisiting the tragedy. Mulvane will forever stand out in my mind as a reminder of what it's like to be an unsuspecting victim of a tornado. I thought I had a tough day on June 12, 2004? Mulvane's Chris Landis—now, she had a bad day. Every time I see a tornado damage someone's home, I replay her incredible story in my mind. The tale goes something like this:

Chris had spent most of her life in Mulvane and was thirty-nine years old in June 2004. She remembers that Saturday morning as beautiful, and early in the day she had gone to a farm auction with her husband, Allen, before he went to work as an overhead crane operator in nearby Wichita. On that particular day, Chris had only one of her three sons at home with her—fourteen-year-old Mitchel. Chris's oldest boy, Joe, was a marine serving in Iraq. Her middle son, Nick, was working at Mulvane's grain cooperative.

The family's house was about two miles southeast of the Mulvane city limits. It was a five-bedroom, 1,600-square-foot home, with a 1,600-square-foot finished basement. The connected three-car garage was built on a cement slab. The Landises had designed and built their cedar-and-stone-walled house in 1997, and it sat on fifteen acres of open land. The basement had a huge window—longer than Chris's four-foot-eleven-inch body—that faced southwest.

Chris rarely thought about tornadoes and never believed one would strike her home. Even though she lived in Tornado Alley, what were the chances that she'd get in one's way?

Early that afternoon, her son Mitchel was somewhere in the house, and Chris was assembling orders for Mary Kay cosmetics on her dining room table. She'd been a Mary Kay consultant for years. She had the TV on, and news warnings occasionally interrupted the daytime programming. Chris thought the warnings were for high-wind advisories, but she couldn't be sure. She wasn't paying a lot of attention. In midafternoon, however, Chris noticed something odd in the sky, and she went outside and looked up. There was one unbelievably tall cloud that sat right above her house. She thought it was hovering unusually close to the ground.

At that very moment, Dean, Joel, and I were bombing around southern Mulvane in Joel's SUV. Our eyes were glued to the very same cloud.

But what was thrilling to us made Chris Landis uneasy. She listened closer to those television weather reports and dragged Mitchel away from

playing video games to look at the cloud that wouldn't go away. She asked her son if he'd ever seen anything like it. He shrugged.

About an hour after Chris first looked at the cloud, she went outside to see if it was still there. It was, and it was changing. The cloud was getting darker, and there was material moving around within the cloud. She'd never seen a cloud like it. Of course, she had no idea that a meso-cyclone was developing overhead, in the supercell thunderstorm that lingered above her home.

Around six P.M., a tornado warning was issued for the area where Chris Landis and her family lived. She began to think about taking the precautionary measure of retreating downstairs. While she still refused to believe that her house could be struck by a tornado, Chris had been trained since childhood to hunker down in tornado weather. She knew that the safest place during a tornado was below ground, where the rotating winds usually had to do more than knock down a wall or two to reach you. The winds would have to suck you out of a hole. Plus, keeping low minimizes the chances of being hit with the debris that gets swung around in a tornado.

Mitchel was slow to cooperate. But Chris finally convinced her young son that, if nothing else, going downstairs with their most valuable possessions was good practice, just in case the day ever came when a tornado might really hit their house. The two of them gathered the irreplaceable family photos that hung on the walls throughout the home and moved them to the basement, specifically to the space under the stairs. Chris couldn't have cared less about the furniture, television, or computer. But she wasn't going to leave any framed family pictures on the walls.

By seven P.M., Chris and Mitchel had brought most of the family photos into the enclosed space underneath the basement steps. At the same time, the phone began ringing off the hook—the calls were from Allen, her son Nick, and various friends. They all wanted to know if Chris and Mitchel were safe and if they were staying in the basement. Everyone was worried. The local television news had broadcast a map showing areas that might be in the path of a tornado, and the Landis home was right in the middle of the danger zone.

As she was making one trip to the basement, Chris looked outside the huge picture window and noticed small funnel clouds extending and then retracting—right in her backyard. She went upstairs, looked out the front door, and saw more of the same. She was still doubtful that her home was in real danger. But by 7:15 P.M., spotters had already reported tornadoes on the ground just southwest of town. Chris began to make her last trips up and down the steps.

The Landises had three dogs and a cat that had to be corralled and put in the basement. Chris and Mitchel got them situated, and then the cat sprinted back upstairs. Mitchel chased it down. Chris forgot a collage of her deceased dad's photos upstairs, and when she went to retrieve it, for whatever reason she decided to momentarily linger and to change out of flip-flops and into socks and sneakers. She also grabbed her purse, which was on the kitchen counter. The phone rang again, but she didn't answer it.

At 7:29 P.M., spotters reported a tornado crossing Kansas State Highway 15, perhaps 1.5 miles from the Landis home.

At that time, Joel, Dean, and I were north of the bright white funnel cloud, watching the fierce tornado and filming its every move.

While the tornado hit two homes just west of the Landis residence, Chris and Mitchel crowded into the storage area underneath the basement steps. Chris held Mitchel close to her. But no sooner had she shut the closet door than her ears began to pop, as if she were on a plane. The huge change in pressure came courtesy of the approaching tornado.

At first Chris heard what sounded like damage being done to her roof. She became irritated at the thought of a hefty repair bill. Then life turned into a strange, horrific dream sequence: Chris heard wind, shattering glass,

and a bizarre tearing of wood, drywall, concrete, and metal. Chris held Mitchel tight, and suddenly the cramped closet became open, airy, and windy. With unreal suddenness, the ceiling above them disappeared. In fact, the tornado lifted away the roof and entire main floor of the house. As the storm raged around them, Chris and Mitchel were bathed in light. The tornado was indeed sucking things out of a hole: Two-by-fours were pulled straight out of the basement's foundation, and drywall was peeled off the studs. The pool table was dragged across the floor. But the tornado, for whatever reason, didn't pick up Chris, Mitchel, or the family photos.

This was the home that I watched being devoured by the Mulvane tornado. From my vantage point, all I could see was the funnel filling up with all manner of debris as it ground up the Landis home. Just above Chris and Mitchel, however, the destruction was playing out in *epic* proportions. The family's new Ford Taurus and fully restored 1969 Ford Mustang Mach I were airborne and being twirled and twisted in the storm. The Landises' large home furnace was sucked up into the rotation and never seen again. A giant metal furnace, reduced to nothing.

When the wind finally stopped and the racket subsided, Mitchel looked up at his mother in the now open-air, destroyed basement and asked her one question: "Is it done?" They stood in that destroyed closet, the door on top of them, for several minutes.

Chris had saved her photographs, the family pets, and her and her son's lives from the fury of a two-hundred-mile-per-hour F3 tornado. But every piece of the family's clothing had to be thrown away. Wood splinters and strands of home insulation were embedded into everyone's shirts, jeans, and sweaters, as if those materials had been knit into the fabric.

Ever since I learned the details of what happened to the Landis home in Mulvane, I always think twice about storms that don't cooperate with me. I sometimes shake my head. How can a storm chaser complain about not capturing the perfect video when some poor, unsuspecting citizen is simply trying to duck a huge meteorological bullet?

. . .

But during that challenging stretch of my life, tornadoes did do me some serious damage. I ultimately realized that I was like a lot of other storm chasers in at least one way. I couldn't successfully juggle chasing and my relationship with Niki. Something had to give.

My fall 2004 chase season wasn't much of an improvement over my spring campaign and my experience in Mulvane, Kansas. While many chasers were notching one intercept after another—my friend Scott Currens saw close to fifty tornadoes that year—I saw next to nothing. Other people's lives seemed to be progressing. Mine stood still. Joel became busier buying and selling real estate. Dean lined up more clients wanting his Web-related skills.

Meanwhile I played househusband and tried to write my thesis. I often found myself in Niki's apartment, calling for Roxie and grabbing her pink leash, making dinners, and brainstorming about how to boost my income. I ultimately borrowed money from my mom and dad, which I hated to do. I always want to be self-sufficient. But I had to eat. I passed my PhD qualifier in August 2004, but even that wasn't entirely good news. Dr. Lamb had seen some of my stock storm-chasing footage on television and heard my voice accompanying the video. Soon afterward, he sat me down in his office, and with a stern look on his face he told me that deserving PhD candidates don't have time to chase storms up one side of Tornado Alley and down the other.

Niki tried a little harder to hide her impatience with my chasing.

"Maybe you could chase the storms that are close. Or go on every third chase," she said one night in February 2005, switching TV stations from the Weather Channel to HBO. "I'd like you to start coming to church more often."

Every time I went to church with Niki and her family, I felt like I was wilting. I hadn't attended church growing up and had no desire to make

it a habit as an adult. In spring 2005 I skipped a big Easter celebration with the Darnaby clan to chase a storm, and Niki was not happy. In May 2005, we'd also agreed that my dad would meet her parents. We were all invited to Niki's folks' house for a cookout.

But the night before the Darnabys' party, I looked at the computer models for Tornado Alley. Conditions looked insane for south-central Nebraska. I called my dad in his Norman hotel room at four A.M.

"Hey, Dad, sorry about the crazy hour," I said from my apartment.

"What's going on?" he said after answering the phone. "You okay?"

"I'm great," I said. "I'm looking at the weather forecast for southern Nebraska tomorrow, and conditions look like they'll be explosive. If we drive up, there's a strong chance that we'll see a tornado. But we'd have to leave soon."

He cleared his throat, apparently trying to shake off the sleep and catch up to my manic thinking.

"What about the party with your girlfriend's folks?" he asked.

"I think Niki will understand," I said. "She knows all about my pent-up energy early in the season. I'm dying to see storms."

"I'll do what you want to do," he said.

My father was a little surprised at how we kept a steady speed of ninety toward the target area outside of Lexington, Nebraska. The trip was five hundred miles from Norman, I explained. We didn't want to arrive late.

At midmorning I called Niki from my mobile phone to tell her that we'd do the cookout another night.

"The moisture's going to make it all the way to Nebraska," I said. "The wind shear will be there."

"So you and your dad aren't coming to my parents' house?" she said.

"There will be lots of other opportunities," I said to her.

"If you say so," she replied quietly.

The storms that day in the hills of Nebraska were incredible. My dad and I saw three tornadoes together and got within a couple hundred yards of an F1. That said, I doubt very seriously that my dad will ever take up storm chasing. A little *too* exciting.

"It was intense," I told Niki in her apartment the day following the chase. "My dad was just blown away. It was like the experience of a lifetime."

"Great, Reed," she said with indifference, her arms crossed. "But I'm really disappointed about you skipping the party at my parents' house. And I'm tired of worrying about you every time you leave to chase some storm."

I apologized. Niki was such a catch—fun, sweet, and caring. But at this point in my life I knew my priorities. Marriage and settling down weren't at the top of the list. Storm chasing and tornadoes were. I didn't want to lose Niki. But I feared that she was done with me because I couldn't put our relationship ahead of the weather.

When I went storm chasing the next week, I called a florist from the road and had flowers sent to Niki. I returned to the apartment complex the next day, and Niki barely acknowledged receiving them.

A week later she told me our relationship was over.

CHAPTER 7

JUST THE TROUBLE I NEEDED

. . .

I wanted to get away, and in August 2005 I did. I took a trip to the Deep South. I visited Louisiana, though I didn't go for the music or Cajun food. Instead I took a wild journey, deploying toward New Orleans to intercept Hurricane Katrina. I went because I'm a storm chaser and am hopelessly intrigued by nearly every type of storm. I also took the trip, however, to get an idea of the kind of extreme weather that could someday resemble the norm in America, let alone the world. I came back with some ideas about the evolution of dangerous weather and deeply sobered by what I had witnessed. We all now recall Katrina as a storm of epic proportions and an unmitigated tragedy. The costliest—and nearly the deadliest—natural disaster in U.S. history threatened to take my life. But I was one of the lucky ones.

Well before pursuing Katrina, I anticipated some of the problems of embarking on such a chase. I knew that more conservative storm chasers would fume when word spread that I'd pursued a severe-weather event that threatened to take many lives and cause unheard-of damage. I realized that I was placing my own life in grave danger by mapping out a collision course with such a violent storm. I acknowledged the hypocrisy of my honest concern for victims of severe weather and my desire to be present at the very moment when a storm might inflict its greatest damage. I realized that people thought I would videotape the hurricane for commercial purposes, even though that was never part of the plan.

But as a seemingly harmless cluster of westbound storms over the Atlantic ocean rapidly evolved from a tropical depression on August 23 to a tropical storm on August 24 to a Category 1 hurricane on August 25, and it was clear to the meteorology community that the storm would continue to intensify, all the chatter inside my head about who would think what stopped. This could be an epic storm. I was a storm chaser. I wanted to check it out.

I needed someone to join me.

"Are you crazy?" said Rick. "Remember Floyd? Never again."

"Reed, come on. You're not serious," said Dean. "This thing could kill you."

"I didn't think your desire to chase could ever surprise me," said Joel. "But you've surprised me. Good luck finding a partner."

I had little choice but to turn to my friendly rival Simon Brewer. I'd known him since we were both meteorology students at OU. We had a lot in common—a passion for storm chasing, commercial storm-chasing Web sites, and the unwillingness to let most other people dictate the wheres and whens of a chase.

But I wanted to chase Katrina, so I could look past any awkwardness. I called Simon and suggested the terms of a pact.

"How about we're rivals for chasing tornadoes and allies for chasing hurricanes?" I said. It was August 26. "I bet you want to chase Katrina too."

Dumb statement. Simon was every bit as enthusiastic a storm chaser as I was. He'd pretty much been waiting for my call.

"Whose car?" he quickly asked in his low voice.

Simon was actually a funny and charismatic guy. I thought we'd get along fine once we both agreed to lower our defenses.

I told him that my car wasn't working—again. But I could provide a lot of the other necessary equipment for chasing hurricanes.

"How soon can you leave?" he asked.

We spent the next two days preparing and packing for the trip. I had chased a few hurricanes since Rick and I pursued Hurricane Floyd in North Carolina in 1999, and in anticipation of the worst—extensive damage to infrastructure, prolonged isolation, and an inability to resupply— I'd already assembled a huge survival kit for such chases. I owned spare gas tanks to strap atop a car; chain saws and axes to cut through downed trees; and helmets, goggles, and waterproof suits to push through virtually any conditions. But I'd never field-tested most of my stuff. I'd chased hurricanes Frances and Jeanne in Florida in 2004, only to have those storms pack relatively little punch once they made landfall.

We also packed our version of ready-to-eat meals: A huge pile of packaged beef jerky, dozens of premixed Slim-Fast shakes, and multiple cases of bottled water. At least it wasn't the bologna I endured when intercepting Hurricane Floyd in 1999. But it wasn't much better.

Like Floyd six years earlier, Katrina began as a series of storms near the West African archipelago of Cape Verde, and as it churned westward over the Atlantic Ocean, it would (like Floyd) ultimately become identified as a Cape Verde hurricane.

While Simon and I prepared for our trip, Katrina was well in motion. It had already struck South Florida on August 25 as a Category 1 hurricane. (Remember, Category 1 hurricanes have sustained winds of 74 to 95 miles per hour on the Saffir-Simpson Hurricane Wind Scale.) A day or so later, after Katrina had inflicted moderate damage on South Florida, it moved over the Gulf of Mexico. It soon intensified dramatically, at one point rising from Category 3 to Category 5 status in just nine hours. Katrina's huge power gain came courtesy of warm water.

How can warm water turn a hurricane from a 130-mile-per-hour

beast into a 155-mile-per-hour monster? It's all about what fuels a hurricane. I carefully explained how hurricanes work in chapter 3, but I'll provide you with a quick refresher:

Similar to tornadoes, a hurricane begins as a thunderstorm, or really a cluster of thunderstorms (known as tropical disturbances). And like tornadoes, these tropical disturbances form because warm, moist air rises in the atmosphere. The rising warm and moist air triggers condensation, which generates more heat, which causes the rise of more warm, moist air and lowers the surface pressure of the tropical disturbance even more. What's a storm's fuel source? Tornadoes live on warm and moist air available to them in the atmosphere, and tropical disturbances gas up on warm ocean waters. The warmer the ocean water, the greater the energy that it provides to a tropical disturbance As a tropical disturbance uses more of that energy, it gains strength, clusters together, attracts wind, and begins to rotate. And then it's potentially on its way to becoming a hurricane.

Very early on the morning of August 28, before Simon and I began our ten-hour drive southeast, I called up the latest information and satellite image of the storm on my computer.

On the satellite image, Katrina looked like a classic hurricane: storm as counterclockwise-rotating buzz saw. At 415 miles across, Katrina was very large. It also had a remarkable, very well-defined, circular hole in its center—the eye of the storm.

A refresher: The eye is the center of a hurricane, and in Katrina it measured approximately 30 miles across (hurricane eyes range from two to over 120 miles in diameter). From a meteorological standpoint, the eye's most significant characteristic is its low pressure, and all of the wind circling the eye is drawn toward this low pressure. In general, the lower the pressure, the stronger the storm, and on that same day that Simon and I were preparing for Louisiana (August 28), the pressure inside

Katrina's eye dipped to 902 millibars. Relative to what we experience on the earth's surface (approximately 1,000 mbar to 1,040 mbar), and the atmospheric pressure inside the eye of other hurricanes (Hurricane Floyd: 921 mbar), the low atmospheric pressure inside Katrina's eye qualified it as one of the most intense Atlantic hurricanes of all time. Meanwhile, on the day we left, sustained winds in Katrina's eyewall—the storm's most violent area, located right next to the eye—were clocked at 175 miles per hour. Katrina's eye also had a beautiful, outward-tapering shape at its top, which is called the "stadium effect" because it resembles the dished shape of a sports stadium. Stadium-effect eyes frequently indicate a particularly violent hurricane.

"I've never seen an eye like that," said my roommate Aaron, looking over my shoulder at the monitor. Weeks after my breakup with Niki, Aaron and I had moved out of the apartment complex and into a much cheaper rental house in south Norman. "You're in for a big ride," he added.

"Sure you don't want to come along?" I asked Aaron with a smile, pushing my desk chair away from the computer and zipping up one of my duffel bags. Aaron didn't even bother to respond, and within an hour Simon and I were on the road in his beat-up white sedan, which he'd just bought used after the red van died. Too bad he wouldn't have his new wheels for long.

"Into the abyss," I said to Simon as he started his car.

Simon smiled a big smile. "Two crazy men on a mission," he said, and then laughed when I put on my helmet and a pair of goggles. He reached behind the driver's seat and grabbed a piece of paper.

"Did you see the National Weather Service's statement issued this morning about Katrina?" he added, and I shook my head. He handed me the page—a printout of the NWS statement. The top several paragraphs read:

URGENT—WEATHER MESSAGE

NATIONAL WEATHER SERVICE NEW ORLEANS LA

1011 AM CDT SUN AUG 28, 2005

. . . DEVASTATING DAMAGE EXPECTED . . .

HURRICANE KATRINA . . . A MOST POWERFUL
HURRICANE WITH UNPRECEDENTED STRENGTH . . .
RIVALING THE INTENSITY OF HURRICANE CAMILLE OF
1969.

MOST OF THE AREA WILL BE UNINHABITABLE FOR
WEEKS . . . PERHAPS LONGER. AT LEAST ONE HALF OF
WELL CONSTRUCTED HOMES WILL HAVE ROOF AND
WALL FAILURE. ALL GABLED ROOFS WILL FAIL . . .
LEAVING THOSE HOMES SEVERELY DAMAGED OR
DESTROYED.

THE MAJORITY OF INDUSTRIAL BUILDINGS WILL
BECOME NON FUNCTIONAL. PARTIAL TO COMPLETE
WALL AND ROOF FAILURE IS EXPECTED. ALL WOOD
FRAMED LOW RISING APARTMENT BUILDINGS WILL BE
DESTROYED. CONCRETE BLOCK LOW RISE
APARTMENTS WILL SUSTAIN MAJOR DAMAGE . . .
INCLUDING SOME WALL AND ROOF FAILURE.

HIGH RISE OFFICE AND APARTMENT BUILDINGS WILL
SWAY DANGEROUSLY . . . A FEW TO THE POINT OF
TOTAL COLLAPSE. ALL WINDOWS WILL BLOW OUT.

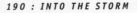

AIRBORNE DEBRIS WILL BE WIDESPREAD . . . AND MAY
INCLUDE HEAVY ITEMS SUCH AS HOUSEHOLD
APPLIANCES AND EVEN LIGHT VEHICLES.

I scanned the rest of the message, which made plenty of other frightening statements. "Livestock left outside will die." "Power outages will last weeks." "Trees will snap." The bulletin ended with the warning "Do not venture outside!"

Sensing that the memo had killed the anticipation buzz, Simon turned on the car radio, and for a long while we tuned in to music, which made for a good distraction. We talked about the coming OU football season and the challenges of selling storm video.

But about five hours into the journey, when we reached Louisiana's Interstate 49, the gravity of this particular storm chase was first felt. Simon and I needed only to look across the road's double yellow line to appreciate the seriousness of what potentially lay ahead. The northbound side of I-49 was bumper-to-bumper with cars driven by evacuees, who were part of the most extensive hurricane evacuation in U.S. history. Surging past all those cars, and sitting in the only vehicle driving south toward the coast, reminded me of a similar moment in my chase of Hurricane Floyd. And I asked myself the same question that I had in North Carolina six years earlier: Was I on a fool's mission?

. . .

Driving down I-49 in Simon's car, I felt sure about one thing: I wasn't taking this trip out of desperation. Shortly after Niki broke off our relationship, I'd vowed to refocus my life on the things that I needed to focus on. Before leaving to intercept Katrina, I'd made good progress on my commitments.

Once my days no longer included Niki, Roxie, or cooking dinner for two, I purposely kept my world small: I increased my efforts for Dr. Lamb

and spent time pursuing tornadoes. I had decided that my life and career would thrive on weather—and weather alone—or bust.

After I passed the PhD qualifier test, Dr. Lamb had objected to my storm chasing, but he'd also offered me rare praise and encouragement. In the fall of 2004 he wrote me an e-mail congratulating me on my success with the test and told me that, given my work ethic and initiative, I could go far as a meteorologist. He said that he was looking forward to helping me earn my PhD.

The unexpected compliments threw a lever inside of me. I poured a lot of time into my master's thesis and had finished a draft by the end of 2004. Dr. Lamb subsequently tore it apart with his trademark red pen, which he used to edit and tell me that my research and writing needed improvement. But instead of feeling discouraged, I went at the revisions with determination.

In July 2005, Dr. Lamb called me into his office a week after I'd submitted some additional data and analysis. I had, for example, uncovered solid reasons as to why indices linking winter temperatures and natural gas consumption were elusive: In northern (cold) regions, accurate indices required factoring in daily maximum temperatures, since the north's minimum temperatures were so cold that they caused residents to indiscriminately heat their homes at a "maximum" rate until the temperatures outside climbed. Conversely, in southern (warmer) regions, accurate indices required factoring in daily minimum temperatures, because the areas' maximum winter temperatures were too warm for heating.

"Smart observations. You're strengthening the work," Dr. Lamb had said in his tidy office, handing me back some pages. Lamb's own papers were neatly arranged on his desk, with a paperweight resting atop each shallow pile. "You'll notice from my suggestions that I believe you're drawing closer. I'm only fine-tuning," he added. When I flipped through the pages, I saw a lot less red ink than I had in the past.

My fate as a storm chaser had rebounded, too.

On June 9, 2005, Joel and I chased together in northwestern Kansas, and as unlucky as I'd been in selling video footage back in 2004, I met with good fortune almost exactly one year later. West of the small town of Hill City, we moved up alongside a storm that spawned not one tornado but two at the same time. I kept moving my camera back and forth between the bright white stovepipe tornado on my left and the dark gray wedge on my right.

The two tornadoes were the product of what's called a cyclic supercell—one storm that's capable of producing multiple tornadoes. Within cyclic supercells, the mesocyclone, or rotating updraft, can produce multiple tight circulations that are called "tornado cyclones." The tornado cyclones are precursors to full-fledged tornadoes, but they frequently become tornadoes in sequence, as one tornado steals the necessary heat and moisture from another. However, on rare occasion, the "handoff" of energy and moisture happens slowly, and two fully formed tornadoes coexist. Such was the case in the Hill City storm. I've never had another intercept like it.

I was also fortunate because both of this amazing cyclic supercell's tornadoes were photogenic, and at one point during the chase I captured the two tornadoes in the same frame. No sooner had the tornadoes roped out, or dissipated, than I was on the phone with the news networks, giving one passionate sales pitch after another. The result was two impressive sales to two different news networks of two different moments in the lifetime of the same storm. I hadn't made such good money in a long time.

Three weeks later I had further reason to believe that the tornado gods were with me. This time I was chasing a storm near the southern Minnesota town of St. James with Dave Holder—a new OU meteorology student and a very game storm chaser. On that particular day—June 29—the wind shear was pronounced. The first tornado that Dave and I saw was a beautiful, light gray funnel that was turning brown as it

plowed up an open field. The second, an elephant-trunk tornado, gener-ated a lot of video sales.

But the third tornado of the day was the most intriguing. Ultimately Dave and I found ourselves directly beneath the funnel, and when the tornado started snapping off tree branches and cornstalks just a few hundreds yards from our position, we realized that we'd better find shel-ter fast. We ducked under Dave's hatchback. Luckily the tornado was rated an F0, which meant it was capable of rotational speeds of only about seventy miles per hour. Its strength was only sufficient to fill our eyes and mouths with dust and dirt.

We coughed and wiped our faces as we crawled out from underneath the car, but we were soon whooping and hollering. That was the first but definitely not the last time I'd survive a moment inside of a tornado.

• • •

Simon and I wanted to find a parking lot. As we drove east—and alone—on Interstate 10 toward Baton Rouge, we reviewed some of our chasing tactics. We'd use the topographic maps of the New Orleans area that I had purchased to situate ourselves at least fifteen feet above sea level. We thought that staying relatively high was one of the keys to avoiding potential trouble in a hurricane that would likely push a lot of water from the Gulf of Mexico into the region's many low-lying areas. A multilevel, steel-reinforced parking structure, we decided, would probably survive Katrina's winds and surging waters. To this day, the approach seems sound. Too bad we got into a whole lot of trouble before we reached a parking lot.

"Did you see that? The lightning?" said Simon with a huge smile on his face. I had just turned on my laptop and looked up from the screen in time to see another pronounced bolt in the distance. "The eyewall is still, what, twenty hours from coming ashore?" he added. "This thing is huge! We're already witnessing lightning?"

This was our first real sense of Katrina's massive size. The lightning meant that the gigantic storm's outer bands of severe weather had already reached shore. The sky above us was already a dull, sunless gray, filled with the blank, contourless sheet of stratus clouds that hide what's to come. But even the unsuspecting sky watcher would have known something was up, because the clouds were moving quickly. Of course, the air was heavy with a tropicslike humidity. Katrina was built out of warm water.

Occasionally Simon and I would pull into a motel parking lot so that I could sneak onto the Internet and track the storm via the motel's Wi-Fi signal. Katrina represented my first intercept equipped with any kind of in-car Internet access, which was proving a lot more convenient than stopping at a public library.

"The hurricane nearly covers the entire Gulf of Mexico on the satellite image," I said to Simon while the car idled outside of a little inn on the outskirts of Baton Rouge. I clicked on another window within the National Hurricane Center's Web site.

"Wind gusts are now exceeding two hundred miles per hour in the eyewall," I read out loud, summarizing the on-screen statistics. "Twenty-eight-foot storm surge headed for populated areas."

I'd never experienced a dramatic storm surge—the huge wall of water that accumulates and grows as hurricane-force winds push ocean water toward shore. I'd seen some of the flooding after Floyd. But I knew what I was about to encounter was different by an order of magnitude. As a kid I remember watching worst-case scenario weather programs about what might happen to New Orleans in a huge hurricane. Now I was about to see firsthand.

"Maybe we need to think about situating ourselves at least thirty feet above sea level," I said to Simon.

"Better start Googling for 'New Orleans parking garages,'" he said.

As the light faded on August 28, however, we faced a concern more

pressing than the hurricane. To prevent looting, southern Louisiana law enforcement had already established a dusk-to-dawn curfew for the coast-line and lowlands. The last thing Simon and I wanted was to call attention to ourselves; we knew the cops didn't want to be bothered or distracted by two Midwestern storm chasers on a counterintuitive mission. I could just imagine what the cop would say: *You want to get closer to the storm?*

We decided to stop for the night in the small town of Covington, forty-five miles away from New Orleans and on the north shore of Lake Pontchartrain.

"Good parking lot—lots of dark corners," said Simon, driving his car into the lot's outer reaches. "You want some beef jerky?" he said, opening a package.

I declined. I'd already had my fill of gas station burritos.

"I'll be happy to get even a little sleep," I said, reclining in the front passenger seat. "I'm already fired up."

We had no intention of entering the motel. Simon had less money than I did—his job at Kentucky Fried Chicken paid just enough to keep up with his schooling, and his storm-chasing habit. As for me, I was still in debt. Besides, I reminded myself as I turned onto my side, I'd had worse moments than sleeping in a car, in ridiculously hot and humid conditions, with another storm chaser. I'd done the same thing in the past with *four* other chasers. The combined stench of so much confined body odor and warm beef jerky was almost unbearable.

I woke before daybreak to steady rain. Wind whistled through the cracks and gaps in Simon's car, and the sky occasionally glowed green with power flashes coming from the distant south and east. Simon was asleep, and I felt lonely, like prey. I figured that the seventy-mile-per-hour, tropical-storm-force winds that were blowing out transformers mounted on power poles were setting the table for bigger winds to come.

I fired up my laptop and—yes!—immediately got onto the Internet. I searched for storm updates. The news was grim: At six A.M., Katrina's eyewall was already hammering the Louisiana swampland parishes with 140-mile-per-hour winds. St. Bernard and Plaquemines parishes, which had been home to tens of thousands of people, were now mostly underwater. You had to imagine that there were already countless deaths, although most of the folks from these parishes had evacuated a day or two earlier.

"Looks like the storm is veering east," said Simon, wiping the sleep out of his eyes and leaning his head over to get a look at my computer screen. "That means we go east."

We still thought that we wanted the full, gonzo storm-chasing experience: We wanted to intercept Katrina at its right eyewall, where the combined wind of the hurricane and the winds that carry the hurricane deliver the greatest force of the storm. We also thought we might get a chance to sit in the low-pressure and eerie eye. Inside a hurricane's eye there can be blue sky above you and no wind, but you can see the intense, impossibly tall thunderstorms ripping around in a circle all around you. They're producing waves of rainfall, and contributing to the compressed air that makes the eye incredibly hot and humid.

Simon fired up the car, and soon we were surging east on Interstate 12 toward the Mississippi border and Gulfport. But we weren't thirty minutes down the road, near the town of Slidell, before we ran into a problem. The highway east was closed in anticipation of Katrina's coming winds and wall of water.

"Now what?" said Simon, taking the exit for Slidell instead of slowing anywhere near the police officer dressed in raingear and standing near the highway roadblock. As we veered away from the roadblock, the cop turned toward the car and gave us a long, suspicious look.

I unbuckled my seatbelt and faced backward in my car seat in order to fish out our maps of the New Orleans area. I found what I was looking for and slid back into the seat. I began searching for alternative routes into Mississippi.

"There's a small road heading east out of southern Slidell, and we can probably link up with other roads all the way to Mississippi," I said, tracing a line on the map.

"How far is Slidell from the coast?" said Simon, driving slowly through Slidell's modest and abandoned downtown. There were absolutely no signs of life. The steady rain outside was punctuated with surging winds and downpours.

"Maybe a couple miles," I said, looking at the map. "The town sits right on the edge of Lake Pontchartrain."

The farther south we went in the small town, the worse the road conditions. We knew it was only a matter of time before the huge waves already coming off of Pontchartrain, a big (approximately fifty miles wide), oval-shaped estuary connected to the Gulf of Mexico, would flood because of Katrina's storm surge. We knew the town was on the brink of disaster. But our escape route wasn't east. The water under Simon's car was nearly a foot deep and getting deeper. We turned around.

"We have to make a quick decision," said Simon. He looked around at the small branches and leaves that were in flight. The wind was now blowing at about fifty miles per hour.

"I say we head back toward the interstate and see if we can find higher ground to our north, either in Slidell or outside of town," I said. "Let's find a concrete structure to wait out the storm."

Simon and I agreed that lowering our expectations—maybe seeing winds of 130 miles per hour in the northern eyewall, and perhaps catching the western portion of a potentially cloudless eye—was better than losing the car, and perhaps our own lives, in floodwater.

"What's that truck doing?" Simon said abruptly.

I looked up from the map and saw a large, rusty dump truck headed toward us, driving south down Slidell's empty, four-lane main street. It was the only other vehicle on the road. The driver was flashing his headlights.

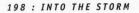

"Is he a looter?" I said as we came within a hundred yards of the truck. "Who's left in this town?"

When we were within seventy-five feet of passing by the truck, it swerved into our lane.

"What the hell?" shouted Simon, and he veered right and went up on the curb. "That guy's trying to kill us!"

The truck just missed us as it blasted by us going the opposite direction.

"Get us out of here!" I yelled, and Simon sped up some. But the deteriorating weather conditions made visibility terrible. Simon couldn't go very fast.

"That same truck is now behind us and closing in," Simon said a couple minutes later, looking in his rearview mirror. "What does this idiot want?"

When the truck was within twenty feet of us, Simon abruptly pulled into a bank parking lot, spun the car around, and pulled back onto Slidell's empty main road heading south.

"Call the cops!" he yelled. But before I could dial 911 a police vehicle appeared with its lights flashing. It was speeding the opposite way down the street, coming toward us.

"Maybe that policeman is looking for the crazy truck driver," said Simon, gripping the wheel. Apparently that wasn't the cop's objective. When the squad car was only a hundred yards in front of us, the driver launched it into a sideways skid, and Simon came to a rapid stop near the vehicle.

All of a sudden four uniformed officers burst out of the car and drew their guns while sprinting toward Simon's car. Despite the driving storm, they surrounded the car with their gun barrels pointed straight at Simon and me.

"Hands up!" yelled the cop who was just on the other side of my window. The rain dripped off the end of his gun barrel. "Now!"

The Katrina intercept quickly became a much different adventure than I'd ever imagined.

"Don't shoot!" I shrieked in a panicky voice. My hands were flat up against the roof of the car. "We're storm chasers! I'm a storm chaser!"

"Out of the car," yelled the cop closest to me. "Both of you."

Simon and I got out of the car just as the huge dump truck came to a stop beside us. A very large, older cop with a mustache and a frown got out of the truck, slammed the door, and strode toward me. His face was bright red and unlikely to be cooled off by the relentless wind and rain. We were all soaking wet.

"Nobody has any business being on these streets right now," said the big cop, and in one fluid motion he grabbed me, swung me around, and slammed my chest down on the hood of Simon's car. He kicked my legs apart.

While the cop searched me, another officer gave Simon similar treatment.

"This one has nothing, chief," said the policeman searching Simon to the big cop searching me.

"You're the police chief?" I said to the cop behind me. "Chief. We're storm chasers."

"I want to find out more," he told another officer while my cheek was pressed up against the car hood. "I don't care what they say. Keep them in a cell until I get back."

Two Slidell officers rode in the back of Simon's car while we drove, following the squad car to the two-story Slidell Police Department station. We were escorted inside, where we surrendered all of our personal possessions before being placed inside a tiny basement cell. Being stuck behind bars was brutal for any number of reasons, but two hurt most: Hearing the howling winds of the storm of the century without being able to see the hurricane was, for me, pure agony. And I was worried that Simon and I would die in that little cell. Everyone ignored us. Would they continue to ignore us when the basement inevitably flooded and we faced the rising waters?

Two hours later the chief showed up and unlocked our cell. He was nice. He'd been patrolling in the borrowed dump truck, he explained, so that he wouldn't get stuck in a flood.

He told us that we "checked out," but I didn't even know if anyone in the station was still able to communicate with the outside world. I also wondered why the officers had spent any time at all worrying about me and Simon. The hurricane of all hurricanes was approaching, and the officers surely had better things to do than deal with a couple of renegade chasers. I felt pretty guilty now.

"Sorry for the confusion, boys," said the chief. "We'd received reports of looting. You two were the only people we saw out there. You were instant suspects."

The chief instructed another officer to give us our belongings and told us that we were free to go.

"Come on! Let's go! You know, before we can't leave," Simon said to me, and we jogged down the department's hallway to the back parking lot where Simon had left his car maybe three hours earlier. But when we ran into the midafternoon daylight, we saw a demoralizing sight. The car was already in about eighteen inches of water, and the level continued to rise.

We no longer had an exit strategy. We didn't have transportation. And we were stuck in a police station, situated at sea level and only two miles from the coast, which was in the path of one of the most powerful hurricanes in history.

Our electronics and other gear, along with all of our supplies, were still in the car. We had no choice but to pull everything out of Simon's vehicle. The water was brown and smelled awful. Alligators and snakes,

for all we knew, were swimming about. I passed a floating red clump of something on my first trip toward the car, and when I bent over to get a closer look I realized that it was a swarm of fire ants. In a split second the police station went from inhospitable to a safe haven.

Simon and I used considerable strength against the weight of the floodwaters to pull open one of the car doors. As the murky water poured into Simon's car we grabbed what we could—our electronic equipment, some clothes and garbage bags, handfuls of Slim-Fast shakes, and a couple of axes and some smaller tools. On subsequent trips we struggled even more to get a car door open and then retrieve what else that we could. Soon the water had risen to our waists. After a while we couldn't shut the door of Simon's car door anymore. So we turned our backs, with full garbage bags slung over our shoulders. The interior of that car soon filled with water. Simon and I essentially moved into the building's dry second floor, which featured a balcony.

The scene from that balcony, which was somewhat protected from the winds blowing out of the northeast, only became increasingly surreal. As the rain poured down and Katrina's surge pushed water farther inland, I watched cars, street signs, and houses disappear as if they'd all somehow dropped into a lake. The small police station itself took on the feel of a houseboat. Simon and I stood at the station's balcony railing and watched tree branches, trash, and furniture float by. We were joined by cops and criminals alike: The chief let the dozen or so inmates in the building's jail out of their cells. Nobody would attempt escape.

In late afternoon the wind shifted directions and intensified. Simon and I stood on the balcony and watched as some of the darkest clouds we'd ever seen approached rapidly from the south. We figured that the storm's northern eyewall was upon us.

When word got out that Simon and I were meteorologists, the inmates and officers had all sorts of questions for us.

What's an eyewall?

When will the wind stop?

Are we all going to die?

I told two dozen fidgety people gathered in the station's second-story conference room to prepare for the worst. Nonetheless, the police officers that only hours before had held us at gunpoint were now glad to have a couple of meteorologists explain exactly what we were all up against.

"The eyewall is the most intense part of the storm," I said. "The wind blows its hardest. The precipitation will be violent."

I went out to the balcony to have another look at the sooty sky. A huge, muscular inmate with a shaved head and a light blue T-shirt with SLIDELL CITY JAIL printed on the back came up beside me.

"If you're going to stand out on the balcony, so am I," he said. "I want to see what hell looks like."

"Debris will soon start flying like bullets," I said.

The eyewall of a huge hurricane is not subtle. In the span of several minutes, the wind accelerated from 75 to probably 120 miles per hour. The police station shook, but with the balcony sheltered from the winds, we were able to watch as sheet metal that had likely peeled off of roofs slammed into structures and telephone poles. A cell phone tower broke in two. Mature trees bent unimaginably, until the upper reaches of their trunks were parallel with the ground. Some of them snapped, and the explosive sound of thick wood breaking could easily be heard over the monstrous, monotone roar of the wind.

There was rain, too. It seemed to come from every direction—down, sideways, up. The undersides of buildings got wet. There were long moments when you couldn't see anything out of the huge windows—the water just poured down. Simon and I were in awe: Physics and the laws of science had all converged to make this unbelievable and terrifying moment possible.

But neither of us felt the urge to celebrate. A couple of Slidell police officers sat on a couch and quietly wept. Inmates and officers looked at

one another emptily. The community that they all knew was now gone under waves of wind and water. Without any way to communicate, everyone in the police station worried about family and friends. Where were they? Were they alive?

The eyewall was gone fifteen minutes after it had arrived. The skies brightened to a dull gray, the wind quieted to a light breeze, and the rain stopped. Simon and I knew that we were in the eye of the storm. We were disappointed, however, that we couldn't see much—no thunderstorms embedded in the eyewalls, no bright blue sky above—because what had once been Katrina's textbook, circular eye had deformed. That can easily occur when friction builds between the storm's winds and land, and/or when the hurricane begins to lose its warm-water fuel source. A deformed eye is an indication that the hurricane is headed off course and weakening, like a railroad train that's starting to slip off the tracks.

But this was Katrina. It was still insane. The storm brought Slidell plenty of misery. The water around us had now risen to the point where all the doors and first-story windows in neighboring buildings had disappeared. Cars floated by in the strong inland current. From the balcony, I scanned the area through my video camera's zoom lens and saw people on the roofs of their homes, while others clung to trees. Many of them screamed for help. It was like a war zone.

I put down the camera and swallowed hard. I knew that the water would rise even more. And the storm wasn't done. Some of those victims wouldn't survive. This *was* hell.

"You a storm chaser, right?" said an inmate with a deep Cajun accent who was standing right next to me.

"Yeah," I replied.

"Y'all got the storm you lookin' for?" he asked.

I had no idea how to answer.

The emotional roller-coaster ride only continued.

One minute Simon showed me the readout from his handheld

barometer—930 millibars, the kind of insanely low pressure one only experiences in the rare eye of a giant hurricane—and the next I saw convicts and cops alike dangerously entering into the waters outside. They wanted to help other victims.

"You have to come back!" Simon yelled from the balcony. "We're in the eye! We're not done! The storm isn't over!"

"Please come back!" I yelled. I knew that many lives have been lost in hurricanes when people mistook the eye of the storm for the end of the storm. When the eye passed and the storm returned, conditions degraded so rapidly that people couldn't retreat to shelter in time.

"Conditions will deteriorate rapidly," I yelled.

Soaking wet prisoners and officers were helping people into bass-fishing boats that now dotted the floodwaters. Most of the boats were driven by citizens.

"Please find shelter," I said to the boatmen as they dropped off entire families at the police station's second story. Many of the survivors were crying.

When I saw the ominous dark clouds approaching again, I screamed from the balcony, begging everyone to take cover. Now Simon and I pitched in, too. We helped people get off the boats and watched them crowd into the second floor of the police station. When I heard the winds begin to pick up, I went to the balcony once more to see if anyone was still in the water near the building. There was no one. But I'm sure there were people in need just around a corner, or just out of earshot.

The horrifying wind now came from the west-northwest and ferociously battered the balcony. We all moved into a windowless area and listened to the roar of the wind, the scratching and screeching of twisted sheet metal that, after having set sail in the gusts, was finally wrapping around something. We waited in that room for what felt like a very long time. I guarantee that everyone in the room was wondering the same thing: if the Slidell police station would peel apart.

When the winds of Hurricane Katrina subsided over Slidell twenty minutes later, Simon and I knew what we had to do. We would assist people as best we could and then, however possible, attempt to evacuate. Our storm chase was unquestionably over. There was a thin line between being helpful and being in the way—being victims. We worried about being the latter.

The water outside was now lapping at the base of the police station's second-story balcony. There was talk of moving everyone in the building to the roof. More and more people showed up at the station on fishing boats.

We helped victims on and off the boats, gave away most of our food, and handed the Slidell police officers everything in our hurricane emergency kit, including our chain saw. When several cops seeking out higher ground to make a command post boarded a large fishing boat, Simon and I asked if there was room for two more. The driver of the boat agreed to give us a lift.

The ride was one strange journey. We puttered north for thirty minutes, practically ducking under Slidell stoplights that used to hang high over intersections. Thanks to the enormous storm surge, we could've reached out and touched power lines.

The officers wanted to take us to a raised city-government building, where they believed displaced victims might likely converge. But when we briefly stopped next to an elevated railroad track that was well above the water and pointing north, my eyes met Simon's.

"We're getting off here," I said to an officer wearing a camouflage-pattern flotation device, and we quickly grabbed our duffel and garbage bags.

"You can't walk from here," he said. "You have no idea what's ahead."

"We'll be okay," I said, and thought to myself that I also had no idea what was waiting for us at some quickly assembled refugee center either. I decided that we'd take our chances with the railroad tracks.

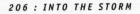

We thanked the officers profusely and then walked, climbed over downed trees, and jumped at every little sound made in the surrounding floodwaters for five miles. I swear, every minute that we were on those tracks, we expected something sinister to come leaping out of the water.

Instead we came upon the dry cement of Interstate 12. Norman was still twenty-four hours away—we'd have to walk, hitchhike, and finally rent a car before we reached home. But Katrina's grip had loosened. We were no longer at the mercy of water or wind. But the true ramifications of that storm would not be known for quite some time.

. . .

Y'all got the storm you lookin' for?

The words from that Slidell prison inmate rang in my head for weeks. In the wake of Katrina's horrific and well-documented tragedy—as much as $100 billion in losses, over 1,800 deaths, and the near obliteration of New Orleans—I wasn't the only one to question our wisdom in chasing Katrina. The storm-chasing community immediately attacked our judgment. What in the world, I kept asking myself, was the takeaway from such an insane experience? What were Simon and I looking for in Louisiana? For the first time ever in my storm-chasing career, I felt regret.

We hadn't been home long enough to empty our garbage bags from the trip south when Roger Edwards, a longtime severe-weather meteorologist and one of the more outspoken and conservative members of the chase community, learned some vague details of our chase.

On August 31, only two days after Katrina struck, Edwards publicly criticized our trip to Louisiana.

"How shameful and sad that the 'extreme video' thrill seekers are bringing such disrepute and greed to my beloved hobby," he wrote. "This is a giant seeping lesion on the face of storm chasing."

Edwards also went on to express anger that his tax dollars went to rescuing Simon and me.

After reading and rereading Edwards's thoughts on my computer screen at home in Norman, I again asked myself: Why did I go? What was the point? Was I just some hopelessly selfish adrenaline junkie? Was I really just greedy? The leading member of the profit-minded weather paparazzi?

We certainly didn't go to Louisiana to interfere with the police, burn taxpayer money, or try to capitalize on tragedy. And watching other people suffer because of a storm turned my stomach, as it always does. Simon and I chased Katrina to see how incredible and intense the atmosphere can become.

But soon after our arrival, we came to a pretty quick conclusion: Most ordinary folk don't know much about what weather can do. The atmosphere can be *very* intense. Simon and I were shocked, time and time again, to discover that many of the Katrina victims knew nothing about the power of the weather. I'm not saying that regular people need to learn terms like *supercell* and *mesocyclone*. They don't need to memorize the Saffir-Simpson Hurricane Wind Scale. Leave those terms to the scientists and us weather geeks. But I do believe that more folks should be able to recognize the skies and cloud structures that serve as a warning of potentially dangerous weather to come. And I think there needs to be more education available on the basics of hurricanes; that way if someone finds themselves caught in one, they don't wander outside when they're in the eye of the storm—with potentially tragic results. And shouldn't everyone who lives where there's severe weather have a $20 weather radio and be taught when might be a good time to tune in? These are some of the many thoughts I had in the wake of Katrina.

I was also looking for something else in Louisiana. In the end, it found me.

Standing on that Slidell Police Department balcony, watching all of that water wash toward me, I wondered—literally—what might become of our world.

The 2005 Atlantic hurricane season, from July to November, had unleashed insane amounts of power before Katrina ever came into existence. Hurricane Cindy had caused flooding in Alabama in early July; Hurricane Dennis struck the Florida panhandle a few days later and was the strongest Atlantic hurricane ever recorded for the month of July (with an incredible central pressure of only 930 millibars); and Hurricane Emily formed on July 11 and became the earliest Category 5 Atlantic hurricane of all time. Four tropical storms and one hurricane later, Katrina developed, incubating and intensifying with unbelievable speed over an exceptionally warm Gulf of Mexico. More Category 5 hurricanes would form during the Atlantic 2005 season—including Rita, which narrowly missed pounding New Orleans a second time—than in any other on record.

The apocalyptic conditions that both preceded and occurred as a result of Katrina were probably explained in part by storm patterns running in decades-long cycles. But the storms' frequency and intensity were also likely due to hot water—similar to the hot water that I'd been studying for years as a graduate student researching the occurrences of rising sea-surface temperatures for Dr. Lamb.

Watching Slidell essentially drown, I wondered if global warming was indeed creating warmer and warmer ocean water—water that could change long-established weather patterns. Like I said before, warm ocean water is one of a hurricane's main ingredients.

I was hardly alone in my thinking. Even back in 2005, many climatologists and other scientists who were much smarter and more experienced than I was had come to similar conclusions. Global climate-change models showed that as global warming continued, we might expect many more enormous hurricanes like Katrina.

Five years later, leading researchers are more convinced than ever that there's a link between a warmer planet and the severity of storms. Early in 2010, a panel of experts from the World Meteorological Organization

authored a study that predicts climate change will have a major influence on altering storm patterns and the resulting hurricanes in years to come. The study states that there will be one-third fewer hurricanes by the end of the current century, but that the surviving storms will feature up to 11 percent greater wind speeds. Eleven percent greater wind speeds, says one of the study's coauthors, translates into approximately 60 percent more damage. That's a scary figure.

Others in the climate community theorize that global warming could have a massive impact on severe weather and threats to humanity around the globe. Countries like Bangladesh and the Philippines, where severe-weather warning systems are poor or nonexistent, could be greatly affected by intensified, hurricanelike typhoons or tropical cyclones. (Imagine a storm even worse than the 1991 Category 5 Bangladesh Cyclone, which reportedly killed over 138,000 people.) Strong tornadoes, some experts say, could come down in Florida in the winter, and Tornado Alley's storm season might lengthen dramatically. One meteorology professor from the Massachusetts Institute of Technology even coined the term *hypercane* and theorized that triple-digit ocean temperatures and a chain of unlikely events could fuel a sort of superhurricane featuring five-hundred-mile-per-hour winds.

Katrina, I'm able to say, hit me with winds that only *felt* like they were moving at five hundred miles per hour. I had experienced some truly scary and sad moments in what was undoubtedly one of the most violent storms of my time. In retrospect, I feel that experiencing Katrina's power wasn't about a thrill, or becoming more intimate with the severe weather that I love. It was about glimpsing the meteorological future.

CHAPTER 8

CHASING FOR AN AUDIENCE

. . .

*M*issing a tornado intercept on May 5, 2006, was one of the best things that ever happened to me. I had deployed to the West Texas panhandle with Joel and three other people. Driving in Joel's white SUV, I thought we were perfectly positioned, just east of a northeast-moving supercell that had a classic "pancake-stack" appearance—multiple, horizontal layers of condensation that form and look a lot like flapjacks in the sky.

We saw the telltale rotating wall cloud and a funnel aloft, thousands of feet in the sky. But something besides a tornado would come out of the clouds, and in turn I'd do something I hadn't done much of before. I'd point my video camera on the chasers instead of what we were chasing. On May 5 I decided to focus on drama, whether it came from the atmosphere or somewhere else. It was a decision I wouldn't regret.

"Look at that clear slot!" I said, craning my neck to stare up through the windshield at the seam in the storm where winds and moisture blow down and around the mesocyclone. I was in the front passenger seat of Joel's idling vehicle. We were on the shoulder of a paved farm road, just east of the Texas–New Mexico border.

I'd seen this cloud structure hundreds of times before, but today was one of those days where I felt like I was seeing such a storm for the very first time. The way the bright white clouds seemed to tuck in, one atop another, was beautiful. Their symmetry was impressive. Their turns around the mesocyclone appeared well-oiled. The whole storm looked as if it had been crafted; this was tornado-making perfection.

There were multiple nipple-shaped clouds hanging down from the hovering storm, and any of them could've represented the beginning of a tornado. The ridiculous amount of wind shear that day certainly made conditions potentially explosive.

"If this storm doesn't spawn a tornado, I mean, what will?" I said giddily, and then soon had an answer to my own riddle. It looked like we might be in for some massive hail.

My computer gave me the news. I'd significantly upgraded my technology since chasing Hurricane Katrina the year prior. Where I'd pursued that storm with a laptop that picked up the Internet whenever I found a Wi-Fi signal, now I had a global positioning unit for whatever vehicle I was chasing in that fed my precise location and mapping information straight into the computer, and a data card that gave me Web access wherever I could secure a good cell phone signal. The technology improvements seriously boosted my abilities to track the storms that I was chasing and find roads and routes for chasing them. Most serious storm chasers now had similar setups.

Luckily I was enjoying plenty of signal strength just outside the tiny Texas-panhandle town of Seminole. The large, green-colored triangle glowing in the radar map on my laptop screen meant that there was a greater than 50 percent chance of the storm spawning severe hail. The radar indicated that it could come down right in our area.

"We might be getting some hail," I warned everyone in the car.

"How good a chance? What kind of hail?" Joel asked with concern. He was sitting in the driver's seat. Three of my friends from the University of Reading, all visiting from the United Kingdom, were in the back. Everyone looked uneasy with the news. Hail was a mixed bag—exciting to look at and listen to as it drummed a vehicle roof, but also capable of reducing a chase to a crawl. In worst-case scenarios, huge hailstones can kill livestock, punch holes in the roofs of homes, and bring down small planes. Hail also destroys vehicles.

Is it a surprise that I personally enjoy a monster hailstorm? I considered it a storm-chasing rite of passage. I, of course, thought that a hail-damaged car should be driven with pride.

"I'd say there's a very good chance of some severe hail," I said with a smile and a nod, and then looked up at the thunderstorm again. There was still no tornado, but now the storm had shifted. It was headed right at us.

Joel put the transmission into gear.

"I want to get farther ahead of this thing," he said, and pulled onto the empty road, driving toward the Texas interior.

Almost immediately we heard a deep thunk from the roof of the SUV. Then another, and another. Several hailstones hit the car, and while they were relatively few and far between, they were gigantic—as big as softballs.

"Uh, the windshield," I said, and the next thing I knew, another huge hailstone hit the top of Joel's windshield and put a big bull's-eye crack in the glass.

"Just lost it," said Sarah, one of my English friends, with her British accent.

More hail hit the car. The impact sounded like someone was standing on the roof of the SUV and going at it with a sledgehammer. The racket and impacts were both exhilarating and scary. Joel had the resigned look of someone who was about to face a major repair bill.

"They're huge," I said, and we all winced as more hailstones came down on the roof.

"Ow! Oh! Ooooo!" I heard from the backseat.

"Let's try and get away," I said, and Joel continued to drive—although

tentatively—down the flat, straight road. There was blue sky in front of us. But the thunderstorm remained overhead.

The hail wasn't a surprise. It's pretty common in supercell thunderstorms: The updraft inside the storm consists of millions of water droplets that cool as they rise into increasingly cold air. In fact, the water droplets "supercool," or remain in a liquid state even below freezing temperatures. Sometimes these supercooled droplets will collide with ice particles high in the storm and immediately bond and freeze to these particles. These small pieces of ice eventually fall due to their own weight, but they may travel only partway back down through the storm before the updraft pushes them up again, where they might collide with more supercooled water droplets and become larger. If the cycle repeats itself enough times—like when updrafts move at a hundred miles per hour or faster—the hailstones can grow to the size of softballs and even beyond. Storm chasers generally try to avoid heavy hail.

But on this day, we couldn't get away. Looking up through the cracked windshield, I could see the rotating mesocyclone forcefully whipping lots of hailstones out the side of the storm, like some pitching machine gone haywire. The hail was pounding the road and putting huge divots in the Texas mud around us.

Another hailstone slammed against the windshield, right at its base and in front of the steering wheel. Pieces of something flew inside the car.

"That's glass," I said, and now even I became uncomfortable with the situation. Joel pulled over. The driving was too difficult while the storm literally threw frozen punches at us. We had no choice but to endure the beating.

"Shut your eyes," I yelled. "Keep your eyes shut! Shield your eyes!"

Predictably, I didn't follow my own advice. I kept my eye pasted to the viewfinder of my video camera. I'd gone from recording the hail falling outside the car to recording the more interesting story that was unfolding inside the car. I filmed the destruction of the windshield. The strained expressions on the others' faces. The blankets they threw over their heads.

There was a shattering noise from the back of the SUV, and I swung my camera toward the sound.

"Oh my God!" said Martin, another friend from England.

"What'd we lose?" I asked, and then spotted the giant hole created by a hailstone crashing into one of the SUV's rear side windows.

"Martin, the bike helmet!" I said, and Martin slipped it on. We'd packed a bike helmet for protection—in case someone wanted to wear it while wandering outside the vehicle during a hailstorm. I never thought we'd need it inside the truck.

I filmed another friend, Ben, tentatively looking out from underneath a blanket. Martin held up his palm, which was covered in small cuts from flying glass.

Then I pointed the camera at myself.

"Very dangerous situation here," I said into the lens while the insanely long and violent hailstorm continued to pound the car. In the background, hailstones bounced off a nearby Texas oil rig.

After the hailstorm finally eased, I took some video of Joel's car. It was destroyed. The windshield was cracked in several places. That rear window was blown out. A door-mounted rearview mirror had nearly been sheared off. All of the bodywork had dents. Somehow the air conditioner had even quit. I'd never seen a vehicle with so much hail damage.

We'd barely begun our seven-hour drive home when I called a couple of news networks. I gave producers an unexpected pitch.

"No, no tornado," I told a producer at CBS News. "It's a video of the most violent hailstorm you've ever seen. Huge hailstones. And there's drama—we're under siege inside the vehicle. The glass is flying. Do you think you might be interested?"

I had no idea if this would fly. As usual, I needed cash.

The producer said she was interested.

By the time Joel pulled his trashed vehicle into a motel parking lot in Lubbock, I'd downloaded the footage from my video camera to my laptop and edited the day's adventures into a brief clip. There was a beginning (the hope of intercepting a tornado), a middle (the insane hailstorm), and an end (our survival and the near-destruction of Joel's vehicle). I didn't pretend to think that I was Quentin Tarantino or Francis Ford Coppola. But I had spliced together more than storm-chasing video. I had a storm-chasing story.

From the motel parking lot in Lubbock, I sent my clip to the Web server that also hosted my Web site. Then I sent the interested producers an e-mail that gave them access to the footage. They were a couple of mouse clicks away from watching, and hopefully buying, my video. Gone forever were the days of stuffing quarters into pay phones, making post-chase stops at network affiliates in one-horse towns, searching for satellite news trucks in the loneliest parts of Tornado Alley. Now all I needed to distribute video of a chase to almost anyone in the world was a Wi-Fi connection. Of course, that's all many other similarly equipped chasers needed, too. Such advances in technology would, in coming years, help create a glut of material in the severe-weather video business. Thousands of people would try to sell footage.

But back on that May 2006 day in West Texas, I was proud of my quick thinking. I took hailstones and turned them into lemonade. I also had another incredible experience under a storm and put some money in my and Joel's pockets (the poor guy had one mauled car). Plus I realized that storm-chasing video didn't always, or didn't always exclusively, have to be about a storm. The footage could involve the people who chase and how they interact with the weather and each other. The drama could hinge on the classic struggle of man versus nature, which in a way was what my life was all about.

• • •

I don't deserve all the credit for my epiphany. Only days before I'd deployed to West Texas with Joel and my British friends, I watched an hour-long documentary about Joel and me and our storm-chasing adventures that our friend had made. The film made me realize that perhaps my crazy obsession with storm chasing could be nearly as entertaining as the tornado footage that I captured.

In 2002, my friend—graduate school student, fellow storm chaser, and budding filmmaker—Ken Cole approached Joel and me to ask if he could document our 2003 chase season as a film project. We said sure. We'd all graduated together with bachelor's of science degrees in meteorology, but Ken had subsequently decided that he wanted to get a master's degree in communications and make films. Joel and I wanted to help our buddy and didn't think Ken's presence with a camera would be a problem. We also didn't know that he'd be such a good filmmaker.

At first, Ken's presence was intrusive. Every time Joel and I turned around to look at the sky, there was Ken with his video camera. He filmed us chasing. He filmed us excitedly pointing at clouds. He filmed us eating. He filmed us climbing out of bed. He filmed us arguing.

By the time we'd become accustomed to Ken and the camera, the 2003 season was over. He'd shadowed us all over Tornado Alley and had interviewed numerous conservative chasers who don't like my intense chasing style. He gathered a lot of material about my friendship with Joel, asking us endless questions about how we chased together so often and still got along.

Then Ken went away. He spent months editing the hundreds of hours of video that he'd captured, and in July 2004 he showed a seventy-five-minute version of his film, which he called *Tornado Glory,* to a full auditorium on the OU campus. Watching myself on the big screen, screaming at the skies while I ran up and down the shoulders of empty

country roads, was strange and pretty embarrassing. (*Do I really act that way?* I kept asking myself.) But the audience paid close attention to the film, which was completely different from the Hollywood blockbuster *Twister:* The moody documentary captured Joel and me chasing, celebrating huge intercepts, bickering, disappointed during blue-sky busts, and saddened when tornadoes caused tragedy. After the show, people applauded and came up to pose questions to Joel and me. They wanted to know about the storms—and what a life of storm chasing was really like.

Ken then showed the documentary at film festivals in Las Vegas and Los Angeles. In early 2006 he pitched a version of the film to Oklahoma City's PBS affiliate. Thirteen hours later, the producers called him, saying that they wanted to broadcast a version of his work. Two days before Joel and I were bombarded with hail in West Texas, an hour-long edit of *Tornado Glory* aired on Oklahoma public television station KOED. A few months later, the documentary went national and pulled great viewership numbers at PBS stations across the United States.

Tornado Glory didn't make Ken wealthy, although it did open doors for him in television and gave him the chance to experiment with other types of films. But the critical success of the film made me think that perhaps I could solidify a real storm-chasing career by putting myself—and not just other chasers—in front of the camera. Apparently people were interested in a guy who could never get too close to the meteorological action.

I wasn't alone in my thinking. In the summer of what turned into an agonizingly slow 2006 chasing season, I received a phone call from a producer at the film production company Natural History New Zealand (NHNZ). The international company produced and sold shows to many television stations. I'd sold tornado footage to NHNZ in the past.

The NHNZ producer who called me, however, wasn't looking for storm video. She told me that the Weather Channel wanted a storm-chasing program in its lineup and had asked production companies like

NHNZ to submit pilot programs for consideration. Would Joel and I, the producer asked, be interested in filming such a pilot?

I confidently responded for both of us: yes. I called Joel afterward and gave him the news.

"Having our own program? Someone paying for our storm chasing?" he said, sounding excited. "I'll fit that into my schedule."

When I spoke to the NHNZ producer again, she said she'd fly out a cameraman soon to film us chasing.

I explained that the process wasn't so simple.

"It's summer," I told her. "This time of year, the jet streams that help generate tornadoes migrate north, out of Tornado Alley. There's nothing to chase."

She was unsympathetic.

"Just find one," she said.

Joel and I scoured the forecasting models online just about every hour.

"We could see something soon in the Dakotas," I said to him over the phone one day in early August. "Decent heat. Wind shear. Dew point should be intense—mid-seventies."

We didn't know if there would be enough cold air aloft to help the thunderstorms fully develop. But we also didn't have much choice.

A few days later, with a cameraman onboard, we left Norman in the dark for a target location in eastern South Dakota, stopping for little more than gas, caffeine, and convenience-store hot dogs.

"You guys always eat like this?" said the cameraman, a chatty guy from California. He sat in the backseat of Joel's new red pickup and looked into the center of his half-eaten hot dog. "This is awful."

The drive brought Joel and me right back to the days of storm chasing with Ken. We answered a ton of the cameraman's questions and sometimes repeated ourselves two or three times for the camera.

"Can you argue about that CAPE stuff one more time for me, but don't look at the camera?" he said as we drove on Interstate 29 through eastern Nebraska.

Unfortunately, CAPE, wind shear, and several other ingredients we needed for a tornado abandoned us that day. When we were still several hours away from our target location, I called up the RUC model—"RUC" stands for Rapid Update Cycle and is accessible on a government-run forecasting Web site—on my laptop.

"CAPE numbers are high, but there's that cap," I said, referring to the platform of stable air that, when in place, sits like a cap and can stop a thunderstorm from developing.

"And RUC always overestimates moisture," said Joel with a sigh from behind the steering wheel.

South Dakota was a blue-sky bust. Joel and I, however, decided we'd come too far to give up. We went another 460 miles north the next day, since conditions for a severe-weather outbreak looked decent around Winnipeg.

We didn't know much about storm chasing in Canada except that some of the country's terrain and weather were highly conducive to the development of severe weather. The Canadian prairies have a lot of the same features as Tornado Alley—a huge western mountain range (the Canadian Rockies) capable of delivering cold, dry air to the eastern flatlands; moist air located in the middle of the country; and warm temperatures flowing in from the south. In fact, the Canadian prairies are in some ways an equal if not better place than Tornado Alley to pursue severe weather. There's enough daylight during Canadian summers to chase almost until midnight. The road network is passable. The air has little haze. And there aren't a lot of other storm chasers—the faithful that exist seem to concentrate around Manitoba. Storm chasing is a born and bred American endeavor that, so far, has reached only fledgling status in a few other parts of the world.

Considering Canada's potential, why haven't American chasers spread the good word north? There are some legitimate hurdles to chasing in Canada. Travel distance is one—not everyone wants to deploy to a target area, no matter how great the setup, a thousand miles away. Canada's radar technology lags well behind radar infrastructure in the United States. Various mapping and forecasting technologies and materials for Canada are limited, and cell phone rates for U.S. chasers jump once they cross their country's northern border. Chasing in Canada is a little like chasing in the days before we had the Web. You have to consistently study the sky.

For Joel, the NHNZ cameraman, and me, that Canadian sky remained a frustratingly bright blue. We drove for hours in virtually every direction and didn't see so much as a raindrop. After surrendering we stopped for ice cream on Lake Winnipeg and then drove 1,100 miles home. We didn't capture more than a gust of wind on tape.

NHNZ producers cobbled together a pilot featuring Joel and me, but the Weather Channel chose another show. I regrouped in Norman, received my master's degree while revving up to pursue a PhD, and tried to forget all about the idea of landing on television. Instead I filled my time during a decent fall 2006 chase season revamping tornadovideos. net and throwing highlights of all my storm-chasing intercepts up for everyone to see on a Web site that I'd never heard of called YouTube. A Web-savvy friend of mine swore that it was a good idea.

• • •

As close as I enjoyed coming to tornadoes, I'd never had the chance to admire one while keeping it at arm's length. Even my intercept of the F4 tornado in Manchester, South Dakota, in 2003 was more of a retreat than a bullfight. But I finally landed the opportunity to spar with an incredible tornado in spring 2007. The game between tornado and chasers, which of course I captured on videotape, made for cliffhanger drama. That

scene would capture the attention of huge TV audiences and be replayed on YouTube millions and millions of times.

The setup in northwestern Oklahoma on May 4 was sublime. A dryline extended north to south across much of southern Tornado Alley, so chasers could expect a blanket of hot air from the west to clash with warm and moist air coming from the south-southeast, which could trigger the creation of supercell thunderstorms. Indeed, the Storm Prediction Center Web site issued a moderate risk for severe weather from the eastern Texas panhandle all the way north to Nebraska, which meant tornadoes could be coming in a whole lot of different places. The threat seemed to be particularly high in western Kansas, and Joel, Ken Cole, and I spent much of the afternoon in Dodge City, deciding which way to deploy.

For a while, the biggest excitement of the day had been a call from Dr. Lamb. He and I were coauthors on a paper to appear in the *Journal of Applied Meteorology and Climatology,* and Lamb needed some figures on consumption of natural gas per capita right away. I furiously researched his questions on the Web for an hour.

Then the atmosphere sprang to life. Late in the afternoon, the National Weather Service issued a tornado warning for Oklahoma's Ellis County, which is in the extreme western part of the state. I looked at the region's conditions on my laptop. Warm and moist air was flooding the region. And conditions were ripe for the air to lift and twist.

"It's two hours away," said Joel after we all heard the storm warning over the radio.

"I bet very few people will be on it. They'll be missing out," I argued. "Let me drive."

I drove south on U.S. Highway 283, and just outside of Arnett we punched through a core of mild hail and saw a tornado on the ground a couple miles away. It was shaped like an elephant's trunk and was narrow and crisp. It was a beautiful white, and raised a brown dust cloud while spinning furiously in an open field set in some rolling hills.

I wanted to get closer.

"Stop sign stop sign stop sign," said Ken, his voice rising in volume and alarm.

I barely slowed for the desolate intersection. There wasn't a car, building, or person around.

"I looked both ways," I said sheepishly.

I quickly glanced at Joel, who was filming the tornado. He usually drove.

"You're getting this, right?" I said, paranoid that Joel wasn't doing justice to one of the most beautiful tornadoes I'd ever seen. Did we have plenty of videotape? Battery power? "Have you hit the zoom button?" I asked.

"I'm zooming way in," he said, his eye on the viewfinder.

"Zoom way out too. It's an incredible tornado," I said.

I drove to within a quarter mile of where the tornado was spinning, but I didn't want to pull over. The road we were on seemed to be leading right to it. Meanwhile the tornado was coming north, right toward us.

"Stop up here on this hill," said Joel.

I blew right over the hill.

"Reed, stop," said Joel.

"We're okay, Joel. Don't worry," I said, accelerating up the next short grade.

I finally stopped in the middle of the road, three hundred yards short of the tornado. It was right off the pavement, virtually spinning in place. Joel and I switched spots. I took the camera from him.

I saw some amazing details of a tornado that day. How it leans one way, then another. How its form expands and contracts, as if it's breathing. How there are seams and openings in its gleaming white skin that allow you to see into its spinning soul.

There was also the tornado's unmistakable roar—a Niagara Falls–caliber roar. That sucker *sounded* like power, like pure energy, intensity, and focus. I've always identified with those qualities.

"Back up!" yelled Ken from the backseat as the tornado started moving directly toward us. Joel began driving the truck slowly in reverse.

"Stop. We're good," I said insistently, and Joel momentarily stopped. I could tell that Ken and Joel felt uneasy. I fought their urge to flee.

The tornado paused for a second. Then, all of a sudden, it charged in our direction.

"Back up!" shouted Ken.

But I'd already jumped out of the truck to stand behind my open door and continue shooting. The tornado couldn't have been more than fifty yards from us. The dust cloud loomed large in my viewfinder. Joel started to reverse and the door slammed into me when I wasn't looking. I dropped my cell phone.

"Don't go," I shrieked.

"Get in and shut your door. Shut your door!" said Joel, and this time he was right to be insistent. I left my phone behind and the tornado sucked it right up.

"That is a strong tornado, Reed," said Joel, shaking his head as he drove backward, the wind rushing through all of the vehicle's open windows.

But I wasn't listening to Joel. I was lost in the thrilling power of the storm. I looked up and saw how the white tornado snaked above us and stood in stark contrast to the dark supercell above it.

"Can you hear that? Listen to the roar!" I exclaimed loudly and in complete joy. The sky framing the torso of the tornado was a perfect blue. The air felt like it had come from a sauna.

Forty-five minutes later we were in Woodward, Oklahoma, in the parking lot of a motel where I found a Wi-Fi signal. I uploaded a quick edit of the Ellis County chase to my Web server's hard drive and called a producer at *Good Morning America* on someone else's phone.

"You know how I always tell you that I have insane tornado video?" I explained to him. "This is beyond insane. This is the whitest, most well-

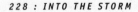

defined, best tornado I've ever seen, and we did a dance with it. We're so close to it in the video that you feel like you can touch the tornado. Or taste it."

I sent him the link to my edit. He watched it and called me right back, and we made a quick deal.

When the video aired, it showcased a great tornado. And quite accidentally, the video also said a lot about the chasers who intercepted the storm. The viewing public watched and asked themselves, who are these obsessed people behind the camera? Who gets close to a tornado and then gets closer still?

Soon my phone rang off the hook with calls from other television producers, and in terms of sales I soon hit an insane jackpot. I ultimately grossed tens of thousands of dollars from this footage.

I made more than money, however, on the storm. Thanks to that tornado, my Web site immediately became synonymous with tornadoes and storm chasing. My name recognition grew.

My agreement with *Good Morning America* had permitted me to "watermark" the footage that ran on the program—that is, my Web site address appeared in the bottom left corner of the video. Shortly after the show ran my clip, the traffic to my Web site resembled a tornado. My site crashed in a storm of overwhelming demand.

Luckily the public could also see a portion of the Ellis County video on YouTube, and the more that people watched, the more my name and "tornadovideos.net" popped up in any search-engine inquiry that included the word "tornado."

YouTube, it turns out, came along at just the right time for me. It was the perfect profile-raising showcase for the tornado video collection that I'd been amassing for eight years. Ellis County was my prize catch: In a matter of days after the May 4 chase, the YouTube clip went viral and notched over a million views, and in the weeks to follow it would notch

millions more. Tornadoes and my extreme brand of storm chasing were going mainstream.

...

Unfortunately, there was another, much darker reason why tornadoes were on the minds of many Americans in early May 2007. Within four hours of Joel, Ken, and I intercepting one of the most beautiful tornadoes in recent storm-chasing history, one of the ugliest tornadoes ever to rotate obliterated the tiny southern Kansas town of Greensburg. President George W. Bush would declare Greensburg and its surrounding lands a major disaster area, and within a week of the catastrophe the president and his press entourage would travel to Tornado Alley to see the damage firsthand. The destruction of Greensburg would attract widespread and long-lived attention.

Eleven people died in the storm, but that number is remarkably low considering the severity of the tornado and the damage it inflicted. One reason more people weren't killed in a town that was essentially destroyed by a two-mile-wide, nighttime F5 tornado? Storm chasers gave the National Weather Service advance warning of the storm's path and potential for destruction. In terms of public service, the Greensburg tornado was the storm-chasing community's finest hour. One of the few positives to come out of Greensburg's demise was the recognition of storm chasers' potential value in terms of increasing public safety.

Joel, Ken, and I crashed in a Woodward, Oklahoma, motel instead of going home on the night of May 4, as we knew that there was more crazy weather brewing nearby. The radar reflectivity image for southwest Kansas was a sea of purple, which can be an indication of explosive thunderstorm activity. If I'd been alone that night, I might have pursued that severe weather too. But Joel doesn't like to chase after dark, and I do understand why. Despite all the technology we had at our disposal, even well-equipped and experienced storm chasers can unwittingly drive straight into a nighttime storm. Retreating to a motel—after a triumphant day of chasing and capturing footage—might have been the decision that saved our lives.

But I have colleagues and friends who will forever be associated with preventing deaths and comforting the shell-shocked at the Greensburg disaster. One such friend is Mike Umscheid. Mike is a storm chaser, meteorologist, and lead forecaster at the National Weather Service office in Dodge City, Kansas—one of 122 weather forecast offices scattered across the United States that are largely responsible for predicting the weather for every square inch of the country.

As darkness fell over Kansas on the night of May 4, Mike saw a huge supercell thunderstorm erupt to life on his radar screen just after seven P.M. The storm was a result of freakish conditions—a strong low-level jet fueling the air with warmth and moisture, and subsequent insane wind shear as well as CAPE measurements over an already high five thousand joules per kilogram (again, strong CAPE indicates that conditions are conducive for air to rise quickly through the atmosphere).

Yet another reason why that night's Kansas sky was so electric? Sometimes supercell thunderstorms split apart but don't die before they run into other supercell thunderstorms. The two can combine and be reinvigorated.

On the night of the Greensburg outbreak, as many as five fragmented supercell storms contributed to the organization of one lone, monster supercell. One of the fragmented storms that helped build the Greensburg tornado had split from the very storm that Ken, Joel, and I had chased earlier in the day.

Sitting at his NWS desk around 7:30 P.M. that night, Mike clearly saw on his radar screen that the gigantic storm had impressive rotating winds. But he couldn't be sure that the rotating winds represented a tornado. Mike's office was a distant forty-five miles west of the action, and more important, his radar can't detect wind rotation on a scale as small as a

tornado's (only the wind shear associated with the mesocyclone). In addition, his radar can't pick up activity that occurs as low in the atmosphere as a tornado. Mike needed eyes on the ground to tell him what was going on.

Now, Mike Umscheid has enormous responsibilities. In his Dodge City office, he has to notify the local media and emergency personnel of potential severe-weather dangers. The media outlets and emergency responders have to trust that what Mike says is worth telling large populations. Cry wolf too many times, authorities know, and people won't listen to any severe-weather warnings.

Such responsibilities make it hard for some NWS forecasters to want to believe all of the anonymous updates about local weather conditions that they get from folks calling their offices. What if someone is overcautious, or worse, playing a joke?

But Mike is a storm chaser himself, and on the night of May 4 he could see on his radar screen that a big storm was heading toward the 1,600-person town of Greensburg. So he listened very carefully to what every storm chaser who called in updates to his office had to say:

The tornado was over a mile wide, warned one storm chaser.

The tornado left power lines and poles strewn across the highway south of town, said another storm chaser.

The tornado crushed homes in outlying areas, said a third chaser.

There were more calls, and Mike kept listening.

Mike soon notified the local media and emergency personnel serving Greensburg of potential severe weather dangers on the horizon.

At 9:18 P.M., Mike issued a warning for "a large and extremely dangerous tornado fourteen miles southeast of Greensburg."

At 9:28 P.M. he issued a warning of a "life-threatening situation."

At 9:37 P.M. he issued a warning to "take shelter immediately if you are in Greensburg."

At 9:41 P.M. he issued a "tornado emergency," a warning so dire that, nationwide, the National Weather Service had issued very few such warnings ever before. The NWS discourages its meteorologists from using the "tornado emergency" alert because it means that there's a high likelihood of a tornado that will cause vast damage and multiple fatalities.

Thankfully, Mike Umscheid listened to the storm chasers. And thankfully, the people of Greensburg listened to Mike Umscheid.

At approximately 9:49 P.M., the power went out in town. Soon folks' ears were popping inside of storm cellars throughout Greensburg, and then there was a brief moment of silence and calm before the tornado unloaded on the tiny, tree-lined streets. Windows exploded, cars folded like paper, brick walls crumbled, and dozens of cows were pulled into the sky and rolled up in airborne barbed wire as a 1.7-mile-wide, 200-mile-per-hour F5 wedge tornado obliterated 95 percent of the town.

• • •

Mike and his network of storm chasers did what they could to brace Greensburg for the apocalyptic tornado. Then the responsibility to help create order out of total chaos in a storm-struck town partially fell to another friend of mine. Randy Denzer is a forty-seven-year-old fireman and storm chaser. Randy happened to be in the right place at the right time that day. Or was it the wrong place at the wrong time?

Like many storm chasers, Randy had waited hours on May 4 for storms to develop in Kansas. He and several friends were ready to write off the day as a bust when other storm chasers called in the evening and said that huge storms were firing south of his location. Randy didn't want to chase at night, but he and his eight chase partners thought that they could keep their distance and perhaps photograph some of the spectacular lightning bolts illuminating a dark sky.

Expectations and plans changed once Randy and the others headed south toward Greensburg on U.S. Highway 183. Their three-car caravan encountered unexpectedly high winds and debris, like flying tree branches

and pink home insulation. What Randy didn't know at the time was that the Greensburg tornado, which had already wreaked havoc there, had turned north and then northwest, crossing Highway 183 before roping out. Randy and the others drove, scared and moving slowly, straight through the outer storm bands of an F5 tornado.

Randy pushed on, but not because he wanted to take pictures. While driving through the blowing winds, he'd received a call from the same friends who had tipped him off earlier about these storms. They said someone with Randy's emergency-responder skills was needed at residences south of Greensburg. Several homes had been destroyed by the tornado, and people were trapped in the rubble.

As Randy's group approached the crossroads leading to Greensburg, he pulled up alongside a man in a truck that was parked with its hazard lights flashing. Randy asked the man if he could help them dig out storm victims south of town, but the man appeared to be in shock. He said he was a local fireman and that he'd been out fishing on his day off when the tornado hit. The fireman said that he'd heard that Greensburg had been crushed. Then he wanted to talk more about fishing.

Randy quickly convinced the fireman that they needed to act. The fireman came to his senses enough to ask Randy's crew to help in Greensburg. Randy himself was a lieutenant in the Austin, Texas, fire department and also trained people to become emergency medical technicians, or EMTs. Among his group of chasers were two additional firefighters and several scientists.

Rolling into town several minutes later, Randy couldn't quite comprehend what he'd encountered. He saw very few buildings and figured that he was on the outskirts of Greensburg. The roads leading farther into town were hard to make out under all of the debris and nearly impassable. Everywhere Randy pointed his vehicle headlights he saw broken power poles, downed electrical wires, shredded building insulation, smashed drywall, broken bricks, and splintered two-by-fours. In other words, complete mayhem.

When Randy and the others finally got out of their cars, they were told that they weren't on the outskirts of Greensburg. They were, in fact, in the center of town, where just an hour earlier there had been buildings everywhere. The air was heavy with the smell of leaking gasoline and propane. When the wind blew, the trees that survived the tornado sounded as if they were loaded with wind chimes. But the branches were actually full of metallic bits of cars and sheet metal that were tinkling in the breeze.

There were other sounds, too—muffled and loud cries for help, from both the walking wounded, some of them only half-clothed, and victims trapped in their crushed cars or stuck in their basements underneath mounds of rubble.

Randy's group did what it could. The nine of them worked alone and with the local authorities to help set up a triage center and a command post. They went looking for rescue equipment at the Greensburg fire station, only to find powder and twisted metal where the fire station once stood. They strapped on some out-of-date safety equipment to search for someone reportedly trapped inside of Greensburg's damaged and fume-spewing power plant, and nearly lost their lives when the compressed air that they were breathing ran dangerously low.

Because Randy was so highly trained, he knew to coordinate his efforts in Greensburg with emergency management. Most storm chasers, even those with the best intentions, are better off asking local authorities how they can help before attempting to provide assistance at a disaster scene. Over my many years of storm chasing, I'm happy to say that I've never encountered a situation like the one Randy did in Greensburg. But I've diligently called in weather reports and occasionally employed my biceps to help lift a fallen tree out of the road.

Randy himself didn't leave Greensburg unscathed. In the weeks and months following the disaster, he displayed symptoms of post-traumatic stress disorder and heard peoples' cries in his sleep. He remembered those who survived, and those who didn't, and how grateful Greensburg's overwhelmed citizens were for his help. But he couldn't get what he had seen out of his head, no matter how hard he tried.

Randy also left the destroyed town with great determination to better involve storm chasers in warning the public of severe-weather outbreaks. Today he's very active in a nonprofit organization called the Spotter Network, which provides precise, online location information from member storm chasers wherever they're pursuing severe weather in the continental United States (via free tracking software loaded into a computer).

When Spotter Network members see severe weather or conditions that indicate severe weather might develop, they're asked to file brief yet descriptive online reports on the Spotter Network Web site. These reports then deliver key details to public servants—like NWS forecasters—who might otherwise not be aware of ground-level weather conditions.

I believe that I have something to contribute to the advancement of storm-warning capability in this country, too. Ever since 2007, I've equipped my Web site, tornadovideos.net, to accept live streaming video from any participating storm chaser—not just me and my chasing partners. The hope is that, over time, a growing network of storm chasers will send live video of the conditions they encounter to my site, and that a widening number of government weather forecasters, emergency services employees, and law enforcement agents will access and use the information to help them make important decisions in protecting people from severe-weather outbreaks. I believe that images will provide reassuring proof to anyone concerned with what's occurring in a local atmosphere.

Hopefully, the Spotter Network and the live-streaming storm-spotting technology on tornadovideos.net, as well as other similar programs, will give the likes of NWS forecasters one, five, or even hundreds of sets of credible eyes on any storm, whether that storm amounts to nothing or another Greensburg tornado. The Spotter Network has already built significant momentum, proving that Randy and his associates are onto something: The organization, which launched in 2006, today has three thousand certified members.

The Greensburg disaster has had another lasting effect: public attention. As ironic as it sounds, May 4, 2007, was the day that little Greensburg, Kansas, both disappeared from and appeared on the map. President Bush returned to the town a year after he saw the damage firsthand, this time to deliver the commencement address for Greensburg High School's tiny graduating class.

Almost a year after that graduation, President Barack Obama mentioned Greensburg and the tornado that destroyed it in an address to a joint session of Congress.

Meanwhile actor Leonardo DiCaprio became the executive producer of a television show called *Greensburg* in 2008 for the Planet Green cable channel. For three years, the program followed the town's careful rebuilding in the wake of the tornado.

As for meteorologist Mike Umscheid, in 2008 he published a study that profiled the Greensburg tornado. Among his findings was that the tornado's mesocyclone, or rapidly rotating updraft, was both gigantic and spinning approximately as fast as the tornado that it spawned. Typically, huge mesocyclones rotate much more slowly. Mike's discovery clearly shows how much there's still left to understand about tornadoes. Because if a huge, high-velocity mesocyclone can occur once—and spawn a two-hundred-mile-per-hour tornado that obliterates a town—one would think that such a storm could appear again.

Just about the only group of people associated with the Greensburg tornado who didn't have a spotlight cast on them in the aftermath of the

destruction was storm chasers, like Randy and the many others who called in weather warnings before the town was hit. Storm chasers unquestionably played a role in saving people's lives, and I consider it a miracle that only eleven people died because of that huge tornado. I consider those storm chasers, some my friends and some complete strangers, the unsung heroes of the Greensburg event.

• • •

Shortly after the Greensburg tornado spun, I witnessed my own unforgettable tornado. I'd made a grueling return storm-chasing trip to Manitoba, Canada, in the summer of 2007. I didn't go because I believed Manitoba would be the chase that vaulted me onto a storm-chasing TV program and into a storm-chasing *career*. But sure enough, Manitoba was my launchpad.

This trip was much different than the Canadian trip I'd taken a year earlier with Joel. That 2006 deployment occurred out of desperation to find a tornado so that we could audition for a TV show. As optimistic as I am, I knew the chances were slim that we'd see something on that trip. The journey turned into a long and agonizing blue-sky bust.

In late June 2007, however, the Canadian sky was begging for attention. The computer models forecasted that a trough, or area of low pressure in the atmosphere ejecting from the Northern Rockies, would soon be moving across the Canadian prairie. The trough would draw moisture northward from the United States and virtually guarantee the presence of the cold air aloft that supercell thunderstorms require as the hot air inside of them blasts skyward. Intense wind shear was also in the forecast. I checked the RUC models online—and found CAPE in the range of four to five thousand joules per kilogram. Numbers half as big excite me.

Dave Holder, whom I'd chased with in Minnesota when we got caught inside the funnel of an F0 tornado, agreed to go with me. We'd drive his car.

"It'll go sixty forever," he said in his typical calm, steady-state voice before we left on June 21. The prime chase day was luckily a full two days later.

Dave, I'm a little sorry to say, is a realist. He didn't underestimate his car's abilities. His little red Hyundai barely maintained the legal speed limit as we made our way north and west through the hot early Midwestern summer. The Hyundai's AC was inoperable, the heater was cranked to take stress off the engine, and the interior featured a thick coat of grime—the by-product of sweat and dust that had accumulated over many long road trips.

When we finally arrived in the farm town of Estevan, Saskatchewan, I was both relieved and excited by the weather reports that I called up via Wi-Fi on my laptop. The favorable conditions had not only held, they'd improved.

We left our crappy motel and surged southeast out of Regina, Saskatchewan, on Canada Provincial Route 33. Deep green grasses bordered the lonely road, and above us the supercell thunderstorms sprouted like weeds. I hoped that Dave and I would see some amazing stuff. An F5 tornado had come down in Manitoba only a day earlier.

The weather teased us. Supercells came and went without spawning a funnel. Finally, late in the afternoon, we sat under a cloud that was round, smooth edged, and tapered—it looked like a black flying saucer. The surrounding sky was a greenish blue-gray, and the fields were filled with yellow canola. Soon, amid lightning and thunder, a triangular, conical tornado formed. It was miles away from our position.

"We need some roads," I said to Dave. Canada's largely empty prairies apparently meant a relative shortage of farm roads. "Can you check out the road situation? We need to find a way to get to that storm."

We scrambled to find a northern route to reach the rain-shrouded tornado. It wasn't the storm that I'd hoped for. The prime atmospheric conditions had led me to believe that we might encounter something truly spectacular. But it was better than a blue-sky bust.

I was driving the Hyundai toward the storm when I noticed a rotating wall cloud to our east. This one was impressive—big and cylindrical, framed by lightning, bright white, and turning underneath a huge layer of dark clouds. You could hear thunder coming from the wall cloud, and the golden yellow canola crops underneath shook in the intensifying wind.

I pulled onto the shoulder of the road. The gigantic wall cloud was only a half mile northeast of us. I pointed at it for Dave.

"Oh yeah," said Dave, who was as understated as I was hyperbolic. "Look at that. Jeez."

We saw little white vortices dancing on the ground that in a matter of moments turned into a full-fledged, bright white wedge tornado.

But our western position was all wrong. The tornado was moving southeast, and I wanted to be out in front of it. It was moving away from us. The lack of roads forced us to drive at right angles, going south before we could go east. I left the driving to Dave so that I could handle the video camera and call Environment Canada, the government-run organization that oversees the country's weather forecasting, to warn the agency of the dangerous storm. I should've also reminded *myself* how dangerous storms like this could be.

We basically entered a horse race with the tornado, and by the time we got close, the tornado was within several hundred yards of us and moving rapidly in our direction. In the heat of the moment, however, I asked to Dave to pull over. Getting out of the car, I glanced at him. I didn't know his eyes could get so wide.

But I couldn't resist. Through the viewfinder, the tornado was a luminescent white, and I watched it swallow a barn. It was terrible luck; there were very few structures anywhere near its path.

When the tornado was perhaps a hundred yards away, I hopped into the car and shouted for Dave to back up and let the tornado cross in front of us. He started backing up, and then I noticed the power lines above.

Big problem. The poles and wires, which could be loosened or freed by the rotating winds, could come down on the car.

Dave needed to go the other direction instead and outrace the tornado. I yelled at him to drive forward, and he threw the car into first. The Hyundai burned rubber.

I could see debris from the barn flying.

"Go! Go!" I yelled.

The tornado, on our left side only yards away and closing fast, kept pace with the car.

I kept filming, and the car struggled forward.

"You've gotta move!" I yelled.

The tornado slowly fell off the pace.

"We got it," Dave finally said, smiling in relief as he put the car into third gear.

When we were several hundred yards east of the tornado, I told Dave to stop once more. The funnel had grown and darkened. It was now a soot-black, half-mile-wide, massive cone that spun crazily. It was like a different tornado. I wanted to get another look.

I jumped out of the car to film it again. I saw dark dirt, pebbles, and cornstalks get sucked into the storm from all around me as the inflow winds grew insanely strong. I crouched behind the parked car to brace myself and filmed as the storm rapidly expanded.

Within seconds I had a terrible feeling that the storm could engulf us. *Nature,* I thought, *might just prevail today.* I could feel the suction of the storm, and I was alarmed. *Did it finally happen? Did I get too close?*

I ran around the vehicle to get back in. But the inflow winds were so fierce that I couldn't open the door.

"Dave!" I yelled, pulling on the door handle. He looked straight at me, his eyes the size of large coins. "Help!" I screamed.

I did, of course, finally open that door, and we pulled away before the tornado pulled us in the other direction. *Oh my God,* I thought, breathing hard, my forehead full of sweat. I was shaking. But I was also on a huge high.

Knowing that we'd intercepted such an insane tornado made the long return trip to Norman far less painful. Once Dave and I crossed the border back into the United States, I downloaded the video to my Web server, made some calls, and closed some big deals. By far, 2007 was my most successful year as a storm chaser. I intercepted almost forty tornadoes and made what I actually consider a living selling video.

But the year wasn't over yet. When I returned from Manitoba, I uploaded my edited footage to YouTube. The response was similar to what I'd experienced after uploading my footage from my May 4 chase in Ellis County—the tornado that I'd teased and taunted. Riding a wave of television exposure and promotion, the YouTube video of my chase in Canada tallied over a million views in just days.

Who, in 2007, was watching all those videos? Not just weather nuts and adrenaline junkies. One viewer was Dr. Brian Fiedler, a well-regarded tornado scientist at Oklahoma University. After watching the footage of my Ellis County tornado intercept, Dr. Fiedler realized that Ken, Joel, and I had come so close to the tornado that our film captured rare imagery that benefitted his academic work. The video illustrates the existence, shape, and motion of suction vortices, the little-known minitornadoes that generally make contact with the ground and often appear *around* and *inside of* other tornadoes. Nobody understands exactly how, when, or why these smaller vortices appear, but scientists believe that suction vortices could rotate at three to four times the speed of the "parent vortex" and cause even more damage to people and property.

After seeing my video, Dr. Fiedler contacted me and wanted to know if he could include a couple still images from our Ellis County chase in one of his recent studies. I immediately said yes. I was eager to help—our work was being deemed scientifically useful. Some other unexpected folks were watching my videos, too. In January 2008, I received calls from executive producers at the Discovery Channel and a production company called Original Media. They were familiar with my crazy work. They asked if I'd be interested in starring, along with Joel and my old friend Chris Chittick, in a Discovery Channel show called *Storm Chasers*. The show featured behind-the-scenes looks at the thinking and adventures of storm chasers, and followed those chasers as they hunted tornadoes in the name of science, great footage, and excitement. *Storm Chasers,* they explained, was already a hit program.

Did I want to think about it? they asked.

For precisely one second. I quickly accepted their offer.

In the fall of 1998, when I was a freshman at the University of Oklahoma, little did I know that I would someday become a "weather celebrity." Back then, sitting in my introductory meteorology classes, I let the more career-minded students dream about the days when they might tell America about the weather while in front of a camera. My head, meanwhile, was in the clouds. That is, the cumulonimbus clouds that turn into tall and intense, tornado-spawning supercell thunderstorms.

But a decade later, I was the one who had the chance to tell a nation about weather, although my opportunity had nothing to do with delivering the five-day forecast. Instead I would get a chance to explain and experience the beauty and brute force of extreme weather in a program that was somewhere between a soap opera, field research, and the X Games. Of course I'd approach *Storm Chasers* the way I always approached storm chasing: with a thrill-seeker's sense of excitement, a scientist's curiosity (I'd earn my meteorology PhD in 2010), and the enormous passion of a man who can never stop chasing.

EPILOGUE

INTO THE
TORNADO

. . .

*T*he next frontier in my quest to unlock the universe's many severe weather mysteries was to get as close as possible to a tornado. Even closer than that, actually. I had to get inside a tornado.

The custom-built storm-chasing vehicle that I drive today makes that possible.

. . .

The handmade machine that is my current chase vehicle or "tornado tank" will unquestionably carry me deeper into unknown territory and well into the future. She was basically born of one simple question: What's going on in there? To me, some of the biggest question marks in tornado science—and I'll get to them soon—will be answered only when scientists can gather data inside of a tornado. So I figured that my vehicle should be capable of taking me there.

Amazingly, for me, the team that I hired to create this storm-chasing vehicle started their modification work with something better than my old Chevy Lumina. Instead, in January 2009, they began the conversion process with a 2008 Chevrolet Tahoe sport-utility vehicle that I had purchased new a year before. That was a first.

When Chris Chittick and I first met with future Dominator team leader Kevin Barton and his brother-in-law, Ben Christie, over beers in a west Michigan bar, they thought we were nuts. *You want to park this truck in front of a what?*

But Kevin is a very talented mechanic who has built and repaired everything from golf carts to race cars. (I knew of him through my connections at the old Grand Rapids, Michigan, golf club where I'd worked during high school and summers in college.) Ultimately my enthusiasm won him over and inspired him.

Kevin and his twelve-man team worked sixteen-hour days in a garage just south of Grand Rapids to ready the vehicle in less than three months for the spring 2009 chase season. When he pulled his creation into my Norman driveway on April 4, I was amazed. The Tahoe had undergone a metamorphosis. It was the wildest vehicle I'd ever seen. It looked like something between a hovercraft, a fighter jet, and an Air Jordan basketball sneaker.

Kevin and I walked around it, and he showed me all the features. A custom-built hydraulic suspension would, with the flip of a switch located inside the cabin, lower the vehicle over half a foot so that it could hunker down in hurricane-force winds. Rubber skirting around the entire body prevented those winds from blowing underneath the car and potentially lifting it skyward. A roll cage made out of 1.5-inch steel tubing went around the outside of the vehicle and attached to it at fourteen different points. Kevin then welded a second steel skin to this cage and installed manually operated Lexan (the same material used in bulletproof glass) windows into the outer skin. He also installed a plastic bubble on the roof to make room for a periscope-style HD video camera. Ultimately we painted the whole thing burgundy.

The official name for this beast is the TVN (tornadovideos.net) Storm Research Vehicle. But we like to call our tornado tank the Dominator.

The Dominator features state-of-the-art data-collecting instruments. Atop the vehicle, an anemometer measures horizontal wind speed and wind direction. Meanwhile a briefcase-sized, custom-built, roof-mounted radar device measures vertical wind speed, or how fast the wind is moving upward in the tornado. The Dominator has allowed me to get closer to tornadoes than I ever have before, and helps me gather more data while doing so.

A lot of the Dominator's futuristic weather-watching accessories came courtesy of Radiance Technologies Incorporated (RTI), which is a Mississippi-based technology company with many ties to the defense industry (my storm-chasing team now works with many of the same engineers at the Tupelo, Mississippi–headquartered Hyperion Technology Group). Folks at RTI had long been fans of *Storm Chasers*, and the company got in touch with me in 2008 to say that they had developed some intriguing technologies that might be adapted to benefit tornado science.

Soon afterward, I visited RTI's Oxford, Mississippi, offices and laboratories. Company engineers showed me a compact radar technology that soldiers used to track the trajectories of fired bullets. The RTI engineers believed that they could manipulate this same technology into a small, bombproof package that I could use to measure horizontal and vertical wind speeds when I was near or inside of a tornado.

Why pour so much thinking and energy into all of this instrumentation? Ground-speed measurements represent something of a holy grail for tornado scientists. Current, conventional radar technologies can only measure tornado speeds that are achieved hundreds or thousands of feet in the air, and it's understood that those aren't the same speeds being achieved at the earth's surface. Meanwhile, tornado "probes," which are overbuilt, stationary cases weighing hundreds of pounds and stuffed with sensors and other equipment, haven't been able to provide definitive answers either. The problem with probes is that scientists must place them on the ground in advance of an oncoming tornado and then hope that the tornado travels right over the device. But hitting the true

bull's-eye—placing a probe directly in the path of a tornado's core flow—has proven difficult if not impossible.

I'm convinced that we need to try harder to measure these speeds—because I think we're underestimating tornadoes. I'm not alone, either. Many scientists believe that the strongest wind speeds inside a tornado are achieved right at the ground, which is significant because those are the winds that directly impact all of us. The vortices that National Weather Service meteorologists and tornado scientists see today and measure courtesy of their radar instrumentation might represent only wolves in sheep's clothing. Inside of what could appear to be a relatively modest tornado can lurk these smaller, dramatically violent minitornadoes that can potentially tear apart buildings, or launch large objects into the air as projectiles, which can then be pulled higher into the sky via intense updrafts. Maybe these are the tornadoes that we always need to prepare for. Maybe these intense minitornadoes should be considered the norm. But so far, we have no idea where they'll pop up inside the larger rotations.

For better or worse, I believe that one of the best ways to learn more about tornado science is to consistently place sophisticated measuring equipment within the tornadoes themselves. And the only way to do that might be via scientists and storm chasers who are obsessed and well equipped enough—using machinery like the Dominator—to put themselves inside of the storm. That would be, to put *myself* inside of the storm.

I am sane enough, however, to explore tornado-intercepting technologies that could do similar data gathering for me. Which leads me back to RTI. During the 2009 storm season, we embraced more than the company's radar technology. RTI also helped us develop a remote-control airplane and its payload. This is no toy. The $30,000, hand-built wood plane with a twelve-foot wingspan (designed by model plane builder Bruce Tharpe of Oregon) can fly at fifty miles per hour for an hour and features two HD video cameras capable of streaming live video, as well as the ability to carry and deploy ten high-tech, parachute-equipped, weather-sensing tornado probes.

The lightweight, foam-encased probes incorporate GPS technology and were designed to record wind speed, temperature, barometric pressure, dew point, and high-definition video. In 2009, the goal for ground pilot Chad Williams was to fly the plane close enough to the tornado so that released probes could parachute, one at a time, into the storm's inflow (the air that the tornado sucks in) and ideally its updraft. Never before had anyone attempted to directly measure such weather variables aloft and inside of a tornado.

On June 15, 2009, Chad, my friend Don Giuliano, and several other members of my plane team launched into action after parking several miles away from a tornado that dropped down near Maxwell, Kansas (meanwhile I was in the Dominator capturing some impressive vertical wind speed data as the same tornado crossed directly in front of us).

Chad flew the plane at an altitude of four hundred feet and managed to land several probes in the tornado's updraft. One of the probes accomplished a lot of what we'd wanted. It was sucked in by the tornado and swept into the updraft, where it was lifted to an altitude of approximately four thousand feet. Its temperature and moisture sensors indicated, even as the probe came out of the rotating winds and down the tornado's trailing side, a consistent presence of warm, moist air. The prevailing wisdom is that the probe should've encountered cooler, dry air in this downdraft behind the tornado, leading me to wonder whether or not we really know everything about the air circulating around a tornado. Certainly one probe doesn't provide reliable answers. But its captured data motivates me to ask questions.

The plane returned intact from that mission, which was an achievement in itself. With the tornado threatening to suck my expensive aircraft into its rotation, Chad was forced to fly the craft several miles away from the storm, which he did from a passenger seat in the team's trans-port truck as the vehicle followed underneath the plane's flight path. That day in Kansas was an intense baptism for both pilot and aircraft.

I have to say that the challenges for me and the rest of my team will only become greater. I want to learn much, much more about tornadoes, and I'm prepared to push myself, my equipment, and fellow chasers farther in the name of tornado science. It has already happened: The Dominator wasn't a year old when it returned to Kevin Barton's garage for reshaping, more horsepower, and a tough, hard, synthetic-elastomer skin that will protect the vehicle from two-by-fours and other debris that tornadoes turn into 150-mile-per-hour projectiles. My engineering corps has also designed cannons that mount to the Dominator and can fire probes straight into the vortex. There's talk of making the Dominator aquatic, too. Yes, a day might come when I can travel on land and sea, intercepting not only tornadoes, but also water spouts and hurricanes over water. Stay tuned.

Custom-made vehicles? Elastomer? Steel second skin? *Inside* a tor-nado?

About all of which I say: What did you expect?

· · ·

Even if I'm on foot, why should I only pursue rotating storms in Tornado Alley? Or go only as far afield as the Canadian provinces? From Australia to India and beyond, tornadoes touch down all over the world. Why not travel the planet in search of such storms? To educate other storm chas-ers, scientists, and emergency service providers? To be a tornado ambas-sador to the world? That's what I'm determined to do whenever possible.

I've already made good on my pledge. After years spent watching tornadoes form in South America's own version of Tornado Alley on radar and television, I rang in the new year of 2010 in the southern hemisphere, where I storm-chased in Argentina. Joined by a media production team (our Argentinian adventure may be featured on television) and an international group of chasers, I spent much of my two-week trip west of Buenos Aires, in an area called the Pampas.

Pampas literally means "plains," and the fertile, low-lying terrain is indeed similar to the Great Plains. The heart of the Pampas, in central Argentina, is flat, sparsely populated farm country that hosts plenty of severe weather. Every year, dozens of tornadoes are reported in the Pampas (many more likely go unreported), and the storms generally strike when North America's skies are tornado-free. For me, that timing couldn't be better.

When I stepped off the plane in South America on December 27, 2009, I knew that I'd gain valuable experience for subsequent overseas deployments. What kind of world was I entering?

The first thing I noticed was something familiar: moist air.

"This is incredible," I said to Chris Chittick as we walked out of Ministro Pistarini International Airport and into a sunny Buenos Aires morning. "It's warm and moist out. Like a spring day in Norman."

Then I inhaled through my nose. "Smells like Tornado Alley, too," I added.

Chris put on his sunglasses. We'd already been up the better part of a day, a lot of it cooped up in airplanes. We were feeling the effects.

Unfortunately, we needed several hours to rent three cars at the airport and to secure the maximum insurance coverage for each of them. Immediately I put "learn to speak the local tongue" on my to-do list for international storm chasing. However, the language barrier did save us from having to give the car-rental agent many specifics of our "sightseeing" trip.

Our group was a twenty- and thirtysomething motley crew that included me and Chris Chittick, cameramen-producers Chris Whiteneck and Robert Seaman, friends and fellow storm chasers Scott Currens and J. R. Hehnly, and safety coordinator and logistics chief Dustin "Bobo"

Feldman. We'd pick up two Argentinian meteorologists later in the journey.

The second thing I became rapidly aware of while abroad was the tremendous impatience of Argentinian drivers. I hadn't driven a stick shift in years, but our rental cars were available only with manual transmissions. My poor clutch skills—next time I'll work on them before leaving—were apparent every time I pulled into one of the numerous tollbooths around Buenos Aires.

"They're honking at you, Reed," Chris Chittick said with an amused smile when I stalled the engine after paying a toll. The line of cars and angry drivers behind me quickly grew. Everyone in back of me laid on their horns. I fumbled with the stick, restarted the motor, and accidentally burned rubber to get our compact, red Ford wagon moving again.

Neither the stick shift nor sleep deprivation was about to slow me down. I'd been studying the South American forecast models for days before our departure, and the date of our arrival looked promising in terms of tornado activity in the western Pampas. A big trough (low-pressure area) was headed there from the Andes Mountains, which meant that wind would be drawn to the region. Meanwhile, Argentina's own low-level jet stream—which, like its Great Plains counterpart, transports warm, moist air—was intensifying as it moved east, out of Chile and into the Argentinian lowlands. Put that all together, and I was hopeful that we'd watch the creation of some rotating thunderstorms.

Not that this particular weather setup was an exception. Like Tornado Alley, the Pampas region serves as a natural intersection for contrasting conditions that together generate thunderstorms. Hot and moist air arrives from the Amazon Basin in the north. The Antarctic Ocean provides cold air from the south. To the west, weather out of the snow-covered Andes helps to provide wind shear and keep cold air aloft. When these conditions ebb and flow just so, the Pampas sort of becomes a Tornado Alley South.

During the 450-mile journey west from Buenos Aires to our target location north of the town of Santa Rosa, however, we were reminded that the Pampas aren't exactly like Tornado Alley. When we stopped along the way, I lost Scott Currens and the compact, silver Chevrolet he was driving (we traveled as a multicar caravan). I went the wrong way down a one-way street. A bunch of Argentine drivers angrily flashed their headlights at me.

Finally I pulled into a gas station and pointed at a pump.

"*Gasolina*," I said, and waited for the attendant to grab the handle.

The attendant shook his head and didn't move an inch. "*Nada, nada*," he said.

Nada? *Doesn't that mean "nothing"?*

"*Gasolina*," I repeated, and this time the attendant spoke to me in Spanish for about fifteen seconds and then shook his head.

"Are you sure that's the right word?" Chris Whiteneck asked me when he emerged from the station's convenience store. He had a fresh cup of good-smelling coffee and a ham sandwich that looked tasty. I'd come to learn the word *jamón* quickly and ate plenty of it during my time there.

"Well, what is the right word?" I asked Chris. He shrugged and walked off to eat his sandwich. Did anyone in rural Argentina speak English?

I looked up into the blue sky. It was early evening, and I could see storms blowing up over a hundred miles to our west. The view was amazingly clear. There was none of Tornado Alley's occasional pollution, or the haze that comes from the dust that blows northward off the Mexican plateau to the United States.

Thirty minutes later our caravan was again complete, and our gas tanks were full (I'd spent twenty minutes pointing at the pump that delivered the wrong fuel—diesel). I drove west like a madman, revved up on the strong coffee and the undying hope of intercepting a tornado on my very first day in South America. But even when my car hit speeds of 160 kilometers per hour—which is about 100 miles per hour—down the flat, eucalyptus-lined highways, I was still passed by the locals. I'd finally found a country where I wouldn't be considered a fast driver.

We reached a thunderstorm at dusk, and because we were in the southern hemisphere, the storm's orientation was exactly the opposite of a Tornado Alley storm. The base was to the south instead of the north, and the inflow came from the south, too. If the thunderstorm were to produce a tornado, it would rotate clockwise. The storm was beautiful—tall, and steel-blue and black, with a well-defined anvil. It obviously had plenty of rising energy.

But the storm was moving north, away from our east-west road. The only north-south route that J. R. Hehnly could find via his satellite Internet connection was a dirt road.

"It's coming up on the right," J.R. announced from the Ford via walkie-talkie. "Maybe a quarter mile."

I didn't want to give up the chase, but I was a little reluctant to make the turn. Optimist that I am, I visualized something going wrong on the dirt road, like one of the cars rolling, or sliding into a ditch the way I had in Kansas in 2004. If we had an accident in the middle of rural Argentina, who would we call? Who would understand me? I could barely buy a tank of gas.

Predictably, the desire to chase prevailed. We followed the rough road and storm for miles, until dirt and mud covered the cars. Just when we thought we could go no farther because of exhaustion and high grass in the deteriorating road, it was the storm that gave out. What had been an incredible cell only minutes earlier was now a withering and harmless cumulonimbus cloud. I didn't know exactly what had gone wrong.

We finally reached a paved road in the day's dying light. Chris Chittick looked over his left shoulder and spotted something between us and the setting sun.

"Look at that," he said, tapping my right arm as he stared out the back of the Ford. "Crazy."

Southwest of us was yet another exploding storm cell. It was 8:30 P.M. We were all going on fumes.

"It's probably a hundred miles away," I said over the walkie-talkie.

"Is anyone falling asleep at the wheel?" asked Bobo. "Still safe to chase?"

We soldiered on, driving south on Argentina's National Route 35 toward the town of Santa Rosa. By the time the storm was due west of our position, the sky was pitch-black. But the cell's intense flashes of lightning delivered good news. We pulled over on the shoulder of the road so that I could relate the details to the camera.

"We've got a potential wedge tornado here just northwest of Santa Rosa," I said, pointing toward the horizon with my left hand and looking into the lens. The flashes of light showed a distinct wedge tornado. "It's very low to the ground," I added.

Subsequent lightning showed that there were likely two tornadoes, both spinning from a cyclic supercell.

We watched the storms for a while and then resumed our drive south into Santa Rosa. But before we arrived at the town, there was further proof of the intense weather. Trees with foot-thick trunks were down and on the road, which was also crowded with emergency-service vehicles. I believe that the vegetation must have been brought down earlier by straight-line, ninety-mile-per-hour winds at the leading edge of a storm. And at the far end of that same storm, I think, were the tornadoes that we'd spotted through the lightning.

We celebrated in Santa Rosa with *empanadas*—small, meat-filled pastries—and *cervezas*. Somehow we all mustered the strength to lift our glasses for a toast. After keeping our eyes open for about forty-eight hours, flying 5,500 miles, and driving another 500 in a foreign country, we could lay claim to having intercepted tornadoes in Argentina. One of the few locals who spoke English told me that each of us was a *cazador de tornado,* which literally means "tornado hunter" in Spanish. It was the rare foreign phrase that I wouldn't forget.

• • •

My sensibilities were the same in Argentina as they would be if I were storm chasing in Australia for cyclones, the Philippines for typhoons, or Tornado Alley: I wanted to get close to the storm. Any *cazador de tornado* who professes to love severe weather yearns to see something more on an exotic storm-chasing trip than a distant lightning-lit wedge. I wanted to feel a South American storm's power. I wanted to watch debris—hopefully vegetation—fly in the "wrong" direction.

The Argentinian storms proved as elusive to me as the country's language. Our caravan drove north toward the colonial city of Córdoba on day two of our trip, and the northeastern city of San Francisco on day three. No tornado intercepts, and we saw nothing on day four, either.

We spent New Year's Eve in the eastern Argentina beach town of Mar del Plata, and if we couldn't find an Argentine tornado, one almost found us. On January 1, when we thought we'd be relaxing on the sand and swimming in the Atlantic, the makings of a supercell appeared right over us.

"See underneath? It's rotating," said Scott Currens, pointing to where it looked as if a wall cloud nearly grazed the water. The two of us stood on the sand, fully clothed with camera equipment in hand, while half the town was crowded onto the beach and enjoying the holiday. "It's rotating pretty strong," he said.

We could see the flat, gray supercell feeding on inflow as the storm sucked in air from the north. I didn't know what would happen next. A tornado? A waterspout (tornado over water) right next to the beach? The partying citizens of Mar del Plata seemed unconcerned, at least until the rain and hail began to fall. Then they ran for cover. In the end, the storm soaked Scott and me, and did little more.

Before we deployed west again to scour every inch of the Pampas, we added two more members to our chase team. Ramiro Saurral and Matías Bertolotti are both around thirty years old, and they're meteorology PhD students at the University of Buenos Aires. In the fall of 2009, when I announced my upcoming chase trip to South America on tornadovideos. net, Ramiro contacted me in his perfect English.

Would I be interested, he wrote in an e-mail, in meeting during our trip? The simple invitation became so much more. Ramiro and Matías were two of the nicest guys I'd ever met. They introduced me to teachers at the university, and meteorologists and officials at the Servicio Meteorológico Nacional, which is Argentina's national weather service. I thought that those were great connections to have should I ever want to perform future field research in Argentina. Ramiro and Matías, meanwhile, joined us for the last several days of South American storm chasing. They were our translators, friends, and valuable storm-chasing advisers. Buying gas got a lot easier with them around.

"Maybe you should be more patient with the storms here, Reed," Ramiro told me one day. We were surging toward the Pampas' eastern Mendoza province, and he was sitting in the Ford's backseat, leaning forward to talk. "The storms here perhaps behave differently than they do in Tornado Alley," he added.

Ramiro was right. The Argentinian storms didn't seem to pack as much energy and immediacy as the storms that I frequently encountered in Tornado Alley. One reason, he explained, could be because the low-level atmospheric cap that would cause Great Plains supercells to build energy until they became explosive wasn't as strong in South America. The Argentinian wind shear, he said, was also more inconsistent. Ramiro and Matías both suggested that we start our chasing earlier in the day and that we stick with potential tornado-producing storms longer than we might in the United States. They said these storms could take a while to develop.

Nonetheless, one day we were too late to get under the two-inch hail that fell near the town of Santa Isabel (I *wanted* to lose a windshield that day). We guessed wrong on another storm, and a beautiful supercell collapsed in front of our eyes east of San Rafael. The forecasting models for the Pampas weren't helping much, either. I'm spoiled by the reams of forecasting data that are available in the United States, which provides relatively pinpoint weather information to meteorologists and storm chasers like me. Argentina, like most places in the world, doesn't have the resources to field observer data from an endless list of weather stations, airports, weather balloons, and even airplanes.

The last chasing day in Argentina was no time to feel sorry for myself. Instead, we got up earlier than usual to chase. I paid less attention to the radar and instead kept my eyes on the sky. When I finally spotted a supercell north of our position near Santa Rosa, we committed to following that storm. I reminded myself that I'd spent years chasing storms without broadband mobile Internet access, constant radar updates, or an instrument-filled Dominator. Maybe one of the lessons I was in South America to learn, I thought, was that I should remember my good meteorological instincts. If I was going to storm-chase around the globe, I'd better be prepared to hunt tornadoes with little more than my knowledge to help me. The equipment might range from the most amazing tornado tank ever built to an old motorcycle, a map, and a compass. I needed to rely on what I always had with me—my knowledge. My fearlessness. My gut.

We finally pulled onto the shoulder of the road just west of the town of San Luis. I parked under one of the most beautiful supercell thunderstorms that I've ever seen. Tall, black clouds had a crisp and stunning white border. The wall cloud was an ice blue. The inflow tail was miles long and looked like the wing of a jet. The air was thick with moisture coming off the electric-green Pampas grassland.

Now this was a language I understood.

I looked up and marveled at the beautiful wall cloud as it rotated clockwise. Then I took a deep breath and waited for the tornado to come down.

ACKNOWLEDGMENTS

I first want to thank my family.

Without my mom, Susan Tolbert, there is *no way* I would be a storm chaser today, let alone a meteorologist making a living, doing what I love, every tornado and hurricane season. As a science teacher with a master's degree in geology, my mom introduced me to science before I knew how to read. While most parents would discourage their children from pursuing a career with little earning potential, my mom has always been supportive and taught me that doing what you love is the only thing that should matter. I'll forever be thankful for a mom who not only always has been there for me, but also encouraged me to follow my passion in everything I do.

I'd also like to thank my sisters, Cortney and Dayna, who have been incredible friends. Dayna was like a younger brother while growing up, catching insects and snakes with me when most neighbor kids were deathly afraid of the things we would pull out of the woods in our backyard. My older sister, Cortney, played a huge role in my interest in weather. Few are passionate enough about weather to record all The Weather Channel's local forecast songs on tape—and that was my sister. I'm actually very surprised she didn't end up as a storm chaser, too!

Though my relationship with my dad was limited after my parents' divorce, I would like to thank him for being hugely supportive in the last several years. I am so proud that he went on a storm chase with me in 2004 when he had no idea what to expect, and very grateful that he helped make the Dominator a reality when most people thought the idea was insane.

I am very grateful to everyone at the University of Oklahoma.

I want to thank my master's and thesis adviser, Dr. Peter Lamb, who taught me not only the process of scientific research but attention to detail and general professionalism. Dr. Lamb also put up with my constant storm chasing over the years when he could have easily found another research assistant with more "grounded" and less demanding interests. Without Dr. Lamb's patience and guidance in both my professional and personal life, there is no way I would even be close to where I am today as a scientist and a storm chaser. I'll be forever indebted to Dr. Lamb and always will have the utmost respect for him as not only one of the most accomplished climatologists of our time, but also as a person. One of these days I'll finally convince him to come along on a chase in the Dominator!

There is no way I would have completed all of my school and research obligations at the University of Oklahoma while storm chasing without Dr. Lamb's secretary and assistant, Luwanda Byrd. When it came time to turn in assignments, I'd often be storm chasing 1,000 miles away from campus and Luwanda would always cover for me.

I also want to thank some of my amazing professors at the University of Oklahoma School of Meteorology—Doctors Lance Leslie, Howie Bluestein, Michael Richman, Brian Fiedler, and Jeff Basara. All of these professors shared their passion for the science of meteorology and conveyed their immense knowledge to their students, myself included. Despite their groundbreaking accomplishments in the field and ongoing important research projects, they always put forth the maximum amount of effort and care in teaching their classes and grooming the next generation of meteorologists for the real word.

I also need to thank Dr. Andrew Mercer, who is one of my best friends, and probably the most skilled meteorologist I've ever known. Andrew and I always sat next to each other during undergraduate and especially demanding graduate classes at OU, and we often worked together on research projects, problem sets, and exam preparation. Andrew helped me catch up after missed classes when I was off chasing tornadoes. He was much better than I was at juggling storm chasing and graduate school, so it's not a surprise that he's already finished his PhD and is teaching at Mississippi State University, while I'm still grinding away at mine!

John Esterheld, James Rogers, and Don Giuliano were my officemates during graduate school. Now Don and John are both working with me on TornadoVideos.net, running the business. Without these guys as friends and officemates, graduate school would not have been nearly as enjoyable.

I, of course, want to thank everyone else at TornadoVideos.net:

Joel Taylor has been my storm-chasing partner for the last decade. Joel is the only friend—and probably the only human being—who would still ride in the same vehicle with me after some of our most dangerous and daring storm chases. He has put up with my constant excitement and intensity, which I'm sure can get pretty damn annoying after a while, especially when we are basically living in our vehicle every tornado and hurricane season. Joel was always supportive of TornadoVideos.net and my effort to make a living as a storm chaser when everyone else close to me said it was impossible and a waste of time. As you've read here, we've had our ups and downs over the years, but I can't put into words how loyal and supportive Joel has been. He's irreplaceable as a best friend and storm-chasing partner. I wouldn't trust anyone else behind the wheel of the Dominator besides Joel "Stretch" Taylor.

Chris Chittick and I have been close friends since our high school summers working at Watermark Golf Club. Chris was always there for me, even if that meant risking our jobs to drive thirty-six hours straight from Michigan to Saskatchewan in a car without air-conditioning to chase marginal tornado setups. In 2000, Chris dropped everything in Michigan, including a well-paying job and a girlfriend, to move to Norman, Oklahoma, and become my partner in a very risky, and likely unprofitable, business venture—storm chasing.

I'd also like to thank Heidi Farrar and Dave Demko, my business partners who keep TornadoVideos.net afloat. They are the hardest workers on the planet, and are also incredibly supportive friends. Both work day and night to keep our business and research moving forward, and there is no way I could do all this without them.

Dick McGowan is one of the best still photographers of tornadoes and anything related to nature I've ever known. Dick provided several of the amazing storm-chasing photos you've seen in this book, and participated in Discovery Channel's Storm Chasers this past season as the trusted driver of our follow-vehicle, the sole purpose of which is to capture the shot of the Dominator driving into the tornado.

Without Dave Holder I would not have seen my first Canadian tornado. Dave was the only friend insane enough to drive from Oklahoma to Saskatchewan and Manitoba for this chase, sacrificing his Hyundai Accent to make the trip happen. Dave is now a trusted guide for our storm-chasing tour company, Extreme Tornado Tours.

I want to thank everyone at Discovery, especially Bill Howard, George Neighbors, Josh Weinberg, Kirk Denkler, and Michael Haas.

Last, this book would not exist without the support of a few key people.

My literary agent, Lisa Grubka, and her coworkers at Foundry Literary + Media made this book possible. Lisa supported the storm-chasing concept from the beginning, and has gone well beyond what is expected of her as an agent to make *Into the Storm* the best book possible. I'd also like to thank Tia Maggini, who introduced me to Lisa, the best literary agent in the world.

I would also like to thank my editor, Carrie Thornton. When we first met with interested publishers about *Into the Storm*, Carrie stood out from the others by far, and we knew right away that she was the editor we wanted for the book. Her passion for producing the best product possible and her enthusiasm for the topic of storm chasing was very apparent during our first meeting, and even more so while working with her on this project. She would personally address any concerns or suggestions I had during the entire process, no matter how ridiculous they may have been, and her top priority has always been my satisfaction with the final product. Thank you, Carrie!

At Dutton, I would also like to thank Lily Kosner, Ava Kavyani, Liza Cassity, Christine Ball, Carrie Swetonic, and Brian Tart. Lily for working through my intense e-mails that typically go way overboard, and Ava, Liza, Christine, and Carrie for working so hard on the publicizing and marketing of *Into the Storm*. And to Brian Tart, Dutton's publisher, for believing in this project.

And *very* important, I'd like to thank my cowriter and now very good friend, Andrew Tilin. Andrew put his life on hold during the last several months, spending hours upon hours in person and on the phone talking with me, as well as even suffering through a few intense weeks on the road while storm chasing in Argentina, to best understand my life as an obsessive extreme storm chaser. When I first read the chapter drafts Andrew was producing, it seemed like I was reliving all the important moments of my storm-chasing career and life in general, both good and bad, with the story being told just how I would have if I had his writing skills. I can say with 100 percent confidence that there is no other writer in existence that could have done a better job, nor could have worked nearly as hard as Andrew Tilin, and I am proud for having had the opportunity to work with him on *Into the Storm,* as well as to gain a great friend.

I'd also like to thank Kevin Barton, Ben Christie, and Terry Rosema for devoting much of their lives over the last few years, designing and building the Dominator and making our storm chasing and research goals possible, as well as Kevin's brother Rob Barton and his wife, Cindy, and all the other friends and family of Kevin who worked so hard on the Dominator in Freeport, Michigan. Also, thanks to the engineers of Hyperion Technology Group for all of their hard work and dedication in building our research equipment like the vertical radar, plane, and cannon system.

Finally, I'd like to thank my girlfriend, Ginger Zee, and all of my friends not specifically mentioned here for their support and understanding during the very demanding book writing process.

GLOSSARY OF METEOROLOGICAL TERMS

Anvil cloud: A wide, high-altitude (up to 60,000 feet), horizontal cloud that frequently develops atop a severe-weather thunderstorm and is blown downstream by fast upper-level winds. An anvil cloud is largely composed of ice crystals and forms as the fast-rising, moist air of a thunderstorm updraft slams into stable "lid" of the lower atmosphere, causing the anvil cloud to spread out horizontally like spilled oil on cement.

Atmosphere layers: The atmosphere consists of several layers—from the ground up: troposphere, stratosphere, mesosphere, and, finally, the thermosphere. Most of the earth's weather occurs inside of the troposphere, which is also called the "lower atmosphere," and is where nearly all of the atmosphere's moisture resides. At the north and south poles, the troposphere extends approximately miles from the earth's surface into the atmosphere. At the equator, the troposphere is approximately miles thick.

Atmospheric pressure: The force placed on any point of the earth's surface by the weight of the air above it (measured in millibars). Air pressure as indicated by a barometer (a mercury-filled device that registers higher readings when air pressure increases). Atmospheric pressure at sea level is

1,013.25 mb (pressure at the earth's surface ranges from approximately 1,000 to 1,040 mb); the centers of hurricanes and tornadoes feature much lower pressures, which is why those storms' winds are drawn inward.

Bear's cage: Storm-chaser slang for the dangerous area located right in the path of the tornado, usually just to its north and northeast and south of the heavy rain-producing part of the supercell. Many chasers are fearful of entering the bear's cage: The potential exists to encounter vehicle-destroying, softball-size hail, or the tornado itself.

Beaver's tail: A wide and flat band of moist, cloudy inflow air that resembles the tail of a beaver. In general, inflow (or "feeder") bands like a beaver's tail move east to west, or north to south, into the updraft of a severe thunderstorm.

Bernoulli Effect: Named after the eighteenth-century Dutch-Swiss mathematician Daniel Bernoulli, the law explains why "fluid" (including air), when flowing horizontally over a given object's top surface faster than it flows in the surrounding air, creates a pressure difference; lower pressure on the top surface than the surroundings. This pressure difference generates a lifting force—the force that's required, for example, to help aircraft wings lift airplanes off the ground. It's also the same lifting force that helps tornadoes to lift roofs off of buildings.

Cap: A layer of warm air approximately 5,000 feet off the ground. The cap acts as a "lid" on the lower atmosphere, which can either prevent storms from developing altogether or just long enough through the day to allow the sun's heating to build instability and generate even stronger storms in the afternoon/evening.

CAPE: Convective Available Potential Energy (CAPE) measures the buoyancy of a parcel of air. Quantified in joules per kilogram, CAPE measurements help chasers know the existing potential for warm air to rise—and thus the potential for thunderstorms to develop—in the atmosphere.

CAPE values of 1,500 J/kg generally catch a chaser's attention. That said, CAPE values ranging from the hundreds to even 10,000 J/kg can contribute to the creation of severe weather. Generally, the higher the CAPE, the more potentially explosive is the atmosphere for severe weather.

Clear slot: The clear slot is a recognizable seam in the thunderstorm of drier air, as frequently evidenced by a patch of brightened sky. The clear slot is also evidence that a tornado is developing.

Condensation: Condensation occurs when moist air rises and cools to a critical temperature called the dew point (defined below), resulting in the tiny liquid water droplets suspended in the air that comprise a cloud. Storm chasers depend on the presence of condensation, or the conversion of a vapor to a liquid, because without it there would be no supercells or hurricanes to chase!

Convection: In meteorology, convection refers to the movement within air by the tendency of hotter (and thus less dense) air to rise, and colder/denser air to sink. Increased convection in the atmosphere means that the air is "unstable," or that it's moving upward and downward. Weather that occurs because of convection—like thunderstorms—is called convective weather. Convective severe weather includes thunderstorms that produce brutal straight-line (nonrotating) winds, large hail, and even tornadoes.

Coriolis force: Named after the nineteenth-century French scientist Gustave-Gaspard Coriolis, the Coriolis force is the curving of winds as the earth rotates underneath them. In the northern hemisphere, the Coriolis force causes the winds to bend right (in the southern hemisphere they bend left; winds directly over the equator don't bend at all). These bending winds contribute to the creation and longevity of midlatitude and tropical cyclones, like hurricanes, and the troughs of low pressure that trigger tornado outbreaks and winter storms.

Cumulonimbus cloud: Cumulonimbus clouds are towering—as high as 75,000 feet—storm clouds that can be precursors to supercell (rotating)

thunderstorms. Cumulonimbus clouds form when hot and moist air rises and condenses in an unstable atmosphere.

Cyclic supercell: A supercell thunderstorm that's capable of producing multiple tornadoes. Within cyclic supercells, the mesocyclone produces multiple, tight circulations that are each potential precursors to full-fledged tornadoes. Cyclic supercells can also have multiple simultaneous tornadoes on the ground at the same time at different life cycles (wedge, stovepipe, and rope, for example).

Damage path: A visually apparent path on the ground created by a tornado. Damage paths include gouged ground cover, broken and denuded vegetation, and the destruction of man-made property.

Debris: Airborne objects caught up in the wind of a severe-weather storm. Debris represents one of the biggest dangers in a tornado or hurricane; stones, branches, and chunks and bits of destroyed structures and cars turn into projectiles that move at the speed of the storm.

Dew point: A measure of moisture content, technically defined as the atmospheric temperature below which water vapor begins to condense. Higher dew points—in the sixties or seventies—are often associated with warmer temperatures and higher atmospheric instability or CAPE, and thus stronger storms, assuming they can break the cap and take full advantage of the heat and moisture.

Doppler radar: A type of radar frequently employed by the National Weather Service and other meteorologists to identify and analyze severe storms and many other types of weather. A Doppler radar dish sends out a beam of energy in the form of a radio wave, then measures the amount of the beam that is reflected back to the antenna—and the time required for that beam to return. Weather that creates "high reflectivity"—that causes a lot of the beam to return to the dish—includes the heavy rain and hail associated with tornado-producing severe thunderstorms.

Downdraft: A downward current of air. Frequently, downdrafts consist of colder (denser, heavier) air, cooled by falling rain and hail.

Dryline: A typically north-south running boundary that separates warm, moist air from hot, dry air, commonly found in the Great Plains. In general, a dryline is the convergence of hot and dry air blowing from the west or southwest with warm, moist air blowing from the south or southeast. Drylines can often generate severe weather.

Eye of a hurricane: The strangely calm region at the center of a hurricane. Eyes range from two to more than 120 miles in diameter, and are areas of tremendous low pressure (all the wind circling the eye is drawn toward this low pressure). Perfectly round and clear hurricane eyes characterize the strongest storms. While inside the eye of such a hurricane, blue sky would be visible above, with a solid-looking, laminar wall of cumulonimbus clouds rotating around.

Eye wall: The wall of intense thunderstorms encircling the eye, or the center, of a tropical cyclone such as a hurricane, typhoon, or tropical storm. The eye wall is the most intense part of a tropical cyclone because it's the convergence point for all of the winds blowing into the center of the storm. These winds fuel the thunderstorms packed into the eye wall, which, in turn, generate more rain, heat, and wind.

Front: A front is a boundary between two different air masses. A cold front is the boundary between cool and warm air when cool air is displacing warm air. A warm front is the boundary between cool and warm air when warm air is displacing cool air. A stationary front is the boundary between warm and cold air where neither air mass prevails.

Fujita Tornado Damage Scale: A widely used scale for rating the severity of tornadoes, developed by meteorologist Tetsuya "Ted" Fujita. The Fujita Scale, or F-scale, is a six-category damage scale that estimates the wind speeds of tornadoes based on the damage they generate. An F0-rated

tornado has estimated wind speeds under 73 miles per hour. F1: 73 to 112 miles per hour; F2: 113 to 157 miles per hour; F3: 158 to 206 miles per hour; F4: 207 to 260 miles per hour; F5: 261 to 318 miles per hour. In 2007, the F-scale was supplanted by a slightly modified damage scale called the Enhanced Fujita Scale, or EF-scale.

Funnel cloud: Funnel clouds are rotating columns of air that can be the immediate precursors to tornadoes when they touch the ground.

Ground probe: A scientific probe—specifically a tornado-data-gathering instrument—that consists of sensors and other recording equipment placed inside a strongly built case. In order to take any meaningful readings, ground probes must be manually placed in the anticipated path of a tornado.

Gustnado: A short-lived vortex in a severe thunderstorm that is generally formed by powerful downdrafts. Gustnadoes are often mistaken for tornadoes—storm chasers often joke that law enforcement officers frequently misidentify these rotational winds, and therefore dub the circular winds "sheriffnadoes." Gustnadoes generally last seconds or minutes, are relatively weak compared to tornadoes, and don't connect to the base of a thunderstorm like tornadoes do.

Helicity: A measure of the "wind shear" in the atmosphere that storm chasers use to decide the likelihood of air to move in a corkscrewing motion (which could lead to the formation of tornadoes). Helicity is derived from the amount of wind shear, or changing wind speed and direction with height through a layer in the atmosphere. Storm chasers believe that helicity values of two hundred or higher in the lowest mile of the atmosphere increase the likelihood of strong tornadoes occurring.

Hodograph: A diagram of lines connecting wind speed and direction values at all heights in a selected cross-section of the atmosphere. Storm chasers use the shapes of hodographs to help them forecast wind shear, which

needs to be present in order for tornadoes to occur. When the lines of wind values comprising a hodograph form a large curve, wind speed and direction changes substantially with height at that location, which means greater helicity encouraging any supercells in that environment to rotate faster.

Hook echo: An indicator of a mesocyclone, and even a tornado or the threat of a tornado, as viewed on radar. The hook echo looks like a hook-shaped appendage on the southwest corner of a supercell thunderstorm. The shape comes from radar picking up the counterclockwise motion of flying debris or precipitation (rain or hail) spinning around the mesocyclone, or rotating updraft, of a supercell.

Hook precipitation: "Hook precip" is the rain and hail that wraps around the backside of a mesocyclone by the storm's rear-flank downdraft. When intercepting a tornado from the west, a storm chaser often has to "punch through" the hook precip to gain visual of the funnel, which of course is very dangerous!

Hurricane: With wind speeds of 74 miles per hour or more, hurricanes are strong tropical cyclones that go by different names in different parts of the world. They're called "typhoons" in the western North Pacific; "tropical cyclones" in the Indian Ocean and western South Pacific; and "hurricanes" in the North Atlantic Ocean, the Caribbean Sea, the Gulf of Mexico, and the North Pacific where it borders the United States.

Like tornadoes, hurricanes are rotating storms fueled by the ascension of warm, moist air, but are much larger in size, and gain much of their fuel from warm ocean water. Before one of these swirling storms is classified as a hurricane, it has to exceed lesser classifications for a "cyclonic" storm that generally forms in the tropics: a "tropical depression" has maximum wind speeds of 38 miles per hour, and a "tropical storm" has wind speeds of 39 to 73 miles per hour.

Inflow: Air getting pulled into a severe thunderstorm by its updraft. Severe thunderstorms and tornadoes are fueled by inflows of moist and warm air. I've experienced inflow winds of 70-plus miles per hour flowing into the mesocyclone of a supercell storm.

Loaded-gun sounding: A "loaded-gun sounding" is storm-chaser slang for a profile that seems particularly likely to produce severe thunderstorms, and potentially tornadoes. Indications are that warm, moist air is gathering energy under a "cap" in the atmosphere, which will gather instability with the heating of the day, typically maxing out in the late afternoon. The hope is that this "loaded gun" will "fire"—the warm, moist air will explode through the cap at "peak heating" when instability is greatest, and turn into severe thunderstorms and possibly tornado-producing supercells during late afternoon into evening. The sounding from Norman, Oklahoma, the morning of the May 3, 1999 tornado outbreak (see Chapter 1) was a classic loaded-gun sounding.

Low-level jet: A fast-moving (up to 80 miles per hour) strip of air that's low (approximately 1,000 feet above the ground) in the atmosphere that is unique to the North American Great Plains. "Jet streams" refer to any of the narrow, fast-moving airflows that exist in many regions of the earth's atmosphere, but the low-level jet is vital to the development of the particularly strong wind shear found in the U.S. Great Plains.

Mammatus cloud: Small, visually interesting clouds with pouchlike silhouettes that appear to hang from upper-level anvil clouds. Mammatus clouds are not reliable indicators of thunderstorm or tornado activity, and are incredibly photogenic and can be rather ominous looking.

Mesocyclone: The rotating updraft of a supercell storm, approximately one to six miles wide, that can give birth to tornadoes when they make contact with the ground.

Mesoscale meteorology: The study of atmospheric conditions that span several hundred horizontal miles, which includes the study of severe storms, tornadoes, and hurricanes.

National Weather Service (NWS): The National Weather Service (NWS) is a part of the National Oceanic and Atmospheric Administration (NOAA). Its mission is to provide weather and climate forecasts to the United States. The NWS has 122 weather forecast offices across the country. Each office forecasts the weather in its area, called the County Warning Area (CWA).

Nowcaster: In storm chasing, a "nowcaster" is a trusted individual who remains in front of a computer and helps direct chasers to the best available targets. Traditionally, nowcasters have operated from their homes or other stationary locations, and communicated with chasers via telephone.

Outflow: Air moving away from a storm, often in the form of cold outflow caused by falling rain and hail. If the outflow is strong enough, it can cut off the storm's warm, moist inflow, causing it to weaken.

Punching the core: Chaser slang for driving through the storm's bear's cage in order to intercept a tornado. Many storm chasers believe that punching the core is dangerous, and refuse to do it.

Rapid Update Cycle (RUC): A computer-based weather prediction model that produces forecasts like wind, CAPE, helicity, and precipitation for the entire Untied States once an hour, up to twelve hours in advance, accessible on the Internet. Storm chasers frequently access the RUC and other forecasting Web sites to help them decide on target areas during storm chases, and to identify regions where the ingredients for tornadoes will be in place.

Rear-flank downdraft (RFD): A downward rush of air that circles around a supercell thunderstorm's mesocyclone. The RFD sometimes carries

precipitation (rain and/or hail), but is typically composed of relatively drier air that lost much of its moisture while descending down the backside of the storm. Scientists theorize that warmer RFD temperatures may be associated with tornado-producing supercells. As the RFD encircles the mesocyclone just right, a tighter area of rotation can develop at its apex. Scientists believe that this "tightened" rotation can result in the birth of a tornado.

Rope out: Storm chasers call these thinner tornadoes "ropes" because of their skinny appearance, and the process of a tornado dissipating is called "roping out." Just because a roping-out tornado looks small does not mean it's weakening. In fact, just the opposite can be true as the diameter of a tornado shrinks; the wind can spin even faster because of conservation of angular momentum.

Saffir-Simpson Hurricane Wind Scale: The Saffir-Simpson scale, which was developed in 1969 by Florida-based structural engineer Herbert Saffir (and later expanded on by Robert Simpson, a former director of the National Hurricane Center), classifies hurricanes in five different categories: Category 1 hurricanes have sustained wind speeds of 74 to 95 miles per hour; Category 2, 96 to 110 miles per hour; Category 3, 111 to 130 miles per hour; Category 4, 131 to 155 miles per hour; Category 5, more than 155 miles per hour.

Scud cloud: Small, low-hanging, ragged formations that are often found beneath cumulonimbus clouds. Different from funnel clouds and tornadoes, scud clouds are not rotating, but their rapid appearance can be the precursor to wall cloud formation.

Skew-T: Many meteorologists and storm chasers diagram a "skew-T" to gauge the instability—and thus the potential for severe convective weather. Using available data from weather balloons, storm chasers and computers will plot temperature and dew point readings against pressure (also a measure of elevation) in the atmosphere. The lines connected between data

points give chasers an idea of the sky's potential to generate thunderstorms, and even tornadoes.

Squall line: A series of severe thunderstorms that merge into a line. Because the thunderstorms of a squall line all compete with each other for the surrounding atmosphere's available warm air, and are typically associated with outflow winning out over inflow, lines of storms generally don't produce tornadoes. Damaging straight-line winds and impressive rainstorms are common with squall lines, however.

Storm Prediction Center: The Storm Prediction Center, or SPC, is a thirty-four-person branch of the National Weather Service located in Norman, Oklahoma. Staffed with meteorologists, the SPC's mission is to issue consistently updated weather forecasts for severe weather (like tornadoes, thunderstorms, and even weather that could create or intensify wildfires). The SPC disseminates its information, among other ways, via its Web site.

Storm surge: The accumulation of water that's pushed toward a shoreline by a hurricane's strong winds. Storm surges can be huge—Hurricane Katrina's was as high as twenty-five feet. Storm surges are often the most devastating part of a land-falling hurricane, even more so than the strong winds.

Straight-line winds: Winds of a thunderstorm that do not rotate.

Stratus cloud: Stratus clouds are frequently uniform and nearly featureless—a drab gray blanket in the sky—and reside in the low levels of the atmosphere. Benign fog is an example of a stratus cloud, but they also generally accompany a hurricane making landfall given the abundance of tropical moisture in the air. During a hurricane, low-level stratus clouds blow very quickly across the sky.

Suction vortices: Miniature tornadoes that often appear around and inside of the larger, parent tornadoes. Nobody understands exactly how, when,

and why these smaller vortices appear, but scientists believe that suction vortices could pack winds at three to four times the speed of the "parent vortex." The presence of suction vortices could explain why one house inside a tornado's damage path can sustain serious damage, while the house next door can remain unscathed.

Supercell thunderstorm: A supercell is the strongest and most damaging form of severe weather, and is defined as any thunderstorm containing a rotating updraft, or mesocyclone. Supercells generally can be classified as low-precipitation (LP) or high-precipitation (HP), and often take on the shape of a mushroom cloud or a UFO. Supercells can produce extreme severe weather such as hail to baseball- or even softball-size torrential rains, and even tornadoes.

Super-cooled rain droplets: Cloud or rain droplets that remain liquid despite passing beneath its "freezing point" of 32 degrees F. Inside severe thunderstorms, water droplets can supercool as they rise into increasingly cold air. By remaining in a liquid state, they can grow (via collisions with other supercooled droplets and ice particles) into large frozen masses, which can grow to incredible sizes and ultimately come down to earth as softball-size hail. I've lost multiple windshields per year from hail stones this large by punching the cores of tornadic supercells!

Synoptic scale meteorology: The study of atmospheric conditions that span horizontal scales on the order of a thousand miles and greater. Also known as "large scale" meteorology.

Target area: A region where storm chasers believe looks most favorable for tornadoes (or hurricanes depending on what form of severe weather is being chased) on a given chase day. The target area may be as small as a group of counties, or as large as a multistate region.

Tornado: An upwardly rotating column of air that emerges from a cloud and contacts the ground. Tornadoes can be narrow or more than one mile

wide, spin at speeds in excess of 300 miles per hour, and last for minutes or hours. Tornadoes come in many forms. Storm chasers frequently describe tornadoes using characterizations like "stovepipe," "elephant trunk," "drill bit," "wedge," and "cone." The Fujita Scale estimates the intensities of tornadoes using the magnitude of their damage (defined above).

Tornado Alley: A nickname for an area in the central United States that roughly overlaps with the Great Plains, where more tornadoes occur than anywhere else in the world. Tornado Alley runs as far south as central Texas and as far north as the Dakotas. It extends west from the eastern edges of the Rocky Mountain states and as far east as Minnesota and even parts of Illinois.

Tropical disturbance: Clusters of thunderstorms at sea that often converge around low-pressure areas. Tropical disturbances can be the precursors for hurricane and typhoon development.

Trough: Troughs are a wave of low pressure and cold air that move east with the upper-level jet stream and can trigger severe weather. Cold air sinks southward to create a trough, or a trench in the path of the jet stream, or river of fast-moving air that exists at high in the Mid-Latitude atmosphere. When a trough passes from the Rocky Mountains into the Great Plains, it pumps warm, moist air northward and upward from the Gulf of Mexico in the strong southerlies to its east, providing the necessary instability for severe weather. Storm chasers will frequently scan the long-range computer forecast models for upcoming troughs of low pressure in the jet stream and assess how active the coming days and weeks will be in Tornado Alley.

Updraft: Upward current of air. Thunderstorms are generally fueled by relatively warm, moist updrafts. A tornado, mesocyclone, and hurricane are all examples of rotating updrafts of different scale, or size.

Vortex: A spiraling flow of any "fluid" (including air). Tornadoes, mesocyclones, and hurricanes are vortices of different scale, or size.

Wall cloud: A signature, block-shaped mass of thick condensation that hangs beneath the updraft base of a severe thunderstorm. Tornadoes frequently come from spinning wall clouds beneath the mesocyclones of supercells. Wall clouds appearing only hundreds of feet off the ground are known as "ground scrapers."

Wind shear: Wind shear is the difference in wind speed and direction between two different heights above the ground. The presence of wind shear can induce part of the lower atmosphere to begin spinning in roll-like patterns.

Photo by Heidi Farrar, TornadoVideos.net

Reed Timmer is a star of Discovery's *Storm Chasers* and one of the most successful and extreme storm chasers in the world. In 2011, he will receive a PhD in meteorology from the University of Oklahoma.

To arrange a speaking engagement for
Reed Timmer, please contact the
Penguin Speakers Bureau at
speakersbureau@us.penguingroup.com.